CYCLING A▮▮▮▮

The Statewide Road Biking Guide

TEXT BY **Christine Maxa**
PHOTOGRAPHS BY **David A. James**

WESTCLIFFE PUBLISHERS
westcliffepublishers.com

International Standard Book Numbers:
ISBN-10: 1-56579-537-7
ISBN-13: 978-1-56579-537-2

Text: Christine Maxa, ©2006. All rights reserved.
Photography: David A. James, ©2006. All rights reserved.

Editor: Dougald MacDonald
Designer: Carol Pando, ÜberInk, 2006.
Production Manager: Craig Keyzer

Published by:
Westcliffe Publishers, Inc.
P.O. Box 1261
Englewood, CO 80150
westcliffepublishers.com

Printed in China by Hing Yip Printing Co., Ltd.

Library of Congress Cataloging-in-Publication Data:
Maxa, Christine.
   Cycling Arizona : the statewide road biking guide /
text by Christine Maxa ; photographs by David A. James.
      p. cm.
   Includes index.
   ISBN-13: 978-1-56579-537-2
   ISBN-10: 1-56579-537-7
   1. Bicycle trails—Arizona—Guidebooks. 2. Arizona—Guidebooks.
   I. James, David A., 1943- II. Title.
   GV1045.5.A6M39 2006
   796.6'409791—dc22

                            2006015242

Please Note: Risk is always a factor when biking on streets and highways. Many of the activities described in this book can be dangerous, especially when weather is adverse or unpredictable, and when unforeseen events or conditions create a hazardous situation. The author has done her best to provide the reader with accurate information about road biking travel, as well as to point out some of its potential hazards. It is the responsibility of the users of this guide to learn the necessary skills for safe travel, and to exercise caution in potentially hazardous areas. The author and publisher disclaim any liability for injury or other damage caused by traveling or performing any other activity described in this book.

The author and publisher of this book have made every effort to ensure the accuracy and currency of its information. Nevertheless, books can require revisions. Please let us know if you find information in this book that needs to be updated, and we will be glad to correct it for the next printing. Your comments and suggestions are always welcome.

Previous Page: *Rider traveling the Bush Highway route*

ACKNOWLEDGMENTS

A big thank-you to Maureen DeCindis and to the veteran road bicyclists she referred me to—Reed Kempton, Richard Corbett, and Eric Prosnier—who gave me great tips, colorful anecdotes, and favorite routes.

Thank you to Jack and Dotti Sieder, who have ridden routes all over the world and led tours all over the state of Arizona.

A thank-you to all the bike shops that helped with information.

Thank you to all the road cyclists who gave information, tips, stories, and favorite bike rides.

To Adrienne Maynes, who allowed her 10-year-old sister to ride her purple and white Schwinn bicycle around our hometown for hours, and to David, who rides around the states with me for days.

—Christine Maxa

To Christine, for her patience and understanding.
To Donna, for her wisdom and encouragement.
To my son, Colin, for his trust and love.
To the Arizona outback, for its quiet beauty and solitude.
It has been all quite unforgettable.

—David A. James

TABLE OF CONTENTS

*Cave Creek Bikeway has a Sonoran Desert landscape
with plenty of trees that offer segments of shade.*

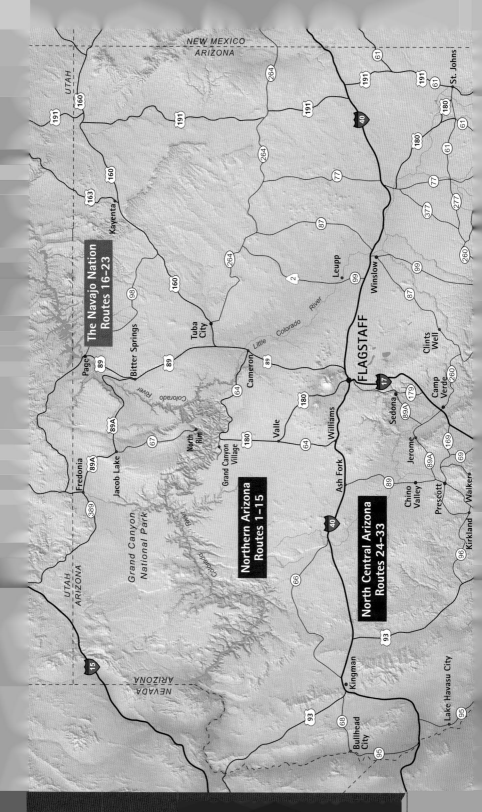

The Navajo Nation
Routes 16–23

Northern Arizona
Routes 1–15

North Central Arizona
Routes 24–33

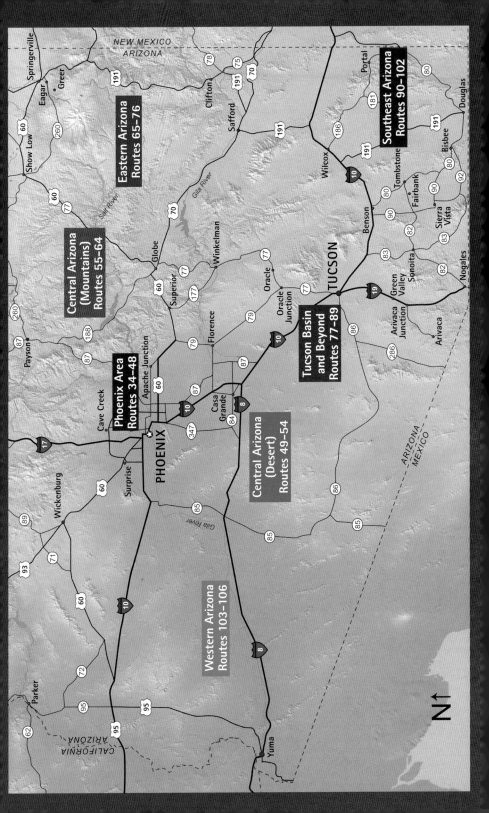

PREFACE

It is generally believed that Arizona consists primarily of unbearably hot and flat desert "wastelands." For large areas of the state, this may be superficially true, although it is very inaccurate to describe anything as beautiful, varied, and teeming with wildlife as Arizona's deserts as "wasteland." Those who really know Arizona can tell you it is a state that enjoys more variety in its topography and climate than any other state except, perhaps, California.

It is also a four-season state—that is to say that regardless of the time of year you are able to comfortably recreate somewhere among Arizona's beautiful mountains, deserts, canyons, lakes, and forests. While the summer temperature may linger in the triple digits on a Phoenix evening, you might want to put on a sweater in the White Mountain town of Greer. In the winter, an afternoon snowball fight on the slopes of Mount Humphreys contrasts with kayaking through warm breezes along the lower Colorado River near Yuma.

In Arizona, your recreation is limited only by your conscious decision "not to"—never by a lack of opportunity. Arizona covers a lot of space, both on the ground and in your mind. Its real beauty lies hidden in the compelling, seductive, timeless architecture of space and silence. It is an ancient cathedral of light and shadow that imprints itself indelibly upon your mind and spirit, softly, quietly, without your even knowing. From sunrise to sunset, cycling Arizona can be an uplifting, rewarding experience that you will never forget.

For these reasons, the author, Christine Maxa, and the photographer, David James, together cycled the routes described in this book, testing their respective views on the beauty, difficulty, or safety of each route. The intent was to make the routes—not merely the book—especially user-friendly and accessible to cyclists at every level of experience and skill, and above all enjoyable and fun!

We hope that we have succeeded and that, from over your handlebars, you will experience one of the most beautiful and magical places on earth.

After a wet winter, Apache Trail roadsides get covered with color.

How To Use This Guide

Arizona, with more than 80 percent public lands, miles of open space, and small towns full of big personalities, is a road cyclist's dream come true. One of road biking's best-kept secrets, this charismatic state has dozens of blue-line highways that travel hundreds of colorful, scenic miles. We have chosen the state's best day-ride routes, averaging 20 to 40 miles one-way, with some century-sized rides (100 miles or longer) that can be done over a couple of days. Most of these routes are scenic and relatively safe (with a shoulder or little traffic). Some will make you tussle with long, steep grades or raise the hair on the back of your neck with hairpin descents. We've covered plenty of beginner routes as well as classic and challenging routes that many experienced road bikers try at least once.

The choice of routes is based on destinations within day-trip range from major population centers, and with convenient access to provisions, food, or lodging. Some of these routes are merely segments of highways between towns; others form loops. Many link up with other routes, as indicated in the descriptions.

The maps at the beginning of each chapter are regional snapshots designed to give you a broad overview of the routes and how they relate to one another. Each route is marked by the route number, with starting and ending points shown in red. If the starting or ending point is a town, it appears as a red circle; when it's outside a town, it appears as a red square. Throughout the book, detail maps provide a closer view of complex areas difficult to depict on the regional maps.

Each route's banner contains:

ROUTE NUMBER

ROUTE NAME

ROAD NAME OR HIGHWAY NUMBER, ROUTE LOCATION, AND/OR START AND FINISH

RATINGS: Route Difficulty • Recommended Experience Level

Route Difficulty Ratings are defined as:

▶ EASY: Flat terrain or easy rollers
▶ MODERATE: Moderate to steep rollers, and/or some blind spots, and/or fast traffic
▶ DIFFICULT: Steep hills, mountainous terrain, and blind spots
▶ VERY DIFFICULT: Consistently steep hills or mountainous terrain and blind spots

Recommended experience levels are defined as:

- BEGINNER: Easy enough for a beginner to cycle
- INTERMEDIATE: Route will be a challenge but doable for a beginner, comfortable to moderately challenging for a cyclist with some hill experience, and easier for more experienced cyclists
- EXPERIENCED: Route not recommended for beginners, challenging for intermediate cyclists

Below the route's banner, the route description continues with:

BRIEF ROUTE INFORMATION

- Interesting highlights
- Number of lanes; type of shoulder or bike lane

Each route description continues with these topics:

DISTANCE: Number of one-way or loop miles, including intermediate turn-around points. Calculating distances can be an elusive target. Maps, odometers and road signs are generally considered accurate, however, inconsistencies do occur. This book tries to maintain the highest possible level of accuracy, but no guidebook, however, can replace common sense and awareness of your environment.

PEAK CYCLING: Best months and/or time of day to cycle the route

ACCOMMODATIONS: Where to find supplies, restaurants, and lodging, including specific suggestions when warranted

SPECIAL CONSIDERATIONS: Specific warnings about the route

STARTING POINT(S): Directions to where the route starts, generally with a milepost (MP) number so you can track your mileage

The main route description follows these introductory topics. We have lavished each route description with helpful information, as well as fun facts, colorful history, and scenic spots to check out. We've added insider tips about the regions and communities the routes travel through. Most of the descriptions contain milepost (MP) numbers to give you a sense of your progress. Turnaround points are often mentioned for cyclists who prefer shorter routes. The route descriptions also contain:

ROUTE PROFILE: A visual representation of the elevation encountered along the ride. The elevation profiles in this guide were designed using topographical software. Because the profiles compress a great deal of distance into a very small space, they at times visually exaggerate the terrain. The elevation profiles should therefore only be used as a quick glimpse of what to expect, rather than an actual representation of every up and down that you'll find on the ground. Your primary sources of information should be route descriptions and maps.

The total vertical gain and loss figures combine all of the ups and downs encountered from start to finish, giving you a calculation of the work ahead, rather than the difference in elevation between the route's high and low points. Note that if your cyclometer or altimeter gives you actual vertical gain, your results might differ from those in the text. Refer also to the table in Appendix A (see p. 276). It shows you at a glance what to expect in each route: mileage, difficulty, and types of terrain and scenery.

A labyrinth of red-rock canyons, part of the Rainbow Plateau, surround Navajo Mountain.

REGION 1

NORTHERN ARIZONA

In northern Arizona, you're cycling some of the state's highest country. Alpinelike forests and meadows around Flagstaff provide a cool backdrop for hours-long rides. Along the rim of the Grand Canyon and in the far northern reaches of the state, you get a taste of country that has always enticed adventure-seekers. Erosion-carved, painted, and utterly breathtaking, this canyoned high-desert country of restless beauty carries a mystique that draws people craving an outdoor challenge—or just a scenic look.

A cyclist looks at the highway that closes the Mormon Lake Loop.

Routes

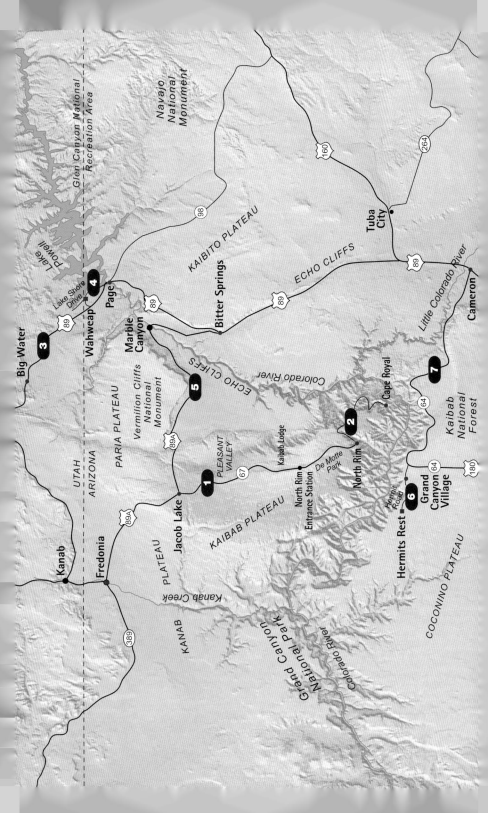

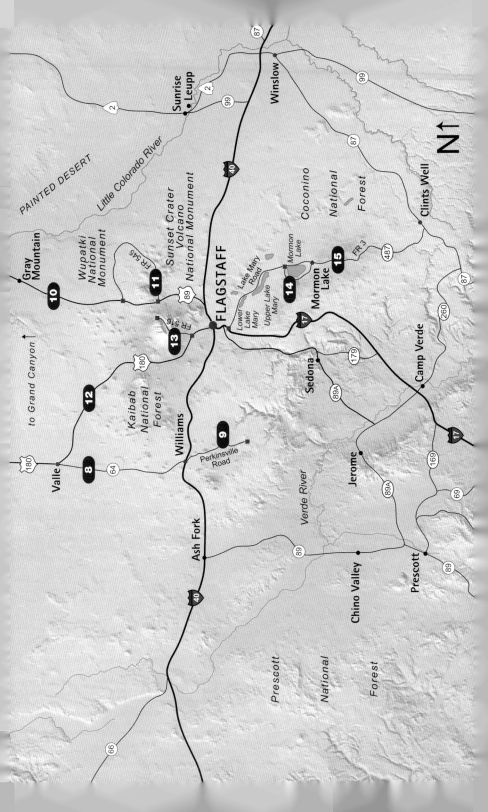

Route 1

NORTH RIM PARKWAY
AZ 67: JACOB LAKE TO GRAND CANYON'S NORTH RIM

Moderate • Beginner

* Travels through national forest and National Park Service land
* Abundant wildlife
* Fall color from late September to early October
* Excellent touring route (two days) or challenging single day
* Scenic, graded backroads adjacent to paved route for hybrid bicycles
* Smooth two-lane highway; narrow shoulder

DISTANCE: 33 miles one-way to the national park boundary;
45 miles one-way to the North Rim

PEAK CYCLING: May 15–October 15

ACCOMMODATIONS: Basic supplies, restaurants, and lodging in Jacob Lake and at the North Rim. Grand Canyon Lodge (888-297-2757), right on the rim in the national park, is the classic spot to stay if you do an overnighter. The lodge's restaurant has food as good as its views.

SPECIAL CONSIDERATIONS: This road closes when the first snows hit, sometime after October 15, and reopens May 15. The National Park Service charges $20 to drive into the park or $10 for individuals on bicycles.

STARTING POINT: Just south of US 89A on AZ 67, between MPs 579 and 580, at the Kaibab Plateau Visitor Center.

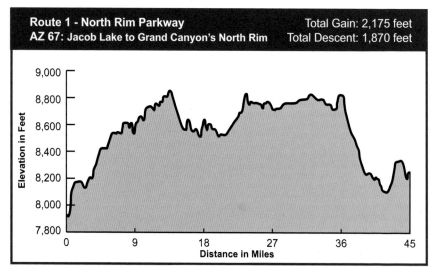

Route 1 - North Rim Parkway — Total Gain: 2,175 feet
AZ 67: Jacob Lake to Grand Canyon's North Rim — Total Descent: 1,870 feet

Flagstaff cyclist Frank Loro calls this route "One of the Seven Wonders of the (Cycling) World." When you consider its smooth surface, genteel rollers, low traffic, and beautiful scenery, you can see what he means. The road has several scenic-byway designations—National Scenic Byway, National Forest Scenic Byway, and Arizona Scenic Byway—and for dessert, Frank points out, "It's all downhill on the way back."

The road starts in a forest of mixed conifers with summer temperatures that hover in the 70s. You might catch the dark blue of a Steller's jay or the red cap of a woodpecker flashing through the woods as you pedal through the forest. The road climbs some comfortable rollers that push you along at a fast speed.

The forest fills with aspen as the road gradually climbs to the edge of "the mountain lying down," the translation of the Paiute Indians' name for the Kaibab Plateau. The aspens will create a pretty gold matrix in the evergreen forest from the end of September to early October. Small meadows appear occasionally as spruce and fir start to dominate the forest.

A string of meadows starts at MP 594: Little Round Valley and then Little Pleasant Valley and Pleasant Valley. During early morning or evening, deer browse the meadows, often unconcerned about human presence. Sprawling De Motte Park at MP 604 leads up to the North Rim entrance station. Just before the entrance, you

Rollers, curves, swerves, and scenery make up the North Rim Parkway.

can stop at the North Rim Country Store for basic groceries and beverages or the Kaibab Lodge for food and lodging.

At the park entrance (a good turnaround point for a shorter ride), the MPs restart and the road surface switches from new, smooth asphalt to an aged surface interspersed with an occasional pothole. You also lose the shoulder, but the superb scenery prevails.

The forest cocoons the road again by MP 3, and then the route starts a more noticeable climb toward the rim. The eastern wall of Thompson Canyon rises around MP 8, and the road makes its final climb out of the canyon—a long uphill grind—and onto the edge of the North Rim just past MP 12. You can top off your water at a public faucet near the restrooms and get electrolyte mix at the general store.

Route 2

CAPE ROYAL ROAD
AZ 67 TO CAPE ROYAL/GRAND CANYON NATIONAL PARK

Moderate • Intermediate

- Ride through mixed-conifer forests; stop at several panoramas of the Grand Canyon
- Abundant wildlife, including possible condor sightings
- Two lanes; no shoulder

DISTANCE: 20 miles one-way

PEAK CYCLING: May 15–October 15

ACCOMMODATIONS: Supplies, restaurants, and lodging in De Motte Park and North Rim

SPECIAL CONSIDERATIONS: Access to this road is subject to weather closures on AZ 67 (anytime after October 15 until May 15). The National Park Service charges $20 to drive into the park or $10 for individuals on bicycles.

STARTING POINT: About 3 miles north of the North Rim on the east side of AZ 67. Viewpoints have parking areas.

Cloistered in a pristine mixed-conifer forest with pockets of meadows, this less-traveled road takes you through the backcountry of the North Rim, across the Walhalla Plateau, to Cape Royal overlook. One big roller after another, powerful panoramas at several viewpoints along the road, and frequent wildlife sightings make this an exceptional ride.

The Unkar Delta viewpoint makes an inspiring rest stop.

The plateau's beauty has always attracted humanity. At the turn of the 20th century, Mormons grazed cattle on the plateau, which they called Greenland Point. When Francois Matthes did a topographic survey of the Grand Canyon for the U.S. Geological Survey in 1902, he suggested Walhalla as the official name.

Though Matthes did acknowledge the area's "rich herbage," Walhalla stuck.

National parks always capitalize on environmental object lessons, and this route starts with a fine example of a basic high-country forest cycle.

Extensive forest fire damage has charred the conifer forest and started the cycle of aspen growth. The aspen forest nurtures evergreens with its cool, moist habitat. Soon the evergreens grow up and overtake the aspens. When fire destroys the forest, the aspens return and start the cycle over again. Here, you might see a flock of wild turkeys meandering in meadows, grouse aimlessly standing along the side of the road, or mule deer grazing nonchalantly.

The route's first long descent takes you to a fork in the road at mile 5. The left road heads 3 miles to Point Imperial, the highest point on the North Rim. To continue on Cape Royal Road, veer right. The road twists through a series of goosenecks for about 5 miles before it arrives at its first viewpoint, Vista Encantada; Roosevelt Point follows in the next mile. Be careful to devote enough attention to the road between these two vistas. The views do not relent, but neither do the bends in the road nor the occasional deep dimples in the surface.

At about mile 15, the route approaches Walhalla Glades. Here, the plateau extends in peninsula fashion into the canyon. The Ancestral Puebloans chose to set up their summer homes here. A viewpoint overlooking the Unkar Delta lies right next to a ruin. Archaeologists have found dwellings and agricultural evidence on the delta at the canyon bottom as well as in the glades.

The scenery goes all-out during the last mile as you pass Angels Window—a natural arch formed in a fin of rock—and canyon views. You might catch a condor soaring above you on the climb. The birds have taken to the cliffs and thermals along the Grand Canyon's rim. Watch, too, for swifts and hawks. You'll have to walk your bike over the mottled parking area to get to Cape Royal's viewpoint trails, but it's worth the trek.

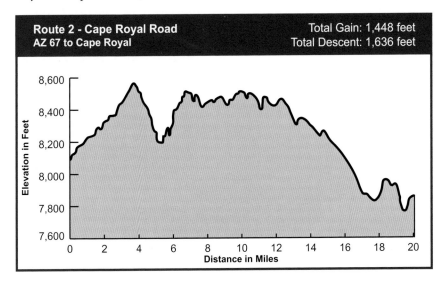

Route 2 - Cape Royal Road
AZ 67 to Cape Royal
Total Gain: 1,448 feet
Total Descent: 1,636 feet

Route 3

BIG WATER
US 89: PAGE TO BIG WATER, UTAH

Moderate • Intermediate

* Travels through a geological time warp to a little town filled with prehistoric relics
* Bureau of Land Management (BLM) visitor center near Big Water is a museumlike source of area information
* Two lanes; medium shoulder

DISTANCE: 15 miles one-way

PEAK CYCLING: April–October

ACCOMMODATIONS: Basic supplies in Big Water; supplies, restaurants, and lodging in Page. Check out the Lake Powell Days Inn and Suites on US 89 and Haul Road (928-645-2800) for comfortable rooms with views at reasonable rates.

SPECIAL CONSIDERATIONS: The Utah segment will have your teeth chattering from the rough road surface.

STARTING POINT: US 89 at the Carl Hayden Visitor Center at Glen Canyon Dam; the first mile marker is MP 550.

The route to Big Water is all about geology.

This route is all about geology and a prehistoric land full of enough dinosaur bones and fossils to make a paleontologist's dream come true. The Grand Staircase Escalante National Monument lies just north of this route; the park is named for a geological stairway of different-colored cliffs rising to Bryce Canyon: the Vermilion, White, Gray, and Pink cliffs. Though the route doesn't enter the monument, you can learn all about it at the BLM's visitor center in Big Water.

As US 89 climbs northwestward through Glen Canyon National Recreation Area, the classic Lake Powell landmarks of Gunsight and Padre buttes, Castle Rock, and Navajo Mountain appear around the Wahweap North entrance (MP 554).

Just over 2 miles later, with Wahweap Bay stretching its long arm to parallel the highway, the route crosses the Utah border (MP 0) and white Navajo sandstone cliffs start to surround the highway. You can detour onto Lone Rock Road, just over the border, and ride about a mile to a viewpoint toward Lake Powell.

At MP 2, the route starts a long climb to the town of Big Water. Almost halfway there, at MP 4, the highway crosses a couple of slot canyons that empty into Lake Powell. These canyons cut through an unusual blue-gray formation of Tropic Shale formed, scientists say, 95 million years ago. The 500- to 1,000-foot-thick sediment, left over from an interior seaway in the Late Cretaceous Era, has the world's best and most continuous record of the era's terrestrial life—the area is packed with dinosaur bones and fossils. The BLM visitor center has a wall-sized mural painted by Larry Felder depicting life the way it might have been during a time frame of 75 million to 95 million years ago, featuring creatures whose bones have been found in the area.

For a small town, Big Water has some interesting history. The town was a sort of sister city to Page during the construction of the Glen Canyon Dam. Page had a saintly demeanor, with several churches constructed for the workers and their families at the town's start. Big Water, on the other hand, catered to the masses via brothels rather than houses of prayer. In 1984, Big Water, then known as Glen Canyon City, was sold for $30,000 to polygamist Alex Joseph. Mr. Joseph had 20 wives at the time. Joseph named his town Big Water because it sounded like an Indian name.

Once you take in the sights of Big Water, which include a market with basics, you can return to Page or continue farther in Utah on US 89. Keep in mind, however, there are no accommodations of any kind until Kanab, more than 50 miles away.

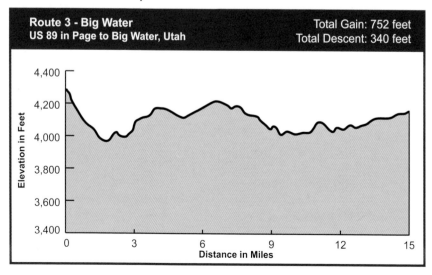

Route 3 - Big Water
US 89 in Page to Big Water, Utah
Total Gain: 752 feet
Total Descent: 340 feet

Route 4

LAKE SHORE DRIVE LOOP
LAKE SHORE DRIVE, GLEN CANYON NATIONAL RECREATION AREA

Easy • Beginner

* Travels along Lake Powell, considered one of the country's most beautiful lakes
* Viewpoint pullouts
* Two lanes; no shoulder

DISTANCE: 10-mile loop

PEAK CYCLING: March–November

ACCOMMODATIONS: Supplies, restaurants, and lodging in Page. The Lake Powell Resort in Wahweap Marina (866-875-8456) has always been a favorite. Ask for a lakeside room for the best views in the area. The lodge's Rainbow Room has a sumptuous breakfast buffet and homemade potato chips so good that some diners have been known to make a meal of them.

SPECIAL CONSIDERATIONS: The National Park Service charges $3 for each individual on a bicycle when entry gates are open. Beginners can double back on Lake Shore Drive rather than take the highway.

STARTING POINT: US 89 at the Carl Hayden Visitor Center at Glen Canyon Dam; the first mile marker is MP 550.

Located on the northern edge of Page, Arizona, once a forbidding mesa the Navajos warned was bewitched and called "the place where trees died of fear," Lake Powell casts its own enchantments on visitors. One look at the aqua waters surrounded by red-rock cliffs under a turquoise sky floating billowy clouds can hook a visitor as fast as the lake's fishermen catch striped bass.

A ride along Glen Canyon National Recreation Area's Lake Shore Drive gives extraordinary panoramas of the lovely area. Early morning or late afternoon make the best riding times. Whenever you go, allow more time than you think you'll need. The views are too good to pass by.

From the Carl Hayden Visitor Center, just west of Glen Canyon Dam, follow US 89 north for a short distance, and then turn right onto Lake Shore Drive. The road drops smoothly to the shore of Lake Powell and heads north with constant views of a classic Southwest skyline, filled with mesas and buttes and crowned by dome-shaped Navajo Mountain along the eastern horizon. The Kaiparowits Plateau stretches across the northern horizon. Navajo Viewpoint comes up quickly to provide a pullout from which to take in the views, including a good look at the back side of Glen Canyon Dam.

An overlook on Wahweap Loop

When you get to a stop sign at about mile 4, you can turn right (east) and explore Wahweap Marina, take a dip in the lake, or have a meal at the Rainbow Room restaurant. To continue the loop, turn left (west) toward US 89. It's about a 2-mile ride to the highway, much of which is uphill. At the highway, you can return the way you came or turn left (south) on US 89 and ride 4 miles back to the Carl Hayden Visitor Center.

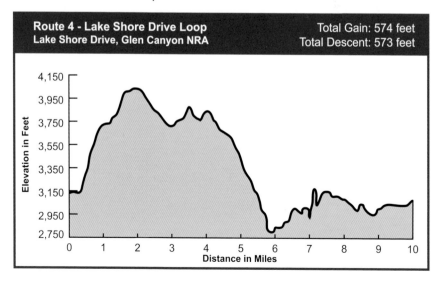

Route 4 - Lake Shore Drive Loop
Lake Shore Drive, Glen Canyon NRA

Total Gain: 574 feet
Total Descent: 573 feet

Route 5

JACOB LAKE HALF-CENTURY
US 89A: Bitter Springs to Jacob Lake

Moderate • Intermediate

- Remote high-desert highway with extravagant geology
- Excellent touring route (two days) or challenging single day; several turnaround points
- Two lanes; no shoulder

DISTANCE: 14 miles to Marble Canyon; 38 miles to House Rock Valley Road; 55 miles to Jacob Lake

PEAK CYCLING: April–October

ACCOMMODATIONS: Basic supplies, restaurants, and lodging at Marble Canyon, Vermilion Cliffs, Cliff Dwellers, and Jacob Lake. Vermilion Cliffs Bar & Grill (928-355-2231, next to Lee's Ferry Lodge in Vermilion Cliffs) has consistently good food, about 100 different brands of bottled beer, and a most unusual staff to serve you.

SPECIAL CONSIDERATIONS: Watch for blind spots between Bitter Springs and Marble Canyon. Less experienced cyclists should start at Marble Canyon.

STARTING POINTS: (1) About 25 miles south of Page, off US 89 at the beginning of US 89A; or (2) about 14 miles north of US 89 on US 89A, at Marble Canyon. Unless you have a shuttle to drop you at the south end of US 89A or permission from the Navajo to park on their land, park at Marble Canyon.

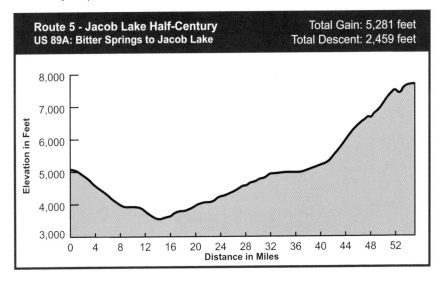

Route 5 - Jacob Lake Half-Century
US 89A: Bitter Springs to Jacob Lake
Total Gain: 5,281 feet
Total Descent: 2,459 feet

With the Echo Cliffs rising to the east and the stratified Vermilion Cliffs angling across the horizon straight ahead, this route shows some glamorous geology on the way to the Arizona Strip—the remote segment of Arizona between the North Rim of the Grand Canyon and Utah. Designated the Vermilion Cliffs Scenic Road, this route travels some of the loneliest but prettiest country in the state.

Crossing the Colorado River on US 89A.

This route features an ever-changing sense of geology. In the first segment, starting at MP 525 between Bitter Springs and Marble Canyon, you get an object lesson of canyons in the making, where flash floods have gouged washes in the red-sand earth. The land dips and heaves like a Tilt-A-Whirl, giving the route mild rollers and curves.

The highway crosses the Navajo Nation during this segment, and several small communities cluster at a distance from the road. Enterprising natives have set up jewelry stands at points along the highway.

The route crosses the Colorado River at MP 537 along a shoulder of Navajo Bridge and then enters the BLM's Arizona Strip District. You can stop at the visitor center to learn about local history and get basic provisions, a meal, or lodging at Marble Canyon or, better, at Vermilion Cliffs just down the road.

The shoulder ends once the road crosses the Colorado River, but the route straightens out and heads toward long, leisurely rollers and long-distance views. The Vermilion Cliffs rise to the north, and House Rock Valley sprawls southward. At MP 542, you pass Vermilion Cliffs. This cyclist-friendly community has food, lodging, and a fly-fishing store. If you crank too fast or blink your eyes too often, you won't notice the handful of homes behind the restaurant away from the road. The last chance to mingle with civilization before route's end comes at a signed geologic spot at MP 547 called Cliff Dwellers.

Any of the three small communities along this stretch of highway makes a good turnaround point for a shorter ride. From Cliff Dwellers to Jacob Lake at MP 570, you're on your own. Along the way, you'll pass a turnoff for House Rock Valley Road on the north side of the highway at MP 565. Condor releases take place 3 miles north of here. The endangered birds almost became extinct by 1987. Through a joint effort of the U.S. Fish and Wildlife Service, The

Peregrine Fund, Arizona Game & Fish Department, Grand Canyon National Park, the Bureau of Land Management, and other partners, condors got a chance to fly in Arizona skies again when six birds were released in 1996. Today, Arizona has more than 40 free-flying condors.

MP 565 also marks the beginning of a long climb up the Kaibab Plateau. A scenic viewpoint between MPs 567 and 568 gives you a chance to catch your breath if you need to. The limestone landscape is subtly attractive, with piñon trees climbing up cream-colored ledges. By MP 573, the route reaches ponderosa pine forest, and it doesn't stop climbing until its end at MP 579 in Jacob Lake. From here, you may continue to the North Rim or return the way you came.

Route 6
HERMIT ROAD
GRAND CANYON VILLAGE TO HERMITS REST
Easy • Beginner

- ◆ Travels the south rim of the Grand Canyon to Hermits Rest viewpoints
- ◆ Mythic Grand Canyon views
- ◆ Two lanes; no shoulder

DISTANCE: 8 miles one-way

PEAK CYCLING: March–October

ACCOMMODATIONS: Supplies, restaurants, and lodging in Grand Canyon Village. If you plan to stay at Grand Canyon, make reservations early. There are several different lodges, as well as campgrounds. The best time to get a room is during the winter months; next best are spring and fall. Once in the national park, plan to take your meals later (breakfast after 9 a.m. and lunch after 12:30 p.m.) to avoid the crowds.

SPECIAL CONSIDERATIONS: The National Park Service charges an entrance fee of $20 per car or $10 for individuals on bicycles. This route allows only shuttle buses from March 1 to November 30 (no private vehicle traffic) and sees little traffic during the winter months.

STARTING POINTS: Grand Canyon Village. If you have to park a vehicle, try the park headquarters lot east of Yavapai Point. From there, you can travel either the road, which has a narrow shoulder, or the paved Greenway for 1 mile to reach Hermit Road at the Bright Angel Trailhead, located at the end of a string of buildings including the Bright Angel Lodge.

Every viewpoint is different along the Hermit Road.

During the spring and fall, this route is one of the best in northern Arizona. With only occasional shuttle bus traffic, you have the road to yourself. But be warned: The shuttle bus drivers run the gamut from courteous with a wave and a smile to passive aggressive. The park service warns that the "shuttles and tour buses have limited sight and maneuverability."

As you can imagine, this route offers some of the state's best scenery. The road is a fun one, with a handful of minor rollers and a border of piñon-juniper forest overloaded with deer. Hot ranger tip: If you head out in the early morning in September, you might hear elk bugling.

All of the five viewpoints have different panoramas, and all are worth gawking moments. Hermits Rest has washrooms and a variety of beverages from coin-operated machines.

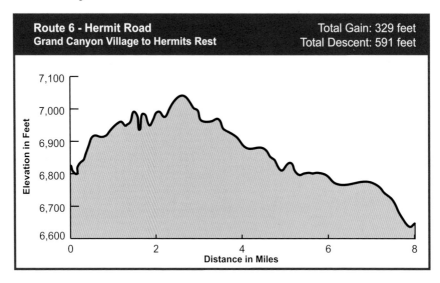

Route 6 - Hermit Road
Grand Canyon Village to Hermits Rest
Total Gain: 329 feet
Total Descent: 591 feet

Route 7

AZ 64 EAST
GRAND CANYON VILLAGE TO CAMERON

Moderate • Intermediate to Experienced

* Travels through several landscapes, from the Grand Canyon to the Painted Desert
* Long downhill screamers
* Two lanes; no shoulder to medium shoulder

DISTANCE: 54 miles one-way

PEAK CYCLING: March–October

ACCOMMODATIONS: Supplies, restaurants, and lodging in Grand Canyon and Cameron

SPECIAL CONSIDERATIONS: If you haven't mastered l-o-n-g downhill screamers, practice before you start this route. A segment of the route travels the Navajo Nation. If you have a hybrid bike and get intrigued by the side roads, you will need a permit to travel off the pavement. The National Park Service charges a fee to enter Grand Canyon National Park: $20 per car or $10 for individuals on bicycles.

STARTING POINT: From Grand Canyon Village, head east on Desert View Drive (AZ 64); the first mile marker is MP 241.

This route takes you from the cool high country of mixed conifers along the rim of the Grand Canyon to the high-desert floor of the Painted Desert. In between, you travel one scenic screamer you might consider an all-around best in Arizona. If the scenery and downhill zooms are not enough, the Cameron Trading Post serves one of the best Navajo tacos on the Rez.

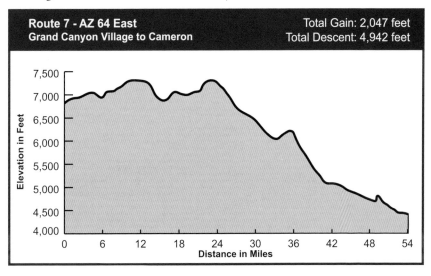

Route 7 - AZ 64 East
Grand Canyon Village to Cameron
Total Gain: 2,047 feet
Total Descent: 4,942 feet

During the first half of the route, you pass several viewpoints of the Grand Canyon. A handful of casual rollers carries you through the first 10 miles. Relatively new pavement starting around MP 251 and a mixed conifer forest give the route a sumptuous feeling.

Your first major descent comes at about MP 255, which drops you into a piñon-juniper forest. Then the rollers get more serious, transitioning into long, steep hills until the grand descent at MP 265—a nearly constant downhill run for about the next 20 miles. Here's where the stunning scenery starts, too. Within a couple miles you can see Mount Humphreys and Bill Williams Mountain. At MP 277, a mile after entering the Navajo Nation, the rough-hewn Little Colorado River Gorge adds high drama.

The highway snakes down to the Painted Desert in the Navajo Nation.

By MP 288, the route lands on the high-desert floor among some deep, ruddy hills. A web of high-tension wires at MP 293 brings a bit of civilization to the route, though you really are in the middle of nowhere. At US 89, just past MP 295, turn left and cycle 1 mile to Cameron for that Navajo taco.

MONSOON SEASON

In Arizona, the monsoon season refers to the time of year when seasonal wind shifts draw moist air from the Gulf of Mexico. An ancient Indian proverb says, "The rains will start a week after the locusts sing at night." Meteorologists say the monsoon season starts when daily dew-point temperatures reach 55 degrees, generally around July 7. The season usually ends sometime around September 13.

Monsoon season isn't nearly as severe in Arizona as it is at Acapulco, at the heart of the Mexican monsoon, where 51 inches of rain falls from June to October. Arizona, lying on the northern fringe, weighs in with a couple inches during this season, a quarter of its annual precipitation, most of which falls during the winter. Nonetheless, if you're out on the road during monsoon season, prepare to take a break when the storm activity strikes: early to midafternoon in the high country and late afternoon to early evening in the deserts.

Route 8

AZ 64 NORTH
WILLIAMS TO GRAND CANYON VILLAGE

Moderate • Experienced

- Travels through open country with far-reaching views to the Grand Canyon
- Colorful spreads of wildflowers in May after a wet winter and during the monsoons in August and September
- Turnaround point in Valle for shorter route
- Two lanes; wide shoulder

DISTANCE: 18 miles (to Valle) to 58 miles one-way

PEAK CYCLING: March–October

ACCOMMODATIONS: Supplies, restaurants, and lodging in Williams, Tusayan, and Grand Canyon National Park. Check out the Grand Hotel in Tusayan (928-638-3333).

SPECIAL CONSIDERATIONS: An alternate route to Grand Canyon from the south is US 180 (see Route 12, p. 39). The National Park Service charges a fee to enter Grand Canyon National Park: $20 per car or $10 for individuals on bicycles.

STARTING POINT: From downtown Williams, head east on Old Route 66 for about 2 miles, and turn left (north) onto AZ 64; the first mile marker is MP 187.

There are two southern approaches to Grand Canyon: US 180 out of Flagstaff is more scenic; this one, with a constant wide shoulder and no blind curves, is safer. We recommend this northward route, especially if you are not traveling in a group.

The route starts out in ponderosa pine country, passing loose-knit forests clustered between long-stretching prairies. During August and September, carpets of wildflowers spread in the low-lying meadows. Development has started to appear in spots along this route, and if you need a quick pit stop there's a gas station between MPs 194 and 195.

By MP 196, the ponderosa pines have transitioned into a piñon-juniper forest. Rollers, which started out nice and comfortable, will start to make you work up steeper and longer ascents. Red Mountain appears to the east around MP 203, and within a couple more miles the rollers calm down and you drop into grasslands.

The route enters the tiny community of Valle between MPs 213 and 214. Totally touristy, this town has some curious shops. One, Flintstone's Bedrock City, is the most notorious. The theme attraction memorializes Fred Flintstone and the gang. If anything, Valle makes a lively pit stop. It also makes a good

End-of-summer flowers spread all along the high country AZ 64 travels.

turnaround point for a shorter ride, or a turning point toward Flagstaff via US 180 (see Route 12, page 39).

Continuing north on AZ 64, the route stays in relatively flat grasslands until about MP 226, when arduous rollers take the road back into a piñon-juniper forest. By now, you are in Kaibab National Forest, and if you are looking for a primitive campsite you might spot one in the next few miles before you get to Tusayan, another tourist town morphing into a residential development. Within another few miles, you reach the entrance to Grand Canyon National Park at MP 238. Mather Point, the first, and incredibly majestic, viewpoint of the canyon appears at MP 240 and the end of this route.

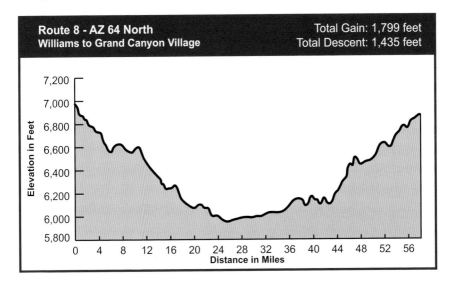

Route 8 - AZ 64 North
Williams to Grand Canyon Village
Total Gain: 1,799 feet
Total Descent: 1,435 feet

Route 9

PERKINSVILLE ROAD
WILLIAMS TO END OF PAVEMENT

Moderate to Difficult • Experienced

* Travels from pine meadows into conifer forests and down to the high desert
* A hybrid bicycle can finish the road and/or explore unpaved side roads
* Two-lane; narrow shoulder

DISTANCE: 11 to 24 miles one-way

PEAK CYCLING: April–October

ACCOMMODATIONS: Supplies, restaurants, and lodging in Williams

SPECIAL CONSIDERATIONS: The last few miles are a steep downhill scream on an old, little-used road. Stay focused to avoid mishaps on chewed-up parts of the road.

STARTING POINT: From Old Route 66 in Williams, go to 4th Street and turn south. This becomes Perkinsville Road; MP 185 is the first mile marker.

This route turns from a pleasant high-country ride to a downhill ripper that lands you in a remote spot in the high desert. It starts on 4th Street and Old Route 66 in Williams, near the bicycle-friendly Java Cycle Coffee House.

As one of the last of the Mother Road's towns bypassed by I-40, Williams has kept one hand on its mountain-man historic roots while entertaining luxury-home living surrounded by national forest. A cozy feel oozes from the

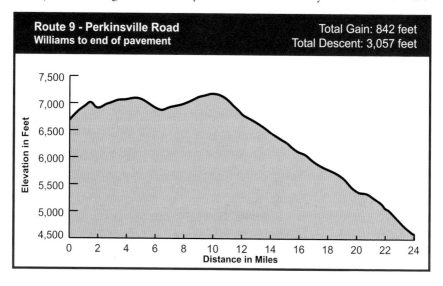

Route 9 - Perkinsville Road
Williams to end of pavement
Total Gain: 842 feet
Total Descent: 3,057 feet

main drag, which has a lineup of classic hotels and restaurants that serve home-cooked meals.

Heading south on 4th Street, it doesn't take long to hit the outskirts of this small mountain town. In less than 1 mile, you pass a canyoned area next to a reservoir and Santa Fe Dam. In the fall, the trees—pine, aspen, and oak—and climbing foliage of Virginia creeper produce great colors. By MP 183, you get into the more typical land-scape of loose-knit ponderosa forest sur-rounding grassy meadows. Your last brush with civilization might occur at the Happy Trails General Store between MPs 181 and 182. At the time of this writing, the store comprised a roadside table dis-playing items handmade by a trio of sib-lings. By publication, they said, they planned to have a real store.

The route definitely turns country when it loses its shoulder and fog line a few miles out of town, but it gains tons of scenery. You can see Bill Williams Mountain, for which the town of Williams was named, rising in the north around MP 179. Bill Williams was one of the most colorful mountain men in the state. The rowdy redhead had a daring nature, an

Perkinsville Road drops into the high desert after rolling through aspen country.

endless well of energy, and a list of eccentric behaviors, from the way he fired his rifle with a wobble to his riding style of wearing his stirrups so short his knees practically grazed his chin. His drunken sprees were legendary.

The road gets as rowdy as Old Bill with crumbly edges and potholes big enough to do some damage if you're not looking. Occasional traffic here consists mainly of recreational vehicles heading to lakes and favorite primitive campsites.

Rollers start at MP 177 and begin to lift you into aspen country. You finally top out around MP 174; panoramic views display the area's volcanic history as you start to make your descent into the high desert. The ascent back up to this forest can be daunting for cyclists less experienced with climbing; if you fit in that group, make your turning point here.

It only takes a few miles to drop into a piñon-juniper forest. This part of the road gets even less traffic than the high-country segment. Vegetation has encroached into the roadside cracks around MP 169. Be careful here: You've got some downhill stretches and plenty of curves coming up that demand your attention.

The deep canyon on the east side of the road at MP 164 is Bear Canyon. Don't dwell too long on the canyon's beauty because a half mile away the road drops like a shot and gets you up to some high speeds. At MP 162, signs give a 1-mile warning of the pavement's end. If you don't have a shuttle waiting at the bottom, take a few moments to gear up for the climb out and return the way you came.

Route 10

US 89
FLAGSTAFF TO PAGE

Moderate to Experienced

• Travels through a variety of life zones and geology
• Direct route to northern Arizona
• Two to four lanes; medium shoulder (none at passing lanes)

DISTANCE: 44 miles to Gray Mountain; 52 miles to Cameron; 68 miles to US 160; 111 miles to Bitter Springs; and 136 miles to Page

PEAK CYCLING: April–October

ACCOMMODATIONS: Supplies, restaurants, and lodging in Flagstaff, Cameron, Gray Mountain, and Page. Check out Lulu's Sleep Ezze Motel in Page (105 8th Ave., 928-608-0273) for a clean room with basic but nice appointments and loads of hospitality at a bargain price.

SPECIAL CONSIDERATIONS: The only direct road to northern Arizona from Flagstaff, this is a fast and high-traffic highway. The road loses the shoulder during passing lanes. The segment between Bitter Springs and Page presents a challenging grade with a very real element of danger from recreational vehicles and trucks. This route is for moderate to intermediate riders between Flagstaff and Sunset Crater National Monument, and for experienced riders on all other portions of the route.

STARTING POINT: From Flagstaff, head north on Business 40 to US 89.

Though this route passes through some interesting landscape and topography, we don't recommend it highly for a pleasure ride, except for the segment between Flagstaff and Sunset Crater National Monument. The route doesn't always present a shoulder, traffic is heavy, and the accident rate is relatively high. Nevertheless, because this highway is the only direct route northward from Flagstaff, we add it for your information.

The first 13 miles from the northern edge of Flagstaff take you through cool, quiet ponderosa forestland. By the turnoff for Sunset Crater National

Monument (MP 430), the San Francisco Lava Field becomes apparent, with cinder hills and lava rocks and boulders. Get ready for a long, fast descent onto the Painted Desert—a high-desert biome full of ruddy earth tones. You get a brief taste of civilization at Gray Mountain (MP 457), and then the route quickly heads

US 89 is the only direct highway between Flagstaff and northern Arizona.

back onto the open road across some lonely and remote country. At Cameron, a popular stopping-off point for travelers on this road between MPs 466 and 467, the route enters an extremely scenic segment. Before heading on, however, take a moment to check out the trading post and restaurant.

As soon as you cross the bridge over the Little Colorado River Gorge, the scenery switches from the ruddy Moenkopi Formation to the elegant but curious Chinle Formation. Typical to the Painted Desert, this formation colors the land with gray, lavender, green, and blue hills. While the Moenkopi Formation contains fossil amphibian skeletons and casts of ancient reptile feet, the Chinle caches fossil trees, petrified wood, and dozens of species of ferns and other plants, as well as dinosaur skeletons. Keep in mind you can't travel the Navajo Nation without a permit or Navajo escort. If you want to

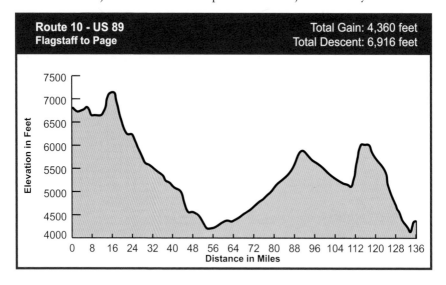

Route 10 - US 89
Flagstaff to Page

Total Gain: 4,360 feet
Total Descent: 6,916 feet

explore the Chinle formation, wait until you hit BLM lands at Vermilion Cliffs or southern Utah.

The route passes US 160, which leads to Tuba City, between MPs 480 and 481. Soon afterward, the most dramatic landscape on this route rises in the east as the Echo Cliffs start around MP 488. The cliffs will accompany you (now on your left), past the turnoff for US 89A at Bitter Springs and all the way into Page.

Though the segment between Bitter Springs and Page is highly dramatic and gives a hyper-thrilling run for southbound cyclists past gorgeous cliffs, it is a dangerous place. No shoulder, steep grades, blind hairpin curves, and lots of RVs make it one of the riskiest rides in the state, a segment where cyclists have lost their lives.

Route 11

SUNSET CRATER LOOP
SUNSET CRATER AND WUPATKI NATIONAL MONUMENTS

Moderate • Intermediate

* Travels through two national monuments—one in the San Francisco Volcanic Field and the other in the Painted Desert
* Passes several Indian ruins
* Two lanes; medium shoulders

DISTANCE: 36 miles one-way or 46-mile loop

PEAK CYCLING: April–October

ACCOMMODATIONS: Supplies, restaurants, and lodging in Flagstaff. Check out Hotel Monte Vista (100 N. San Francisco St., 928-779-6971) for a spirited time. Resident ghosts sometimes show up in the hotel lounge and rooms.

SPECIAL CONSIDERATIONS: The National Park Service charges $5 for up to seven days' visit.

STARTING POINTS: About 13 miles north of Flagstaff on US 89, at the signed turnoff for Sunset Crater, or 23 miles north on US 89 at the signed turnoff for Wupatki.

Sunset Crater

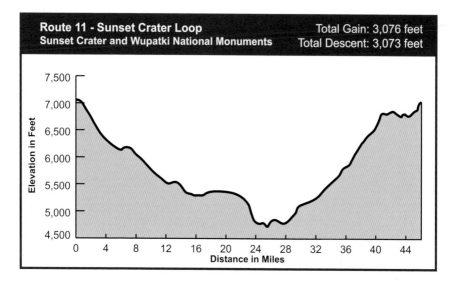

Route 11 - Sunset Crater Loop
Sunset Crater and Wupatki National Monuments

Total Gain: 3,076 feet
Total Descent: 3,073 feet

When nationally recognized bicycle expert and Tucsonan Richard Corbett first planned the Great Arizona Biking Adventure (GABA), which travels from the Grand Canyon to Tucson (hosted by the Tucson chapter of GABA), he discovered the Sunset Crater Loop. It ended up being his favorite route in the state.

"The route has incredible 50-mile vistas, and it's an important part of history," Richard says. "More importantly, it's just a fun route."

The route starts at a parking area just outside Sunset Crater National Monument, travels through the lava flow produced by Sunset Crater, and descends to the Painted Desert past a number of Indian ruins in Wupatki National Monument. Along the way, it passes right by the San Francisco Volcanic Field's youngest volcano, Sunset Crater. The 1,000-foot-high crater, with its distinctive ruddy-cinder top, shows itself early in the route, rising in the distance from Bonito Park; in August, this park fills with sunflowers and skyrocket.

The route heads right for the Bonito Lava Flow, located a few miles from the entrance gate at around MP 30. After passing Sunset Crater, the route starts a series of downhills, gliding past a cindered landscape laced with enchantment. Here's where the vistas and fun come in. The surrounding landscape looks untouched from the time of its formation: Cinder hillsides slope casually like swells of the sea, their ruddy brown or jet-black colors contrasting austerely with gaunt stands of ponderosa or dots of wildflowers.

The salmon strand of Painted Desert glows across the horizon at about MP 26, and the route takes a screaming plunge into a piñon-juniper forest. The route drops 2,200 feet and the forest opens into a sea of sage pouring into the Painted Desert. By MP 22, the downhill levels to a coast with a few residual rollers, and the black cinders of the volcanic field start to meld with the Painted Desert's red sand.

At first blush, the windswept landscape lacks any noticeable relics from humanity. Basalt mesas, formed from older volcanic eruptions, rise from the ruddy Moenkopi sandstone formation. The forces of erosion have crumbled these mesa tops into broken slabs. But some mesas have exquisitely mortared pueblos still standing upon them. After piecing together information from tree-ring data gathered at Sunset Crater and Wupatki, scientists concluded that Sinagua Indians left the Sunset Crater area when the volcano erupted, then returned with several other Indian cultures to settle the Wupatki area. The Indians finally deserted the Wupatki area after 200 years with no trace as to where or why they fled.

The first ruin in the area, Wupatki Ruin, and the monument's visitor center lie at MP 14. The route's interlude of pleasant grades ends at MP 11 with an austere climb up Doney Mountain. The grade relents by MP 9 and even levels out for a couple of miles.

After Citadel Ruin, right next to the road between MPs 5 and 4, a couple of climbs take you out of the monument to US 89. If you don't have a shuttle planned, you may return the way you came or turn south (left) and climb 14 miles back up the four- to six-lane highway (with shoulders) to the Sunset Crater turnoff around MP 430.

LIGHT UP LIKE A CHRISTMAS TREE

Arizona state law (ARS 28-817, Bicycle Equipment) states: "A bicycle that is used at nighttime shall have a lamp on the front that emits a white light visible from a distance of at least five hundred feet to the front and a red reflector on the rear of a type that is approved by the department and that is visible from all distances from fifty feet to three hundred feet to the rear."

Eric Prosnier, who commutes 25 miles one-way to his job with Arizona Department of Transportation, says cyclists should "light up like a Christmas tree" whenever they ride at night. Eric wears reflective material wherever he can on his body, a flashing-red rear light, and a powerful light on the front of his Eddy Merckx bicycle. Even if you don't plan to ride at night, outfitting your bike for a night ride will safely get you where you want to go in the event you ever find yourself in the dark.

Route 12

SAN FRANCISCO PEAKS SCENIC ROAD
US 180: FLAGSTAFF TO VALLE

Moderate • Experienced

* Travels a forested route with mountain panoramas
* Scenic cycling route to the Grand Canyon
* Two lanes; no shoulder

DISTANCE: 51 miles one-way

PEAK CYCLING: March–October

ACCOMMODATIONS: Supplies, restaurants, and lodging in Flagstaff. Check out the Starlight Pines Bed and Breakfast (928-527-1912 or 1-800-752-1912, 3380 E. Lockett Rd.) in Flagstaff. It is correctly described as "Victorian-style with an edge" by friendly innkeepers Richard and Michael.

SPECIAL CONSIDERATIONS: This road sees heavy traffic in the summer.

STARTING POINT: From Santa Fe Avenue and Humphreys Street (US 180) in Flagstaff, go north on Humphreys Street, following signs to the Snowbowl turnoff; MP 223 is the first mile marker.

Hands down, this is the most scenic of the southern routes to the Grand Canyon. It travels snaking rollers with beautiful panoramas. Two lanes and little to no shoulder make it a bit treacherous during summer, when recreational vehicles sway and impatient drivers carelessly pass. However, if you cycle this route in the early hours of morning, you'll feel like you're the only one on the road. Watch for elk!

The route starts climbing past the Snow Bowl Road into loose-knit ponderosa forests that slowly gather groves of aspen. Rollers just intensify the scenic quality of the route. Watch

US 180 twists between aspen-fir forests and open meadows.

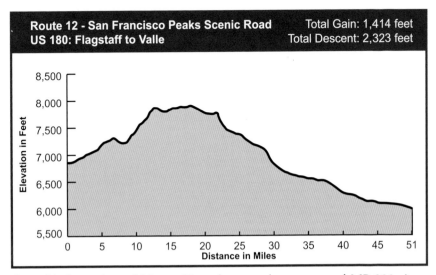

Route 12 - San Francisco Peaks Scenic Road
US 180: Flagstaff to Valle

Total Gain: 1,414 feet
Total Descent: 2,323 feet

for a fabulous view of Mount Humphreys to the east around MP 233. A few miles later you might catch a glimpse of some elk in Kendrick Meadow on the west. On the other side of the highway is the Chapel of the Holy Dove. This makes a good turnaround point for a shorter ride.

From the meadow, the route starts its drop into the high desert, slowly at first and then the downhill gets more intense, and you drop from the lofty aspens into a pygmy piñon-juniper forest in no time. Look for distinctive Red Mountain to the west at MP 247. By MP 255, the scenic-highway status ends, and you have no trouble figuring out why as the road gets a little rough, with tar sealing old cracks and a landscape of flatlands, red sand, and sparse trees. Nonetheless, the high desert keeps its appealing atmosphere.

The community of Valle shows up at MP 260. Containing everything for the tourist, Valle has curio shops, quirky camping, and campy eateries. Buy at your own risk.

From Valle, you may return the way you came or follow Route 8 (see p. 30) south on AZ 64 to Williams or north to Grand Canyon.

Route 13

SNOW BOWL ROAD
US 180 TO ARIZONA SNOWBOWL

Difficult • Experienced

♦ A nonstop climb up Arizona's highest peak

♦ Two lanes; no shoulder

DISTANCE: 7.5 miles one-way

PEAK CYCLING: May–October

ACCOMMODATIONS: Supplies, restaurants, and lodging in Flagstaff. You can start your ride directly from the England House Bed and Breakfast (928-214-7350 or 817-214-7350, 614 W. Santa Fe Ave.), an exquisitely-crafted stone house with cool antiques and art

SPECIAL CONSIDERATIONS: Watch for patches of black ice during springtime. Locals suggest practicing on Mars Hill, the mile-long road up to Lowell Observatory (located at the end of West Santa Fe Avenue), before tackling this route.

STARTING POINT: About 7 miles north of Flagstaff on US 180.

No one said it would be easy," Jim Koubeck says of riding up Mount Humphreys, his favorite training route, "but it sure is pretty." Jim rides with his friend, Tom Lamica, who races. While Tom trains to race, Jim rides for his sanity, explaining that "it oxygenates the brain and heart."

The average time to cycle the route ranges from 35 to 50 minutes. Top riders will finish in less than 30 minutes.

The road starts on the uphill and never stops until you reach the parking areas for two popular hiking routes, one that contours the south face of Mount Humphreys and the other that climbs to the top of the 12,633-foot mountain. Since these trails lie in the Kachina Peaks Wilderness, bicycles are not allowed.

Snow Bowl Road travels from a mixed conifer forest into an alpine meadow.

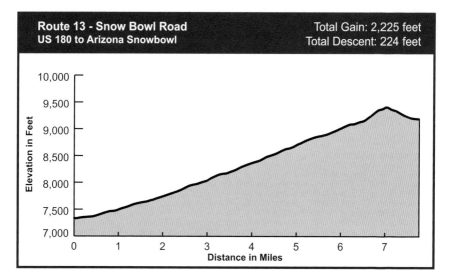

As the road makes its ascent up the mountain, the forest vegetation transitions quickly from young ponderosa pines into mixed conifers by mile 2. In another 0.5 mile, the route starts its hardest segment. At mile 4, double S-turns have you winding through thick aspen forests. The forest turns gold with autumn color from the end of September through the first week of October. At this point, the temperature has dropped several degrees since the route's start. For every 1,000 feet, the temperature drops about 5 degrees, and by the time you finish the air temp will measure about 20 degrees lower than when you started.

Subalpine meadows start appearing at mile 5.3. Watch out for cinders scattered onto the route at the cinder-surfaced pullouts around the meadows. (The city of Flagstaff uses cinders for road material and for spreading on ice instead of salt.) Black ice, a thin sheet of ice on the roadway that you can't see until you're right on it, sometimes forms on this route, especially during April and May as snowmelt or rain freezes during the night.

At the end of the route, you get a good look at the heart of the San Francisco Volcanic Field across the meadow spreading before Mount Humphreys. The San Francisco Volcanic Field, with the San Francisco Peaks in its heart, harbors over 600 volcanoes, most of them cones that rise in flat grasslands. Before you head back down to the "flatlands," stop at the clearing overlooking the landscape spreading to the west to see some of the lesser volcanoes in the area.

Route 14

MORMON LAKE LOOP
MORMON LAKE ROAD AND LAKE MARY ROAD

Moderate • Beginner

- ◆ Travels around northern Arizona's largest natural lake
- ◆ Major hangout for elk (which bugle in the fall), bald eagles in the winter,
  and bikers in the summer
- ◆ Two lanes; narrow shoulder

DISTANCE: 15-mile loop or 7 miles one-way to Mormon Lake

PEAK CYCLING: May–October

ACCOMMODATIONS: Supplies, restaurants, and lodging in Flagstaff and Mormon Lake. Mormon Lake Lodge (928-354-2227) has cabins, and its restaurant serves steaks that are so good people travel miles to savor one. The bar can get pretty rowdy when cowboys gather from around the Southwest for rodeos and other contests.

SPECIAL CONSIDERATIONS: Bring rain gear for summer thunderstorms.

STARTING POINTS: From Flagstaff, drive 20 miles south on Lake Mary Road to MP 323, and turn right (west) onto Mormon Lake Road; or drive 8 miles farther on Mormon Lake Road to Mormon Lake village.

Cyclists usually make a day out of this loop, starting from Flagstaff or just on its outskirts, where a bike lane begins on Lake Mary Road (see Route 15, p. 45). Beginners and families can whittle down the route to follow this version—which rings Mormon Lake—and still get a taste of the beautiful meadows and lakes in the area.

In the town of Mormon Lake (population 50 to 5,000, depending on the time of year), you can find food, beverages, and lodging along the one-block downtown area. During the summer, the town bustles with campers, equestrians, fishermen, hikers, cyclists, and bikers.

The epitome of Mormon Lake: a cabin, snow-topped Mount Humphreys, and a well-pooled Mormon Lake.

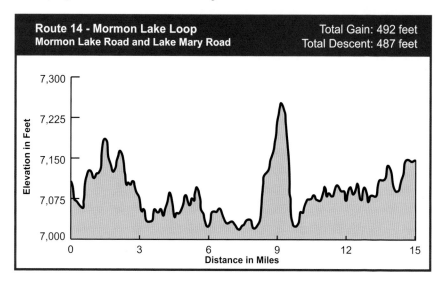

Route 14 - Mormon Lake Loop
Mormon Lake Road and Lake Mary Road
Total Gain: 492 feet
Total Descent: 487 feet

If you start right in Mormon Lake Village, you get a choice of how long you want to ride: Heading north you will travel 8 miles to Lake Mary Road; south will bring you in 2 miles to the highway; a loop around the lake totals 15 miles. This route starts at the lodge and heads north.

The road along the lake presents shallow rollers and forests. One large meadow practically swallows you into insignificance. After a spate of wet weather or a particularly wet and snowy winter, these areas come alive with birdlife lured by pooled groundwater. Around 235 species of birds have appeared at Mormon Lake and its surrounding lakes—this amounts to 45 percent of all bird species seen in Arizona. Spring and fall migrations present the best birding, but more than 100 species breed in the area.

Mormon Lake is also known for its wintering eagles, as 30 to more than 100 eagles each year come here from points north as far as Alaska. The raptors start arriving in November and will stay as late as April.

When the route reaches Lake Mary Road, turn south (right). Within 1 mile, near MP 322, watch for the Douglas Morrison Overlook on the right. This great pullout gives a panoramic view of Mormon Lake with Mount Humphreys rising in the background. Back on Lake Mary Road, it's another 5 miles to the southern access to Mormon Lake Road, near MP 318. Turn right onto Mormon Lake Road, then cycle 2 miles back to Mormon Lake.

Route 15

LAKE MARY ROAD
FLAGSTAFF TO CLINTS WELL

Moderate • Intermediate

- Travels along a chain of meadow lakes surrounded by forests
- Two lanes; bike lane from MP 338 to Mormon Lake

DISTANCE: 15 miles one-way from Canyon Vista Campground (where bike lane starts) to Mormon Lake; 21 miles from Flagstaff to Mormon Lake; or 55 miles from Flagstaff to Clints Well

PEAK CYCLING: May–October

ACCOMMODATIONS: Supplies, restaurants, and lodging in Flagstaff, and supplies in Clints Well. Check out Montezuma Lodge (928-354-2200), about 4 miles off the highway on Mormon Lake Road, to rent a retro cottage.

SPECIAL CONSIDERATIONS: Bring rain gear for summer thunderstorms.

STARTING POINTS: (1) In the town of Flagstaff, head south on South Milton Road and turn right (west) onto Forest Meadows Street, and then left (south) onto South Beulah Boulevard, drive a few blocks, and turn left (east) onto Lake Mary Road; or (2) continue on Lake Mary Road for 6 miles and park at Canyon Vista Campground, where the bike lane begins.

Once you are traveling along the bike lane, the route heads, uninterrupted, to the Promised Land for which the Mormons searched when they came to this area from the Arizona Strip in the 1870s. The Mormons correctly called the area Pleasant Valley and raised cattle here. The lakes did not appear until the 20th century, when underground channels filled with sediment and groundwater collected in the valley.

The combination of green, sprawling meadows separated by

Cyclists along Lake Mary Road.

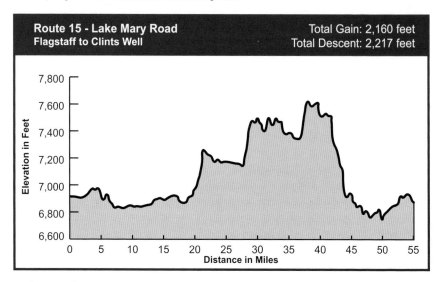

Route 15 - Lake Mary Road
Flagstaff to Clints Well

Total Gain: 2,160 feet
Total Descent: 2,217 feet

colonies of ponderosa pines, blue lakes, and colorful carpets of wildflowers still creates a pleasant and soothing atmosphere. The continuous wave of rollers adds to the perfection.

After you pass the scenic spread of Upper and Lower Lake Mary, the Mormon Lake Road turnoff comes up at around MP 323. If you plan to tour Mormon Lake, turn right (west) where a sign reads "Mormon Lake Village"; otherwise, continue south on Lake Mary Road.

The Douglas Morrison Overlook near MP 322 makes a good observation deck to view the lake's visiting bald eagles in winter. Mormon Lake has the largest number of wintering bald eagles in the Southwest.

From Mormon Lake, you start a 29-mile roller-filled ride through ponderosa forestland interspersed with meadows where wildlife is rife. Uninterrupted by residential or business traffic, the route trends downward with fun glides from Happy Jack (MP 305) to route's end at Clints Well.

A mini-mart/gas station at Clints Well (a spot on the map rather than a real town) is busy most of the year with hikers, hunters, bikers, and fishermen. You can pick up some quick carbs there, then return the way you came.

Ride in the Beauty !...
Page, Arizona

REGION 2

THE NAVAJO NATION

I n the Navajo Nation, you're cycling one of the most charismatic landscapes in the state, if not the country. The Navajo Nation takes you into another world. Its inhabitants call this high-desert country, stretched between four sacred mountains in three states (Arizona, Colorado, and New Mexico), "the Glittering World." This region stretches from Page eastward to the New Mexico border. On the south end, it curls just south of Cameron around the Coconino National Forest east of Flagstaff. It's a red-rock wonderland of open space, shifting sands, magnificent buttes and mesas, and legends wonderful enough to celebrate humanity and dark enough to raise the hair on the back of your neck. Those who live on the Navajo Nation say these legends are all true. Once you cycle here, you'll have a chance to decide for yourself.

As the route nears Kaibito, the landscape fills with lucid sandstone formations

ROUTES

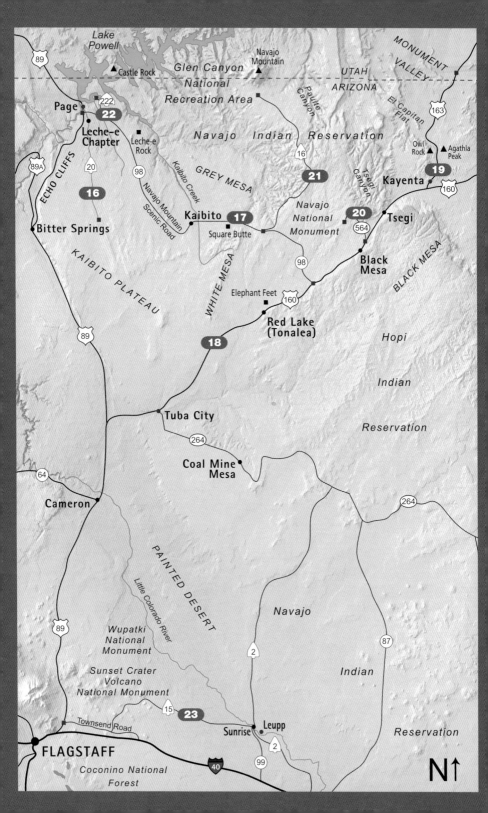

Route 16

COPPERMINE ROAD
NAVAJO ROUTE 20: PAGE TO END OF PAVEMENT

Moderate • Beginner

◆ Travels through a scenic and remote area of the Navajo Nation

◆ Excellent road with fun rollers

◆ Two lanes; no shoulder

DISTANCE: 14.5 miles one-way

PEAK CYCLING: March–May; September–November

ACCOMMODATIONS: Supplies, restaurants, and lodging in Page. Check out Fiesta
Mexicana Family Restaurant (125 S. Powell Blvd., 928-645-4082) for the perfect
post-ride dinner and margaritas. If you like hot dogs, you haven't lived until you've
had a Rez Dog (a hot dog wrapped and fried in fry bread). Get them at Leche-e
Flea Market on weekends.

SPECIAL CONSIDERATIONS: This road travels isolated land. Be sure you are well-equipped.
Road gets little use after Leche-e Chapter House.

STARTING POINTS: (1) Start right in town, at Lake Powell Boulevard and Coppermine
Road; or (2) follow Haul Road 1.5 miles east from US 89 to Coppermine Road; or (3)
start at intersection of AZ 98 and Navajo 20 (Coppermine Road). MP 1 is the first mile
marker.

You don't have to travel far from Page to get out in the "middle of
nowhere." This road, which travels down to the chapter house in Leche-e
(pronounced Le-**chee**-ee) and several
miles beyond, will take you right to
"remote." Add some enchanting
scenery and lots of fun rollers even
beginners can handle, and you have
one excellent ride.

Jerry Kocjan, who has cycled the
roads and trails of Page for the last
20 years, says the Page area is "one of
the best-kept secrets waiting to be
revealed." The hills around Page, especially on this route, helped Jerry train
several times for El Tour de Tucson,
the country's largest cycling event.

*Coppermine Road heads into Navajo sandstone
swells and cliffs.*

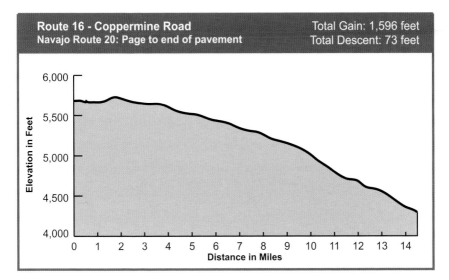

Route 16 - Coppermine Road
Navajo Route 20: Page to end of pavement
Total Gain: 1,596 feet
Total Descent: 73 feet

You can't go any distance from Page without encountering some climbs, nor can you get very far without a drop-dead panorama of the surrounding landscape and its trademark landmarks, such as Gunsight and Padre buttes, Castle Rock, Navajo Mountain, Marble Canyon, Vermilion Cliffs, or beloved Lake Powell. All these vistas appear during your return trip on this route.

Starting on Navajo 20 (Coppermine Road), the route climbs for almost 2 miles. Watch for an exceptional chasm near the top of the climb, then have fun on the 2-mile downhill. You'll pass the Leche-e Chapter House along the way. After that, you have little traffic and lots of open space. Sand dunes, mesas, and the distant Vermilion Cliffs create interesting scenes.

The 2-mile-long rollers repeat themselves until about mile 10, then it's one big downhill to the pavement's end, just past MP 14 near a ridge of white Navajo sandstone full of hoodoos, alcoves, and crossbedding in a sea of sagebrush. The ride back, starting once again on an uphill, looks upon the landmarks of Page and Lake Powell around MP 9. From there it's an easy pull back into town.

Route 17

NAVAJO MOUNTAIN SCENIC ROAD
AZ 98: US 89 TO US 160

Moderate • Experienced

* Travels along unusual red-rock formations in the Navajo Nation
* A designated scenic drive
* Two lanes; wide shoulder

DISTANCE: 36 miles to Kaibito; 42 miles to Square Buttes;
   66 miles to end of route at US 160

PEAK CYCLING: March–May; September–November

ACCOMMODATIONS: Supplies, restaurants, and lodging in Page; basic supplies in Kaibito.
   The trading post in Kaibito has fried chicken.

SPECIAL CONSIDERATIONS: This highway gets widely traveled; shuttle support recommended for cyclists planning the whole route; no supplies available after Kaibito.

STARTING POINT: From US 89, head east on AZ 98; or, from Lake Powell Boulevard in
   Page, head south on Coppermine Road for about 1 mile to AZ 98.

This route keeps wowing you from its start with extraordinary scenery. After passing Antelope Canyon and Navajo Generating Station just beyond MP 300, you're on your own with no sign of civilization until the town of Kaibito. Blankets of blackbrush darken the high-desert floor that stretches to landmark Leche-e Rock. Sand dunes ripple in other areas. By MP 310, you get a momentary break from the long-pulling rollers that ultimately carry

Scenery starts from the first mile on the road to Kaibito.

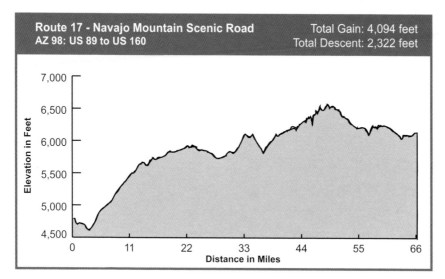

Route 17 - Navajo Mountain Scenic Road
AZ 98: US 89 to US 160

Total Gain: 4,094 feet
Total Descent: 2,322 feet

you to higher country. By MP 321, the route has risen into piñon-juniper country and begins passing some spectacular and odd rock formations along the Kaibito Plateau. The turnoff for the town of Kaibito is at MP 331; if you need food or beverages, turn at the signed road to the Kaibito Market—your last chance for any provisions, including fried chicken.

As you continue along the route, White Mesa on the south runs along the horizon as a pale sandstone wall with jutting turrets, pinnacles, and extravagant formations. At MP 340, look for Square Butte. A wonderland of sandstone then dips down into the Kaibito Creek drainage, where the scenery only gets more beautiful. This makes a good turnaround point for cyclists without shuttle support.

After a few major climbs and dips, and a major curve southward, the route ends at US 160. Straight ahead, you can see Black Mesa, where the Navajo mine coal to power their generation plant just outside of Page. Dził Yíjiin, Navajo for "Mountain Which Appears Black," got its name from the coal beds that appear on the hand-shaped mesa. If you plan to continue east alongside Black Mesa, the next food and lodging is 22 miles away in Tsegi (see Route 18, p. 54).

Route 18

US 160
TUBA CITY TO KAYENTA

Moderate • Experienced

- ◆ Travels past beautiful Navajo sandstone scenery in the Navajo Nation
- ◆ Major east-west route across the Navajo Nation
- ◆ Two lanes; narrow to medium shoulder

DISTANCE: 72 miles one-way

PEAK CYCLING: March–May; September–November

ACCOMMODATIONS: Supplies, restaurants, and lodging in Tuba City, Tsegi, and Kayenta.
    You can pick up basic provisions at trading posts in the small communities along
    the route. If you stay at the Anasazi Inn in Tsegi (928-697-3793), be sure to ask
    for a room in the main building. The restaurant here is a classic all-night diner, a
    Native American version of an Edward Hopper scene.

SPECIAL CONSIDERATIONS: This route has a variety of road conditions and shoulders.
    The route is heavily traveled, and it's best to ride in a group for more visibility.
    The route travels extremely remote segments, so bring a repair kit, food, and
    enough water.

STARTING POINT: From US 89 west of Tuba City, head east on US 160.

This route, one of the only major routes traveling across the Navajo Nation,
sees a large amount of traffic. We don't highly recommend the route, but
it's the only choice if you are cycling across the Navajo Nation. We have

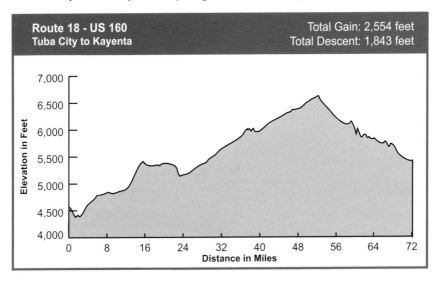

Route 18 - US 160
Tuba City to Kayenta
Total Gain: 2,554 feet
Total Descent: 1,843 feet

only included the segment to Kayenta. Beyond that, there is no lodging and little in the way of restaurants before you reach New Mexico or Utah. This entire route presents plenty of open space and rollers. Some segments have relatively new surfaces; others have bumps and mottled shoulders.

The beginning of the route passes some wonderful formations before you enter Tuba City. There is a motel north of the road, as well as a campground. Watch for the Elephant Feet—two monoliths—around MP 347 in the town of Red Lake. Starting at about MP 373, the route shows off some exquisite scenery. Here the route travels along Black Mesa to the south, heading toward the magnificent Tsegi Canyon system of Navajo sandstone, full of Indian ruins. Keep in mind you cannot travel off the highway in the Navajo Nation without a permit or Navajo escort.

You may notice a railroad line alongside the road. Electric trains ship coal from Kayenta Mine to the Navajo Generating Plant just outside of Page. Near Tsegi, at MP 383, coal from Black Mesa Mine gets powdered and mixed with water before entering the world's longest coal-slurry pipeline; the coal runs 273 miles in three days between Black Mesa Mine and Mohave Generating Station at Laughlin, Nevada.

Between Tsegi and Kayenta, the route travels classic Navajo countryside full of slickrock, sandstone cliffs, and interesting formations. If you're planning to travel past Kayenta to the Four Corners area, US 160 continues 72 miles farther to reach Colorado; or, just before the border, US 64 branches off toward New Mexico. If you have no shuttle, stay the night in Kayenta to safely travel the remaining distance.

US 160 is the access across northern Arizona on the Navajo Nation.

Route 19

MONUMENT VALLEY
AZ 163: Kayenta to Monument Valley

Moderate • Intermediate

◆ Travels along the world-renowned Monument Valley

◆ Two lanes; no shoulder

DISTANCE: 29 miles one-way

PEAK CYCLING: March–May; September–November

ACCOMMODATIONS: Supplies, restaurants, and lodging in Kayenta, Monument Valley
Navajo Tribal Park (campground), and Goulding's in Utah, a short distance from
the park. Goulding's Lodge has excellent Navajo tacos.

SPECIAL CONSIDERATIONS: The route travels extremely remote segments. Bring a
repair kit, food, and enough water. Monument Valley Navajo Tribal Park
charges $5 per person to enter.

STARTING POINT: From US 160 in Kayenta, head north on AZ 163.

As soon as the four-lane road that travels 2 miles through the town of
Kayenta whittles down to two lanes, this route starts displaying the
landscape made famous by Hollywood. And it doesn't stop. The hilltop
around MP 398 gives you a taste of the scenery clustered in Monument
Valley Navajo Tribal Park 25 miles ahead.

The route slips through the gatepost formations of Agathla Peak on the
east and Owl Rock rising on the west, with the Porras Dykes in the eastern

*At the end of summer, wildflowers color the high desert
floor of the Navajo Nation.*

foreground. The road
heads onto Capitan Flat,
and around the bend from
MP 406 you get more
glimpses of Monument
Valley.

Mystery Valley shows
up first, around MP 408.
If you explore this off-the-
beaten-path valley (only
available through special
tour or Navajo escort), you
enter a world of Navajo

RIMS, TUBES, AND TIRES

The main mantra in road biking—lighter means better—often interferes with other considerations, especially regarding rims, tubes, and tires. If you whittle down the weight in any of these components to gain more speed, you open doors to other problems.

For instance, lighter rims get damaged easier. Highway cyclists encounter all kinds of messy road conditions, such as holes, stones, and wide cracks, that can weaken the rim's integrity. Since the lighter the rims the more they cost, replacing one can set you back several hundred dollars. Also, the lighter the rim the fewer spokes it has. Losing a spoke could be disastrous with a lighter rim, but unnoticeable in a heavier one.

Light tires and tubes get punctured more easily. When you're cycling in a state where thorns, spines, and stingers reign in the flora and fauna, punctures happen. The panacea of thornproof tubes adds weight—enough to sway road cyclists away from them. If you're not racing, however, a more rugged tire and thornproof tubes might make sense.

sandstone pocked with arches and cliffs that swirl with crossbedding. You can sign up for a tour at Monument Valley.

You can see the tribal park's trademark Mitten Buttes at MP 416. When you cross the state line into Utah, cycle another 1 mile to reach the turnoff for Monument Valley Navajo Tribal Park. From here, you can turn right and travel 3.5 miles to reach the park; turn left and cycle about 1 mile to reach Goulding's Lodge, where you can get a perfect Navajo taco; or return the way you came.

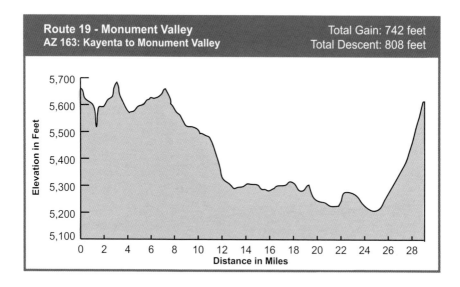

Route 19 - Monument Valley
AZ 163: Kayenta to Monument Valley
Total Gain: 742 feet
Total Descent: 808 feet

Route 20

NAVAJO NATIONAL MONUMENT
AZ 564: US 160 TO NAVAJO NATIONAL MONUMENT

Moderate • Intermediate

* Travels along an extraordinarily scenic canyon system full of Indian ruins
* Two lanes; no shoulder

DISTANCE: 9.5 miles one-way

PEAK CYCLING: March–May; September–November

ACCOMMODATIONS: Supplies, restaurants, and lodging in Tsegi and Kayenta;
campground and picnic area at the monument

SPECIAL CONSIDERATIONS: The route travels remote countryside. Bring a repair kit,
food, and enough water. Entrance to Navajo National Monument is free.

STARTING POINT: From US 160, head north on AZ 564 at MP 375.

Some of the best-preserved Indian ruins lie inside Navajo National Monument. The 8-mile hike to the Keet Seel ruins is a memorable experience. Another alternative for exploring this moody but beautiful country is to cycle the short span of road along Tsegi Canyon. You can get glimpses of the canyon below from viewpoints along the way to the monument.

Slabs of slickrock swirl along this route, and long rollers have you working hard on the uphill and zooming on the descent. By MP 379, a piñon-juniper

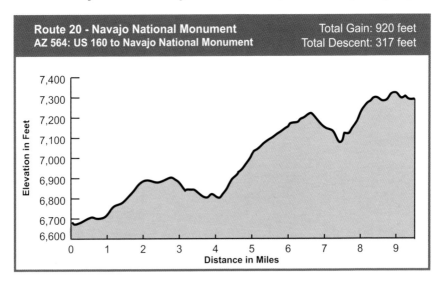

Route 20 - Navajo National Monument
AZ 564: US 160 to Navajo National Monument
Total Gain: 920 feet
Total Descent: 317 feet

Winding through Navajo sandstone, the road to Navajo National Monument makes a scenic ride to a special spot on the reservation.

forest cloisters the road and sage scents the air. In September, you might see Navajos gathering pine nuts from trees alongside the road.

The Tsegi overlook between MPs 383 and 384 gives a stunning view of this tremendous canyon. The route ends at the monument's visitor center—a unique pit stop honoring antiquity!

ROADWAY DEBRIS

One of the biggest downfalls, literally, for cyclists is roadway debris. In Flagstaff it's cinders, the element used by the city instead of salt on snow and ice. Navajo or Hopi nation roads have sand that drifts across their roadways during dust storms. Most other Arizona roads have plain old gravel. Debris often appears at intersections with unpaved backroads. Whatever the scatter encroaching on the path of cycling, it can be treacherous, especially on high-speed turns.

Chris Coolman, a bicycle racer who works at the Bike Barn in Phoenix, advises that when gravel appears on the roadway, cyclists "should stay as straight as possible." The smooth tires on a road bike can't grip like treaded tires. The gravel acts like ball bearings and can cause the cyclist to skid.

"Don't make any sudden movements," Chris adds, "or you'll probably end up on your butt. But if you're flying down a hill and come to a curve, you just kind of pray."

Route 21

NAVAJO MOUNTAIN ROAD
NAVAJO ROUTE 16: AZ 98 TO END OF PAVEMENT

Moderate • Intermediate

◆ Travels along a historic, isolated area of the Navajo Nation

◆ Two lanes; medium shoulder

DISTANCE: 25.5 miles one-way to pavement's end

PEAK CYCLING: April–October

ACCOMMODATIONS: Supplies, restaurants, and lodging in Page; basic supplies at Inscription House

SPECIAL CONSIDERATIONS: This road travels isolated land. Be sure you are well-equipped.

STARTING POINT: From AZ 98, 52 miles southeast of Page or 14 miles northwest of US 160, head north on Navajo Route 16.

Naatsis'áán, the Navajo name for Navajo Mountain, means "Head of the Earth." The highest point on the Navajo Nation, one of several sacred mountains in the Navajo religion, rises 10,388 feet above sea level right on the Arizona-Utah border. At the northwestern foot of the mountain, in a side canyon off Lake Powell, spans world-famous Rainbow Bridge. You can see dome-shaped Navajo Mountain from points along Lake Powell.

Navajo Mountain is the most isolated community of the entire Navajo Nation. This route takes you 10 miles past this backcountry community—as far as the pavement will take you. In the last 10 years, the paved road has been extended from about 15 miles to 25 miles, and the last 5 miles are the newest and smoothest. The "young" road, filled with great rollers and hardly any traffic, makes a perfect cycle ride.

The route starts out in a lackluster stretch of piñon and juniper trees. After Inscription House Trading Post (MP 5) you practically have the road to yourself.

The road to Navajo Mountain crosses some of the most remote land on the Navajo Nation.

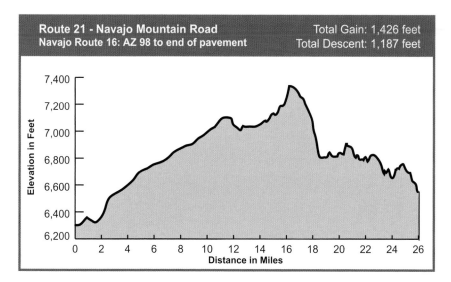

Route 21 - Navajo Mountain Road
Navajo Route 16: AZ 98 to end of pavement

Total Gain: 1,426 feet
Total Descent: 1,187 feet

Watch, however, for horses munching forbs along the roadsides. The trading post, located on Bá Há Joó Bá Lane, is named after a ruin composed of four living quarters and granaries and one kiva built around the same time as Betatakin and Keet Seel ruins, located less than a dozen miles to the east. The whole area is loaded with ruins.

The landscape starts to turn scenic by MP 10. Crossbedded slickrock rises by the route while Paiute Canyon digs deeply to the east of the road. The rollers get intense at MP 17, with some grades dropping in the double digits. At the same time, fingered canyons stretch toward the road from the west, with a beautiful backdrop of buttes and pinnacles behind them along the hazy horizon. With Navajo Mountain growing closer, the canyons slicing into the mountain's base begin to articulate.

The MPs end at mile 18 where new pavement recently has been laid, extending the good road several more miles. The road settles down to moderate rollers, and the scenery only gets better. The pavement, however, abruptly ends at mile 25.5. Perhaps in a few years more pavement will be laid on the route to Navajo Mountain. Until then, return the way you came.

Route 22

ANTELOPE POINT
NAVAJO ROAD 222: PAGE TO ANTELOPE POINT

Easy • Beginner

* Takes you from the city to the isolated outback of Page
* Travels past slickrock formations of Navajo sandstone
* Two lanes; medium shoulder

DISTANCE: 10 to 11 miles one-way

PEAK CYCLING: March–November

ACCOMMODATIONS: Supplies, restaurants, and lodging in Page

SPECIAL CONSIDERATIONS: You may cycle all the way to Lake Powell; however, the National Park Service charges $10 per individual to pass through the entrance gate to Antelope Point, and it only adds 1 mile to the ride.

STARTING POINTS: From US 89, head east on AZ 98; or, from Lake Powell Boulevard in Page, head south on Coppermine Road for about 1 mile to AZ 98.

It's a bunch of rolling hills with great scenery," says Rob Barnett about cycling the area around his hometown of Page. "It's great riding here."

Rob has cycled around Page since 1990. Riding a Trek 2300 carbon-fiber road bike, he participates in charity rides around the state. When he goes to

Antelope Point Road swirls through Navajo sandstone formations.

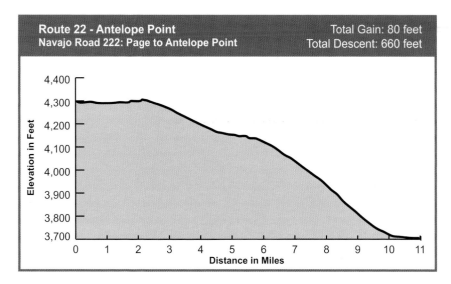

| Route 22 - Antelope Point | Total Gain: 80 feet |
| Navajo Road 222: Page to Antelope Point | Total Descent: 660 feet |

events in the desert, such as the Tour de Farm in Phoenix, he has more stamina and energy because of the hills and higher altitude in Page.

"Riding in altitude makes a big difference," Rob says. "When I go to a flatland event, it's so easy."

Antelope Point is one of Rob's favorite rides. Starting from the city of Page, this route reaches the outback countryside in a matter of minutes. However, since you never get far from Page's apron strings, the route is always within the safety net of civilization.

The scenery starts as soon as you head east on AZ 98. If you start from US 89, you pass Navajo sandstone haystacks and crossbedded cliffs. By Coppermine Road, between MPs 297 and 298, you hit the outskirts of town, a mile from the Navajo Nation. Just before the Navajo Generating Plant at MP 299, turn left (north) on Navajo Road 222. This three-stack plant burns coal from Kayenta Mine, about 80 miles away via the electric-powered Black Mesa & Lake Powell Railroad.

Once you get the electric plant behind you, the 6-mile road becomes isolated in a red-orange world of Navajo sandstone cliffs and formations. The chunky expanse of the Kaiparowits Plateau stretches across the northern horizon. At about mile 3 of Navajo 222, you can see the giant gash of Marble Canyon to the west.

The entrance to Antelope Point Marina comes at about mile 5. You can pay to continue another 1 mile to Lake Powell or return the way you came.

Route 23

ROAD TO LEUPP
TOWNSEND ROAD AND NAVAJO ROUTE 15 TO LEUPP

Moderate to Difficult (return) • Intermediate

◆ Travels through lava fields outside Flagstaff into the Painted Desert on the Navajo Nation

◆ Two lanes; good shoulders along most of the route

DISTANCE: 37 miles one-way

PEAK CYCLING: April–October

ACCOMMODATIONS: Supplies, restaurants, and lodging in Flagstaff—if you can wait. We recommend you try T-Bows 2 Bar 3 Historic Restaurant (5877 Leupp Road, 928-714-0678) for a tasty meal befitting a road biker's appetite after a route such as this.

SPECIAL CONSIDERATIONS: If you're doing a round-trip, be sure you have the stamina for the ascent back into Flagstaff.

STARTING POINT: About 3 miles north of Flagstaff on US 89, turn right (east) onto Townsend Road.

Located on the Little Colorado River, the little town of Leupp (pronounced "Loop") has seen settlements since the 1800s. The area lies along a historic travel route. As you ride your cycle from the cinderlands of Flagstaff down to the color-streaked mesa land on the Navajo Nation, you not only transition from one landscape to another but also from the fast-paced convenience

The road to Leupp drops from cinder-coned forests into the Painted Desert.

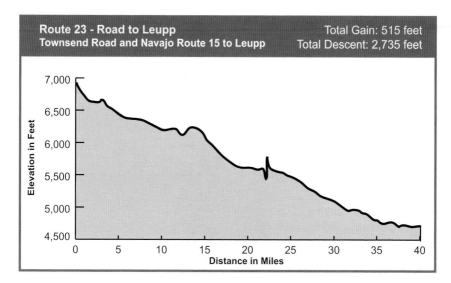

Route 23 - Road to Leupp
Townsend Road and Navajo Route 15 to Leupp
Total Gain: 515 feet
Total Descent: 2,735 feet

called the American Way to the remote and timeless way of life of the Navajo Nation.

The route starts out around MP 423 on Townsend Road with soft banks and rolling hills leading you from the edge of town into the middle of nowhere. Watch for prairie dogs along the road, standing statue-still with tiny paws dangling from rotund bodies. The critters play an important environmental role, as their tunnels provide a megapore system to help disburse water in this arid land.

As the route heads farther out of town, it drops from high-country pines into piñon-juniper vegetation by the time it turns northeast onto Navajo Route 15 at MP 428. Now the route gets a wider shoulder, but it is not as smooth. A series of long, steep rollers give the route some kick as it heads past a scenic spread of cinder cones to a promontory (about MP 435); you can see Crater 6830 on the west side of the highway and the Painted Desert in the distance.

At MP 438, the route leaves Coconino National Forest and runs across a checkerboard of private and state lands for another 5 miles until it enters the Navajo Nation. Starting at MP 0, the route runs like a ribbon across expansive views of a land that rises and falls like long, shallow waves. At MP 9, the road drops into a landscape of red sand mesas crinkled by erosion. In the distance, shadows of mesas and buttes reminiscent of Monument Valley loom along the horizon.

In the town of Sunrise, you reach the Little Colorado River and the end of this route at MP 15; the town of Leupp is just to the southeast. Stop at the West Sun Food Mart at MP 14 if you need basic supplies before you head back to Flagstaff.

© David James - 2006

Jamax Enterprises[T.M.]

www.jamaxfoto.com

REGION 3

NORTH CENTRAL ARIZONA

The central regions of Arizona brew with dips and swells of mountain ranges—some displaying violent volcanism, others jagged with precipitous peaks, and still others, in this north central region, characterized by rounded ridges that test your hill climbing and valleys that epitomize pastoral life. The grasslands make ideal cattle country, though ranching here is more often a gentlemanly quest than a way to make a living. Small towns that roll up their sidewalks early on weeknights make popular day-trip and weekend getaways. With that in mind, you'll always have a place to put your saddle.

ROUTES

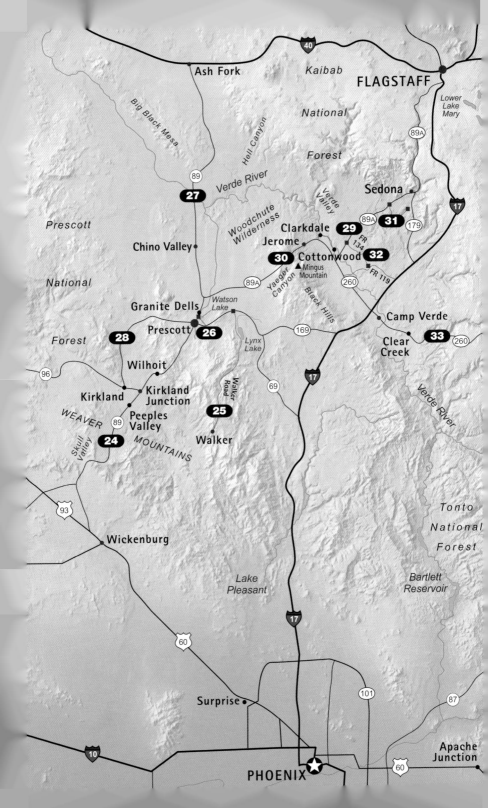

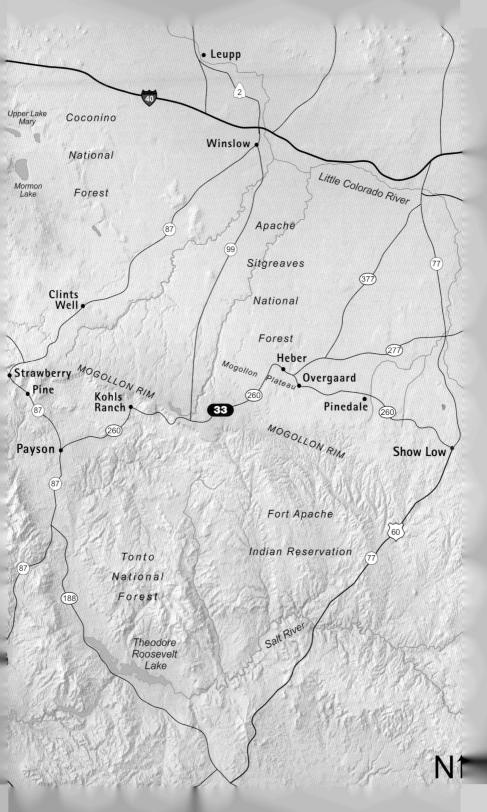

Route 24

WHITE SPAR ROAD
AZ 89: PRESCOTT TO WICKENBURG

Moderate to Difficult • Intermediate to Experienced

* Screams down the Bradshaw Mountains through Prescott National Forest into scenic ranch country, then lands on the desert floor in western Wickenburg
* Two lanes; occasional shoulder

DISTANCE: 13 to 61 miles one-way

PEAK CYCLING: All year; lower half in early morning

ACCOMMODATIONS: Supplies, restaurants, and lodging in Prescott and Wickenburg. Check out the Hassayampa Inn (122 E. Gurley St., 928-778-9434), one of Prescott's classic hotels. It carries the élan of its early days in the 1930s but with modern amenities, and its lounge is a jazz source. If you love jazz, catch a comfort-food dinner with a French infusion at 129 1/2 An American Jazz Grille (129 1/2 N. Cortez St., 928-443-9292).

SPECIAL CONSIDERATIONS: Cyclists planning to ride the northern half of this route should have experience with mountain grades. Difficulty ranges from moderate/intermediate on the lower portion to difficult/experienced on the upper portion.

STARTING POINT: From downtown Prescott, head south on Montezuma Street about 1 mile and veer right onto AZ 89, White Spar Road.

This route takes you from downtown Prescott's Whiskey Row to the Western town of Wickenburg. It is popular with Prescott cyclists, many of whom loop it with the Iron Springs Road (see Route 28, p. 79). Most cyclists who do this loop start on White Spar Road, which switchbacks down more than 1,000 feet in a few miles to the town of Wilhoit; then they head west on rolling Thompson Valley Road at Kirkland Junction, then northward at Kirkland back up to Prescott on the reasonable climbs of Iron Springs Road. Prescottonian Paul Walrath prefers to do this loop in reverse.

"Most people hate it," Paul says of the climb up the switchbacks. "I like it. You have to work to get up to the top."

From Prescott, the White Spar route enjoys a nice shoulder as it travels through the mile-high city's business district. In about 1 mile, at the outskirts of town, the route takes on the look and feel of a forest resort town, with lodges, specialty shops, and restaurants interspersed in the pines. At MP 309, the shoulder disappears and the road rolls with the mountain peaks and valleys.

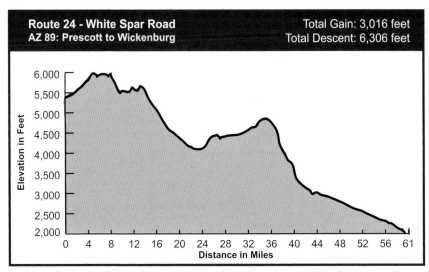

Route 24 - White Spar Road
AZ 89: Prescott to Wickenburg

Total Gain: 3,016 feet
Total Descent: 6,306 feet

A few miles later, the roadway yawns with widened curves and occasional passing lanes to the highpoint at MP 305. From there, it's a rollicking ride downhill on a switchbacked route with some quirky grades.

At MP 302 the tread of the road degrades to bumpy vibration. While negotiating double S-turns, you will probably keep pace with most vehicular traffic. Some cyclists ride right in the middle of the road; this not only avoids the chance of vehicles squeezing you off the already narrow roadway, it's also your rules-of-the-road right. If you have the pluck, this road will ask you to use it.

Around MP 298 a narrow shoulder appears for cyclists who like to ride the white line. A decent shoulder accompanies you into the town of Wilhoit at MP 295. You might be ready for a pit stop at the country store in Wilhoit or a libation at the Burro Inn, which advertises "the last drink in nowhere." This is a good turnaround point if you're training or, like Paul Walrath, just plain like the workout of climbing back up the mountain.

Continuing southward, the route drops into rich grasslands and rolling hills. You come to the handful of buildings at dot-on-the-map Kirkland Junction at MP 289. To loop back to Prescott via Iron Springs Road, turn right (west) onto Thompson Valley Road. Cyclists continuing to Wickenburg should stay on AZ 89.

When the route drops into Peeples Valley at MP 283, you pass through one of the more pastoral spots in the state. The lush landscape hosts Black Angus cattle and meticulously manicured horse ranches. By MP 278, the road widens to four lanes as it enters Yarnell. Only a few blocks long, this town shows its sense of humor in the clever store and restaurant names: Buford's Buzzard's Roost serves natural barbecued foods; Brand New Dead

Things sells arts and crafts made of materials gathered from the desert; and DnA's restaurant caters to the local residents and bikers. The Ranch House Restaurant draws the locals, but we recommend Cornerstone Bakery for incredible homebaked treats and sandwiches (both establishments close by 2 p.m.).

By MP 276, you'll understand Yarnell's slogan—"Where the desert breeze meets the mountain air"—as you start switchbacking down to the desert floor. This descent is docile compared to the screamer from Prescott because of the road's excellent engineering—a far cry from the original roadsite. Oldtimers still talk about vehicles careening around corners when their brakes went out. Along the way, you get fantastic

AZ 89 winds down Yarnell Hill.

views of the Weaver Mountains' jagged ridgeline. Watch for the occasional pothole in the wide shoulder while on the downhill.

By Congress, around MP 267, you're in the creosote flats of the desert. Though the road has no shoulder, it has plenty of flat segments and hardly any blind spots as it gradually drops into the town of Wickenburg. At MP 259 you reach US 93 and the end of White Spar Road. Turn left (southeast) onto US 93 to continue 6 miles to Wickenburg. The route continues its gentle downhill, giving you a soft landing into town.

STOP SIGN? WHAT STOP SIGN?

Some cyclists develop the nasty habit of not stopping at stop signs, especially on side streets where there's little traffic. It's one of the most-ignored traffic laws, says Tucson Regional Bicycle Program Manager Richard Corbett.

"There are a lot of reasons to stop," Richard explains. The most beneficial one is that it makes cyclists stronger. The more important one is that it sets a good example. Richard says adults generally can safely run stop signs, but the younger kids that are watching don't have the same perceptual prowess that adults do. Adults' senses are better attuned to quickly monitoring the situation with their hearing, peripheral vision, and cognition. Kids haven't developed that ability.

Route 25

LYNX LAKE
WALKER ROAD: AZ 69 TO WALKER

Moderate • Beginner

- ◆ Travels through ponderosa pine forests and past a mountain lake to a mountain town
- ◆ Two lanes; narrow shoulder

DISTANCE: 10 miles one-way

PEAK CYCLING: May–October

ACCOMMODATIONS: Supplies, restaurants, and lodging in Prescott. Lynx Lake Store has basic provisions and a restaurant that serves breakfast and lunch.

SPECIAL CONSIDERATIONS: If you drive a car to Lynx Lake, you will need to purchase a $2 day-use permit to park. Wednesdays are free.

STARTING POINT: From Prescott, drive about 3 miles east on Gurley Street (AZ 69), and turn right (south) onto Walker Road.

You enter the pines right away on this rolling road, and the forest and its sweet smell give the route a special appeal. The mountain lake near mile 2, Lynx Lake, makes a nice diversion. This man-made lake was named for Lynx Creek from which it's formed. The creek originally had the name Oolkilsipava River, and this complicated name got changed into its simpler version by a prospector named Sam Miller in the party led by Joe Walker

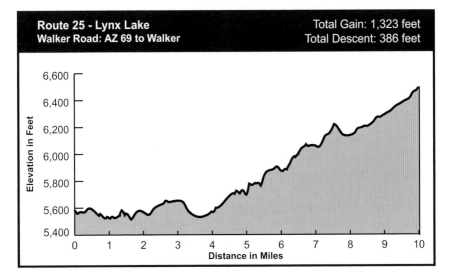

Route 25 - Lynx Lake
Walker Road: AZ 69 to Walker

Total Gain: 1,323 feet
Total Descent: 386 feet

(who founded Prescott). Miller accidentally found gold here. He also, the story goes, found a lynx. When Miller went to pick up the cat, it sprang on him. Miller killed the cat and renamed the river.

Despite its wildcat history, Lynx Lake makes a peaceful place to cycle. A half-mile ride from the north-shore entrance brings you to the lakeshore. The south-shore entrance, about 1 mile farther on Walker Road, winds through the forest for almost 2 miles to the lake and a campground.

Back on Walker Road, the route continues several miles through the forest to the mountain town of Walker. Now the epitome of a mountain cabin community, the town was started by prospector Joe Walker. Mining kept it alive for decades. The town's post office opened December 15, 1879, and closed September 30, 1940. The town, which had around 2,700 residents, now consists of summer cabins. The fire station still stands, as well as a giant charcoal kiln nearby.

The pavement ends at Walker. If you have a tour bike, you can continue another 6 miles to White Spar Road; otherwise, return the way you came.

The road to Lynx Lake is scenic and relaxing.

Route 26

PRESCOTT PEAVINE TRAIL
WATSON LAKE TO AZ 89A

Easy • Beginner

◆ Travels through the unique granite formations of the Granite Dells

◆ Multiuse doubletrack

DISTANCE: 4.6 miles one-way

PEAK CYCLING: March–October

ACCOMMODATIONS: Supplies, restaurants, and lodging in Prescott. The Rocamadour Bed and Breakfast (928-771-1933), located in the Granite Dells, is one of the exceptional bed and breakfasts in the Prescott area—well-appointed rooms in a scenic location, and run by thoughtful innkeepers.

SPECIAL CONSIDERATIONS: The route's tread is made of hardpack gravel appropriate for road bikes.

STARTING POINT: From Gurley Street in downtown Prescott, go east to AZ 89, and then turn left (north); go about 2.3 miles to Prescott Lakes Parkway and turn right; cross a bridge and turn left (north) onto Sun Dog Ranch Road; go 0.1 mile to parking area on left.

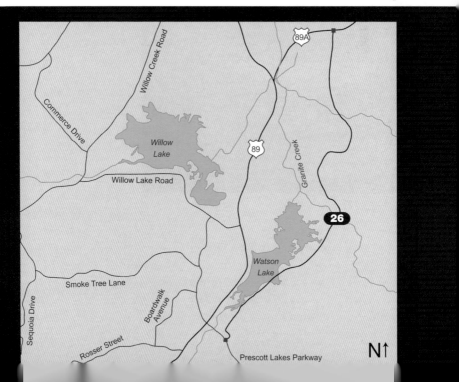

From wetlands to grasslands with the Granite Dells in between, the Prescott Peavine Trail takes you into some of the most scenic areas around Prescott. This is a popular route with Prescottonians that takes users around the edges of the mountain town on an old railroad bed called the Peavine. With a name inspired by the twisting curves it negotiated, the Peavine Railroad ran between Ash Fork and Prescott, then southward around the Bradshaw Mountains to Skull Valley, west through Date Creek, close to the gold-infested environs of Congress and Wickenburg, and into Phoenix. The city revived this 4-plus-mile segment as a multiuse, barrier-free path that works fine for road bikes.

The trail heads right toward the Watson Woods Riparian Preserve. This small (125-acre) wetlands preserve is just a remnant of the cottonwood-willow forest along Granite Creek that originally made its way 4 miles into Prescott. The marsh flows into Watson Lake, and the route follows right along with it, edging the blue-watered lake well past MP 1. At mile 1.5, you get a glimpse of the magic of the Granite Dells when a channel gives you a window to the lake with Granite Mountain rising in the distance.

Just past the Boulder Creek bridge, at MP 2, the route gets a scruffy look to it from the dominant vegetation of scrub oak, mountain mahogany, piñon, and oak trees. This lasts until MP 3, when the route starts to rub shoulders with the magnificent granite formations that comprise the Granite Dells.

Long-term weathering of natural cracks in the granite produced the balancing rocks, hoodoos, and joint planes. This labyrinthine landscape made a great place for outlaws to hide. Its beauty lured Hollywood stars as a respite. Movies were made there, too.

After a junction with the Iron King Trail, the route starts to get a look at the stretches of

Peavine Trail cozies up to a channel in Granite Dells.

prairies that attracted ranchers to the area. The grasslands, a blend of Great Plains short-grass prairies and Great Basin grasslands, attract pronghorn antelope.

A cluster of cliffrose bushes gathers around the trail at about mile 3.5. In May the yellow clusters of blossoms from this cousin of the rose waft a sweet aroma. The route ends on an overpass above AZ 89A. Someday the trail may connect with the Chino Valley's Peavine Trail. Until it does, return the way you came.

Route 27

WILLIAMSON VALLEY ROAD
AZ 89: Chino Valley to Ash Fork

Moderate • Intermediate

• Travels through gorgeous, less-traveled countryside full of open space and wildlife
◆ Colorful spreads of wildflowers in May after a wet winter and during the summer monsoons in August and September
◆ Two lanes; shoulder most of the way

Distance: 22 to 38 miles one-way

Peak Cycling: March through October

Accommodations: Supplies, restaurants, and lodging in Prescott

Special Considerations: You may start the route in Prescott (and add 16 miles), but with the heavy flow of traffic and development, we recommend waiting until Chino Valley.

Starting Points: From Gurley Street in downtown Prescott, go east to AZ 89, and turn left (north); go about 16 miles to Chino Valley. If you want your ride to be a total backcountry experience, go beyond Chino Valley to the national forest boundary around MP 341 and park on one of several side roads along the highway. To start in Ash Fork, head south on AZ 89.

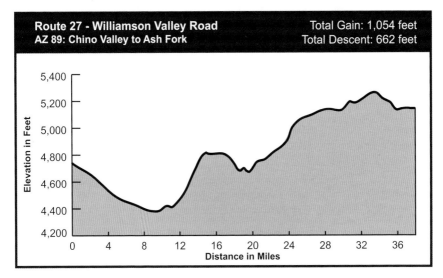

Route 27 - Williamson Valley Road
AZ 89: Chino Valley to Ash Fork
Total Gain: 1,054 feet
Total Descent: 662 feet

Traveling through undeveloped high-desert grasslands with little traffic, this route brings you in touch with the magnificent feeling of pure open space. It's a favorite of Don Reeves, a road cyclist from Chino Valley.

"There is a lot of wildlife," Don says. "It has a good, wide shoulder for the most part, and it's challenging enough with some climbs, some downhills, and pure enjoyment."

Don has seen deer, elk, coyotes, bear, and even a bald eagle along this route. From one point you can look across the landscape to the east and see the red rocks at Sedona. Several sandstone quarries are visible from the highway as well.

Don, a former Phoenician, used to race and cycle in Phoenix. He has a heroic road biker's story to tell.

"I was actually hit on my bike down in Phoenix and left for dead," Don says. "I broke 17 bones in my body, had a punctured lung, was in a coma for some time, and now have a titanium rod that runs from my knee to my ankle. The docs said if I hadn't been in the shape I

Williamson Valley Road travels through remote national forest land.

was in from riding, I would have surely not lived to talk about it."

Bicycling, however, played a major role in Don's recovery. His son used to take him around on a tandem. When he could once again ride single, he returned to racing. Don now lives in Chino Valley, where life is several notches slower than in Phoenix, and he leads bicycle trips for Yavapai College Elderhostel.

"I guess it doesn't matter if you race and are addicted to that sound when the pack is working in perfect sync," Don muses, "or if you cycle alone on a Sunday morning and celebrate each peak. Cycling gets into your soul."

This route gets off to a great start, as it only takes a couple of miles outside Chino Valley to get into the backcountry of rolling grasslands. After a few bends in the road, you head into Big Black Mesa and Prescott National Forest at MP 341. Scenic Hell Canyon country appears around MP 346, and from there you travel through open countryside where you're apt to see some of the wildlife mentioned earlier.

AZ 89 ends at Ash Fork (MP 363) on Old Route 66. You can either continue west to follow this historic route or return the way you came.

Route 28

IRON SPRINGS ROAD
PRESCOTT TO KIRKLAND JUNCTION

Moderate • Intermediate

- Travels from the pine forests of Prescott National Forest to historic ranchland in Skull Valley and high desert near Kirkland Junction
- Two lanes; shoulder part of the way

DISTANCE: 26 miles one-way

PEAK CYCLING: March–October

ACCOMMODATIONS: Supplies, restaurants, and lodging in Prescott

SPECIAL CONSIDERATIONS: Blind spots and no shoulder on part of the mountainous downhill can challenge less experienced cyclists.

STARTING POINT: From Gurley and Montezuma streets in downtown Prescott, go north on Montezuma and continue as it bends into Whipple Street and then Whipple turns into Iron Springs Road. If you're driving, there's a parking area along the road at Granite Basin Road just past MP 215, where this route starts.

This great route takes you from pine-forested mountaintops into lush and moody Skull Valley, then winds around the high desert to the old communities of Kirkland and Kirkland Junction. The route starts with a marked bike lane and takes you through Prescott National Forest. At this point, you

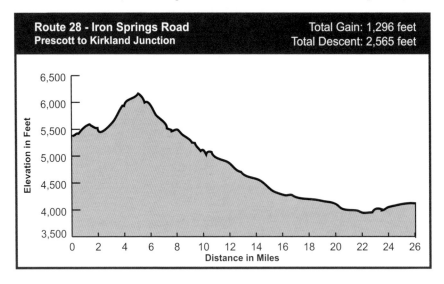

Route 28 - Iron Springs Road
Prescott to Kirkland Junction

Total Gain: 1,296 feet
Total Descent: 2,565 feet

are eye-level with the pine-covered peaks and you're climbing. Then climbing some more. By about mile 4, you experience your just desserts when you zoom on the downhill.

In another mile, you're well on the other side of the ridge and heading into the grasslands that lured cowboys to the area. Granite boulders start to stack up along the roadway, and panoramas of the valley come into view. Rollers have you rising and falling with the landscape, which turns emerald after wet weather. Watch for stalks of Palmer's penstemon with elongated clusters of pretty pink flowers in May. Apache plume bushes show white flowers around that time, too. In late summer, yellow composites color the rolling hillsides.

At MP 12, the road narrows, exits the national forest, and loses the shoulder. Within a couple miles, ranches start to appear, and by MP 16 you pass the Skull Valley Cemetery. Though you're heading into an old, established community, you're in the boonies where wildlife makes frequent appearances. Deer, javelina, raptors, and rattlesnakes appear alongside, above, and upon the road.

Skull Valley, lush, lovely, and shaded by giant cottonwood trees, hardly matches its ignoble name. Stories about the genesis agree the name comes from a number of skulls that were left lying pell-mell on the valley floor after a battle. Explanations for how they got there, and to whom the bones belonged, differ. The Anglo version says skulls and bones remained from a battle that felled more than two dozen Maricopa and Yavapai Indians. Indians claim they were white men's bones.

Unless you stop at the old gas station, Skull Valley fast becomes a memory, as it's only a few blocks long. The tiny community makes a good turnaround point for a shorter ride. To continue on the route, keep cycling south, and by MP 18 you begin a winding coast into Kirkland. Along the way, attractive and anomalous volcanic tuff formations appear. The tuffa stone from this area was made into blocks that built Phoenix's capitol building.

At MP 25 the route rolls into Kirkland, the hub of activity for the ranchers in the area in the late 1800s. The Kirkland Bar Steakhouse Hotel is listed on the National Register of Historic Places. You can cut this route short by making Kirkland your turnaround point, or you can continue 4 miles to dot-on-the-map Kirkland Junction. If you do, watch the cattle guards, as some of them have uneven placements and can cause damage if they're taken too fast. At Kirkland Junction, return the way you came or continue on White Spar Road (see Route 24, p. 70) northward to Prescott or south to Wickenburg.

Route 29

JEROME-COTTONWOOD-CLARKDALE SCENIC ROAD
AZ 89A: SEDONA TO JEROME

Moderate • Intermediate

* Travels through scenic red-rock country
* Passes through historic towns
* Two to four lanes; wide to no shoulders

DISTANCE: 29 miles one-way

PEAK CYCLING: March–October

ACCOMMODATIONS: Supplies, restaurants, and lodging in Sedona, Cottonwood, and Jerome. In Sedona, the Cowboy Club Grille (928-28202499, 241 Hwy. 89A) serves up generous portions of High Desert cuisine. Troia's (928-282-0123, 1885 W. Hwy 89A) has classic Italian food in a fresh, casual environment. The Surgeon's House Bed and Breakfast (800-639-1452) in Jerome has a lively, artsy interior and sanctuary-like yard. Owner and innkeeper Andrea serves a great breakfast with colorful stories of life (then and now) in Jerome. The Haunted Hamburger (410 Clark St., 928-634-0554) in Jerome will satiate the heartiest of post-ride appetites.

SPECIAL CONSIDERATIONS: The last mile to Jerome requires hill-climbing experience.

STARTING POINT: From the intersection of AZ 179 and AZ 89A in Sedona, go west on AZ 89A; MP 374 is the first mile marker.

Long before Sedona became a new-age mecca, romantic getaway, and title-bearer of most beautiful city in the United States, it was an ordinary cowtown, along with nearby Cottonwood. On the other hand, mining town Jerome had a lively reputation in its heyday, and it still keeps some semblance of one, especially on Halloween. This cycling route connects this historic string of cities, from Sedona to Jerome. It's a great route not only for history but also for scenery, as it includes Sedona's red-rock country. Cyclists who want to do an overnighter have many great spots to stay and places to eat.

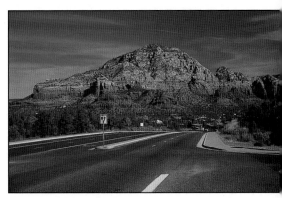

The western edge of Sedona marks the beginning of world-renowned scenery.

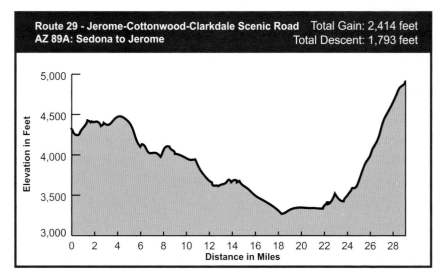

The route starts out on a very busy, shoulderless, four-lane stretch of highway in Sedona. There's a sidewalk cyclists not comfortable with the flow of traffic can use. The sidewalk ends at MP 370. A nice, wide shoulder takes over at MP 366. The route enters an engaging piñon-juniper landscape of rolling hills. Watch for Page Springs Road at MP 362; this canyon road makes a great cycle ride (see Route 32, p. 87).

Continuing on this route, start downhill into the Verde Valley at MP 360. A few miles of downhill brings you into the town of Cottonwood, where the route loses the shoulder. Follow the signage near MP 353 toward Jerome and Prescott. At MP 351, the road narrows to two lanes with a wide shoulder. In another mile, the route comes to the town of Clarkdale, where you might feel like you've entered a time warp.

Looking like it hasn't aged a day since the 1960s, small-town Clarkdale's big draw is its architecture. The buildings, ahead of their time when built, housed workers at a mine in Jerome. Check out the Clarkdale Antique Emporium and Old Fashioned Soda Fountain, built in 1946. You'll need the carbs for the upcoming hill climb.

When you get to the stop sign at the end of Clarkdale, about MP 349, take a left. Then get ready to climb to the final destination, Jerome. This is a 4-mile ascent that gets pretty tough. The road narrows substantially in the last mile. Just hold steady in the traffic and keep climbing.

The highway winds right into town, giving you a look at its decades-old architecture. Shops, art, food, and spirits (both libations and the post-flesh-and-bones variety) make interesting diversions. When you're ready to depart, return the way you came or continue on AZ 89A to Prescott (see Route 30, opposite).

Route 30

MINGUS MOUNTAIN SCENIC ROAD
AZ 89A: JEROME TO PRESCOTT

Difficult • Experienced

- Travels a wild mountain road with striking panoramas
- Shows great autumn color in October
- Two lanes; no shoulder

DISTANCE: 32 miles one-way

PEAK CYCLING: March–October

ACCOMMODATIONS: Supplies, restaurants, and lodging in Jerome and Prescott. Check out Prescott's Hotel St. Michael (205 W. Gurley St., 928-776-1999). The historic hotel has lots of character and reasonable rates, and its café serves great coffee drinks and meals, with the best seats in the town for people-watching.

SPECIAL CONSIDERATIONS: This route requires hill-climbing experience.

STARTING POINT: From downtown Jerome, follow the main road as it wends through the town, then turn right (south) toward Prescott onto AZ 89A; MP 344 is the first mile marker.

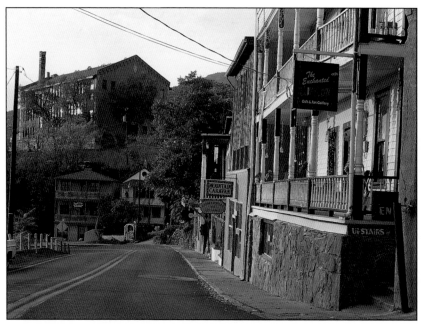

The road to Jerome, a scenic descent north into the center of town.

I f you're looking for a challenge, this route through the Black Hills around Mingus Mountain will meet it. Along with a memorable bout of climbing, the route includes soulful high-desert scenery along the highway and inspiring panoramas of northern Arizona; in October, it throws in a lagniappe of exquisite fall color—gold from Arizona walnut, box elder, and velvet ash trees in the roadside canyons and fiery reds from maples on the upper reaches of Mingus Mountain. It's a favorite for the area's experienced cyclists, especially those in training.

The route has you working right away as it winds via a narrow road through the hills of Mingus Mountain, with spectacular views of the Verde Valley each time the road switchbacks eastward. You leave all views of the Verde Valley behind around MP 340 when the route crosses to the other side of the ridge and drops into a bowl that holds Potato Patch Recreation Area and a campground in the Woodchute Wilderness. The road generally follows Yeager Canyon from MP 335 onward. The continual downhill will have you braking to manage the tight curves for the next 2 miles; the curves start to relax in another mile when the scenic route ends. Then, it's a long, gradual drop into Prescott Valley. You finally hit the flatlands by MP 328, but the fast run lasts until MP 320. The route enters Prescott Valley's town limits at MP 325. Watch for a fork in the road where you veer right to stay on AZ 89A. The road widens to four lanes with a wide shoulder and exits. It's fast-moving but in great shape, with a lot of shoulder space. Be careful, though, of entrance ramps.

AZ 89A ends just past MP 319. To continue on this route, take AZ 89 into Prescott. A few miles later, turn left onto Williamson Valley Road and follow it a few miles farther to Iron Springs Road in Prescott. Now you can turn left and head into downtown Prescott or turn right and continue on the Iron Springs Road (see Route 28, p. 79).

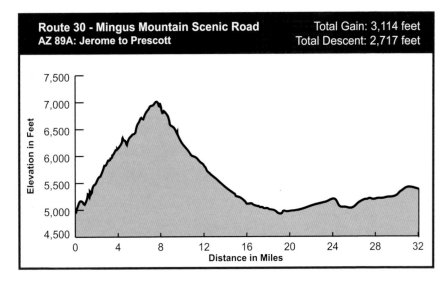

Route 30 - Mingus Mountain Scenic Road
AZ 89A: Jerome to Prescott

Total Gain: 3,114 feet
Total Descent: 2,717 feet

Route 31

RED ROCK CROSSING
RED ROCK ROAD: AZ 89A TO END OF PAVEMENT

Moderate • Intermediate

- Travels through an extraordinarily scenic section of Sedona's red-rock country
- Visits Crescent Moon Ranch Picnic Area at Red Rock Crossing, where much-photographed Cathedral Rock stands
- Two lanes; no shoulder

DISTANCE: 5.5 miles one-way

PEAK CYCLING: March–October

ACCOMMODATIONS: Supplies, restaurants, and lodging in Sedona. Check out Sedona Rouge Hotel (2250 W. AZ 89A, 928-203-4111). Its restaurant, Reds, serves gourmet comfort food. Its spa has some of the best therapists around.

SPECIAL CONSIDERATIONS: Crescent Moon Picnic Area charges $1 for bicycles to enter, $7 for cars.

STARTING POINT: From Sedona, go west on AZ 89A about 5 miles to Upper Red Rock Loop (just past MP 370), and then turn left (south).

From the first moment you start pedaling, the dazzling scenery shows up and doesn't quit. Hyper-scenic and full of twists, turns, and rollers, the road requires your full attention. If you want to gawk at the scenery that

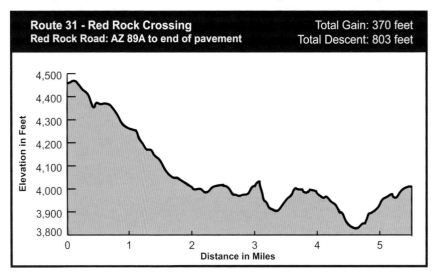

Route 31 - Red Rock Crossing
Red Rock Road: AZ 89A to end of pavement
Total Gain: 370 feet
Total Descent: 803 feet

made Sedona famous, stop at a pull-out. There's enough traffic and tricky road topography to make taking your eyes off the road potentially tragic.

The world-renowned Cathedral Rock formation comes in view early, within the first mile, and it remains in view throughout the route. When the road forks at Chavez Ranch Road, veer right; then take another sharp bend to the right in another 0.5 mile to join Forest Road 216. For the next mile, until the pavement ends, the scenery switches from elegant formations to country-lane residential. Halfway, you pass the entrance for Crescent Moon Picnic Area. At the pavement's end, return the way you came. Or, if you have a tour bike, you can continue another 5 miles as the road bends like a horseshoe back to AZ 89A.

Route's end—Crescent Moon Recreation Area.

BLUE SKIES

Blue skies aren't necessarily friendly skies. The Arizona Sun Awareness Project says Arizonans have the highest rate of skin cancer in the United States—the second highest in the world. In the summer, as little as 15 minutes' exposure at noon can burn unprotected skin. Take extra precautions if you have the following characteristics:

- light skin type
- red or blonde hair
- light blue, green, or hazel eyes
- melanoma in your family history
- irregular moles
- an abundance of moles

If you're bald(ing), be sure to protect your skin under the ventilation slots of your helmet:

- Regular sunscreen may be too greasy and will make your helmet slide around. Try an alcohol-based and waterproof product (bonus points if marked: "Does not sting eyes").
- Wear a bandana in cooler weather.
- Attach screening in the vents.
- Put a thin napkin between your noggin and the helmet.

Route 32

PAGE SPRINGS ROAD
AZ 89A TO CORNVILLE ROAD

Easy • Intermediate

◆ Travels through lower Oak Creek Canyon shaded by a riparian forest

◆ Two lanes road; no shoulder

DISTANCE: 7 miles one-way

PEAK CYCLING: March–October

ACCOMMODATIONS: Supplies, restaurants, and lodging in Sedona. Check out Keiser's West restaurant (2920 W. AZ 89A, 928-204-2088) for excellent comfort food with a special twist, at reasonable prices.

SPECIAL CONSIDERATIONS: This road has no shoulder.

STARTING POINT: From Sedona, go west on AZ 89A about 8 miles to Page Springs Road (Forest Road 134), and then turn left (south).

Every area, no matter how popular, has a secret spot tucked away in its back pocket. This road, short and sweet, shows a secret side of world-famous Oak Creek. Compared to the swaggering scenery, gooseneck bends, and rollers on the highway that define the upper part of Oak Creek Canyon, this road through the lower part of the canyon looks every bit like a country lane winding demurely past cozy homes, riparian vegetation, and vineyards.

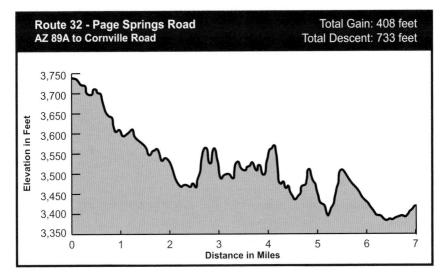

Route 32 - Page Springs Road
AZ 89A to Cornville Road
Total Gain: 408 feet
Total Descent: 733 feet

This road is also much safer. AZ 89A traveling through Oak Creek Canyon between Sedona and Flagstaff is a dangerous route. Though it is truly one of the most beautiful routes in the world, we don't recommend it because it's so hazardous. A combination of blind curves, recreational vehicles, and impatient drivers who don't respect cyclists or know that the law requires three feet of space if they plan to pass a cyclist makes the route a deadly one. If you must cycle it, do so in the very early morning to avoid the traffic.

The Page Springs route is far more user-friendly. Close to perennially flowing Oak Creek, the route is a birder's paradise, especially during spring and fall migrations. The Audubon Society identified the riparian area along lower Oak Creek as an Important Bird Area.

The route starts in high-desert rolling hills of sandstone topped with basalt, so familiar to the area around the Verde River. Page Springs Road squirms through this countryside for a couple of miles before dropping into the Oak Creek drainage. The riparian vegetation of cottonwoods, sumac, and velvet ash turns pretty in autumn, usually peaking in late October.

About 3 miles into the route, you pass Arizona Game and Fish Department's Page Springs Fish Hatchery, the department's largest hatchery in the state. Though the raceways where the fish are raised have protective chain-link covers, some predators, especially skunk and raccoon, still like to try their hand at purloining a trout or two. Black-crowned night heron, great blue heron, and belted kingfisher stalk the creekwaters.

Just past the fish hatchery the route enters Arizona's hot new wine country. Oak Creek Vineyards & Winery's Zinfandel, Syrah, and Chardonnay vines

Ranches along Page Springs Road.

line the terraced slops of the canyon. Javelina Leap Vineyard & Winery just started. Page Springs Vineyards & Cellars plans to bear fruit by 2006.

At about mile 5, the route leaves the lush canyon behind as it climbs back into the open country of mesquite and juniper. The route ends at Cornville Road (Forest Road 119). You may return the way you came or continue on a loop heading west on Cornville Road to AZ 89A.

Route 33

MOGOLLON RIM WEST
AZ 260: CAMP VERDE TO SHOW LOW

Moderate to Difficult • Intermediate to Experienced

- Travels a 2,000-foot-high wooded escarpment across Arizona
- Makes a great several-day tour
- Two to four lanes; no shoulder to wide shoulder

DISTANCE: 156 miles one-way

PEAK CYCLING: March–October

ACCOMMODATIONS: Supplies and restaurants in Camp Verde, Strawberry, Pine, Payson, Christopher Creek, Heber, and Overgaard. If you're in the mood for some fine dining, check out The Torreon Grille in Show Low (corner of AZ 60 and AZ 260, 928-532-8000). This well-kept secret is located in master-planned Torreon but is open to the public.

SPECIAL CONSIDERATIONS: The diversity in elevations requires you to pay attention to the time of day that you cycle some segments. During the summer, cycle the far western end in early morning.

STARTING POINT: Route starts at I-17, exit 285 (Camp Verde); MP 226 is the first mile marker.

This route, with is diversity in vegetation and elevation, makes an interesting several-day tour. However, you can break it up into segments for day trips. Whatever way you approach this route, which spans one of Arizona's most popular summer destinations, you'll probably agree with Western writer Zane Grey's thoughts when he first experienced the Mogollon (pronounced "Muggyown") Rim. His poetic prose met its match as he "saw a scene that defied words.... For wild rugged beauty, I had not seen its equal."

The route starts out in a comfortable manner, with four lanes, a wide shoulder, and large, long rollers. By MP 231, you start climbing up the escarpment in stair-step fashion. The challenge of this route lies in the grade. While many mountain roads have switchbacks to add a degree of relief from the steep grade, this segment has an unrelenting grade that slogs up the Mogollon Rim for a couple dozen miles. This, of course, makes for an eternal screamer on the way back.

The layer of basalt that caps much of Arizona's high country appears around MP 239. Within a couple of miles, the route straddles some interesting formations upon Thirteenmile Rock Butte. A sign signals the General George Crook National Recreation Trail, which generally follows this road.

Continuing eastward, the road eventually rises into a ponderosa pine forest, which it travels for several miles. Though in the forest, this road is wide enough to soak up the sun. Keep that in mind when planning the timing of your ride.

At MP 278, turn right onto AZ 87/260 to continue on this route. The relatively clean, roomy shoulder narrows into a cinder-covered strip here. Plus, the road takes a long, winding dive into the Verde River valley. Ride defensively in this several-mile stretch to the town of Strawberry at MP 271.

Still dropping, the route continues to the next tiny town, Pine, at MP 268. Within a couple of miles, you start a string of rollers that have more downhill than up. This segment is fast, full of curves, and has only a sliver of a shoulder as it drops to the East Verde River at MP 258. As in all canyons, what goes down into them must climb out, and it's a long, steep climb (albeit a scenic one, where fluted limestone stacks upon blushing sandstone outcroppings) out of this one into the town of Payson (MP 255).

It takes a few miles to get through Payson. Watch for the turnoff for AZ 260 just before MP 252. By MP 254, the road starts heading out of town and climbing back up into the ponderosa forest. Wide shoulders, a product of the road-widening project started at the turn of the century, make this

Dropping into the East Verde River drainage along AZ 260.

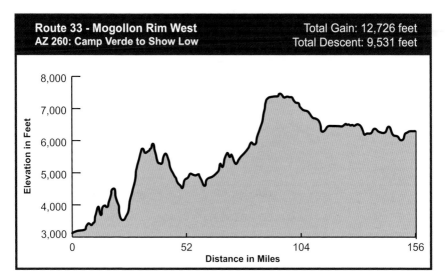

Route 33 - Mogollon Rim West
AZ 260: Camp Verde to Show Low
Total Gain: 12,726 feet
Total Descent: 9,531 feet

a more comfortable segment to cycle. Uphill-heavy rollers have you gaining elevation quickly. At MP 269, and several miles into the forest's shade, the road starts a pleasant stretch of rollers. Add to that the wide shoulder and scenic panoramas, and you have one of the best segments of this rim road. This area is one of the most densely populated with elk in the state. On early September mornings you might hear their high-pitched bugling.

A mile after the Young Road, at MP 286, you start to see remnants of the disastrous Rodeo-Chediski Fire of 2002. The road, new and smooth, travels casual rollers spiked with demanding hills before it levels off for a ways at MP 296. You start to approach the town of Heber on the downhill. A few miles later, the route approaches the town of Overgaard. By MP 310, you're back on the open road.

Several miles of long curves and perfect rollers pass a heavy burn area after MP 315. The community of Pinedale (MP 326) gives a moment of civilization without the services, as does Linden, located in scenic ranch country. You get your pick of food and lodging in Show Low. The city limits start around MP 337, but the business district doesn't start until MP 340. To continue on AZ 260 east of Show Low, see the Mogollon Rim East route (Route 65, p. 170).

REGION 4

PHOENIX AREA

The Phoenix Valley is crisscrossed with bike lanes that give you a chance to string together your own routes. This chapter features bikeways, routes that travel through scenic areas, and popular training routes.

ROUTES

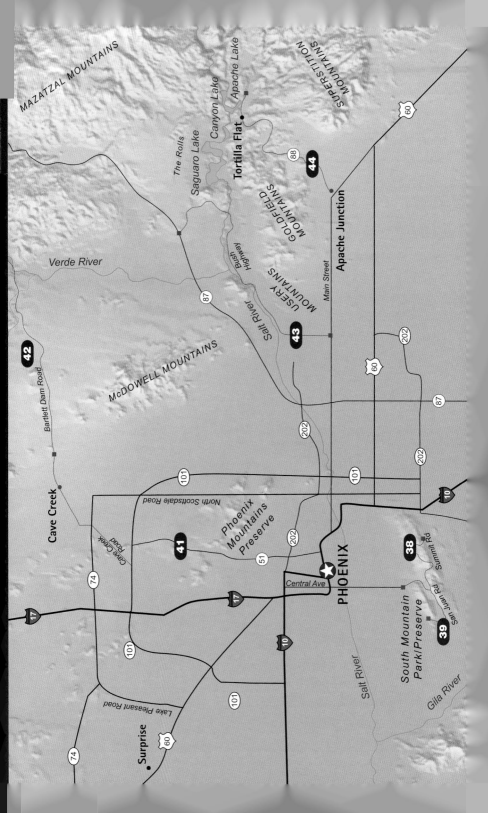

Route 34

CAVE CREEK BIKEWAY
ARIZONA CANAL TO GREENWAY ROAD

Easy • Beginner

◆ Travels along the Cave Creek greenway
◆ Multiuse bikeway

DISTANCE: 8 miles one-way

PEAK CYCLING: October–April; early morning in warmer weather

ACCOMMODATIONS: Supplies, restaurants, and lodging in Phoenix

SPECIAL CONSIDERATIONS: Older bikeways maps of metropolitan Phoenix show this route connecting with Cave Creek Road. It does not. Rather, it ends just south of Greenway Road.

STARTING POINTS: South access: Arizona Canal Bikeway, just east of I-17.
North access: just south of Greenway Road on 19th Avenue.

This bikeway, an easygoing route on its own, adds miles to a cycle ride on the Arizona Canal Bikeway (see Route 35, p. 96) or makes a nice commuter route from northern Phoenix. Starting from the Rose Mofford Sports Complex parking lot, the route travels a pleasantly landscaped path along the Cave Creek wash. Underpasses take you across major thoroughfares. Benches, a playground, and restrooms are located near the northern end of the bikeway, north of Thunderbird Road.

Cave Creek Bikeway has a Sonoran Desert landscape with plenty of trees that offer segments of shade.

Route 35

ARIZONA CANAL BIKEWAY
24TH STREET TO 75TH AVENUE

Easy • Beginner

◆ Travels a paved segment of a multiuse path along the Arizona Canal

◆ Scenery evolves from city residential to a greenway that attracts birds all along the way

DISTANCE: 13.2 paved miles one-way

PEAK CYCLING: October–March; early mornings in warmer weather

ACCOMMODATIONS: Supplies, restaurants, and lodging in Phoenix and Glendale

SPECIAL CONSIDERATIONS: Parts of the greenway on the western end might flood during wet weather.

STARTING POINTS: East end: 24th Street just north of Camelback Road. West end: 75th Avenue between Bell and Greenway roads. See map on page 98.

An ancient canal system set up by the Hohokam Indians, residents of the Valley from 100 B.C. to A.D. 1450, kept villages in the Salt River Valley well watered. Their irrigation system, the most sophisticated in pre-Columbian North America, networked more than 300 miles. Centuries later, the Valley's founding father, Jack Swilling, resurrected the Indians' canal system in the area of Tempe and Mesa. The northern and western portions of the Salt River

Arizona Canal across from Cortez Park lagoons.

Valley had no Indian canals to restore, so in the 1880s the Arizona Canal Company built this one. The company sold the canal to the federal government in the early 1900s, and the Salt River Project (SRP) currently manages the canal.

This route travels the paved segment of the 38-mile canal, past a variety of parks, pleasant urban settings, and landmarks. In late spring, paloverde trees glow golden with blossoms. In summer, desert willow trees exude a sweet perfume from their pink trumpet flowers. Small colonies of ducks hang out all along the canal. Killdeer, with their drone-whine, dive in the sky. In the spring, the killdeer will cause a ruckus and feign injury if you get too close to a cluster of eggs they laid on the ground.

Underpasses take you through most of the major intersections, except for three. A crosswalk takes you across 7th Avenue. The next crossing occurs at 23rd Avenue, right after the intersection with the Cave Creek bikeway; this road sees little traffic. The last, and most complicated, street crossing comes at 54th Avenue and Cactus Road, and the most efficient way to cross here is counterclockwise.

Once past this busy double crossing, the path takes a pastoral turn. Horse property appears, a greenbelt attracts waterfowl, and Thunderbird Paseo Park offers rest areas and restrooms. Below is a mileage chart to gauge your distance.

Section	Cumulative Mileage	Section Mileage
24th Street to Maryland Avenue	0.8	0.8
Maryland Avenue to Glendale Avenue	0.7	1.5
Glendale Avenue to Northern Avenue	0.5	2.0
Northern Avenue to Central Avenue	1.0	3.0
Central Avenue to 7th Avenue	0.7	3.7
7th Avenue to 19th Avenue	1.0	4.7
19th Avenue to I-17	1.0	5.7
I-17 to 35th Avenue	1.0	6.7
35th Avenue to 51st Avenue	2.5	9.2
51st Avenue to 67th Avenue	2.5	11.7
67th Avenue to End (75th Avenue)	1.5	13.2

Route 36

INDIAN BEND BIKEWAY
TEMPE TOWN LAKE TO PIMA ROAD

Easy • Beginner

- ◆ A lushly landscaped multiuse bikeway passing through parks laced with lagoons
- ◆ Great place for bird-watching
- ◆ Scenic north-south crosstown route for the east Valley

DISTANCE: 12 miles one-way

PEAK CYCLING: Mid-October–April; early morning in warmer weather

ACCOMMODATIONS: Supplies, restaurants, and lodging in Scottsdale. Check out Hotel Valley Ho (6850 E. Main St., 480-248-2000) in Scottsdale. The 1950s resort, recently remodeled with a mix of retro and chic knitted with Wi-Fi, makes cool lodging. Café Zuzu, its restaurant, has soul-satisfying ultra-comfort food. Its slogan ("Good Eats Here") says it all. Check out its VH spa, too; its very cool Quantum Biofeedback Treatment helps you reach greater potential—from better road biking to off-loading a vice.

SPECIAL CONSIDERATIONS: This route floods after heavy rain.

STARTING POINTS: North access: Pima Road just north of Indian Bend Road. **South access:** Priest Drive just south of 202 Freeway (parking lot located under the freeway) along Tempe Town Lake. Several other access points in between.

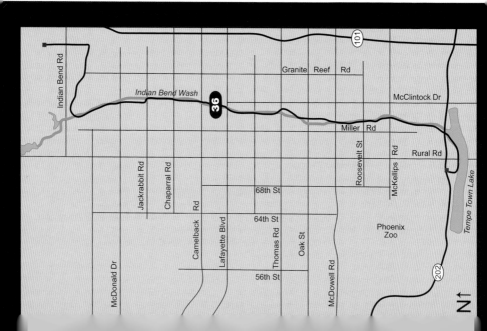

Landscaped with lakes, ponds, grass, and golf courses, this route looks more like a California park than a ride through the desert. After a 2-mile ride along Tempe Town Lake, the bikeway bends northward and heads into its Disney world of wetlands and green grass, aptly named the Scottsdale Greenway. The route takes you through parks landscaped to soothe and comfort the harried soul.

Indian Bend Wash parts from its water world oasis and returns to the desert on its eastern end.

What seems like a grossly inappropriate use of water at first blush actually turns out to be a creative attempt to manage floodwaters in the midst of dense development. Indian Bend Wash, a major drainage in the Valley, floods regularly. The Indian Bend Flood Control Project merely followed the natural flood course, confined the watercourse with structural elements, and enhanced it with recreational opportunities.

The lushest part of this project lies in the 4.5-mile-long greenbelt. The grassy swale swells from 600 to 1,000 feet wide to handle a 100-year flood (a major flood with a mathematical chance of occurring once a century). The well-manicured grassy areas protect the landscape from erosion caused by fast-moving floodwaters.

A string of ponds starting in El Dorado Park attracts several species of waterfowl, including a flock of displaced Canada geese—opportunistic snowbirds that never went home—and a variety of ducks. You might also catch sight of an elegant great egret or a great blue heron patiently waiting in the shallows for a meal. Farther north, Chaparral Lake, in Chaparral Park, is part of Arizona Game and Fish Department's urban fishing program. The department stocks the lake with trout in the winter and catfish in the warmer weather.

The route bends east at about mile 10 and comes back down to the realities of a desert landscape. If you need a pit stop, watch for restrooms at about mile 11.

At Pima Road, you may turn left (north) to follow the route to its uneventful end about 0.5 mile farther, just past Indian Bend Road, or return the way you came.

Route 37

SKUNK CREEK
SKUNK CREEK LINEAR PARK

Easy • Beginner

* Travels through urban open space
* Multiuse doubletrack
* Excellent family route

DISTANCE: 3.8 miles (Sunset Park to Arizona Canal) to 4.5 miles (51st Avenue to Arizona Canal) one-way; add 0.25 mile if starting point is 75th Avenue

PEAK CYCLING: October–March; early morning in warmer weather

ACCOMMODATIONS: Supplies, restaurants, and lodging in Phoenix

SPECIAL CONSIDERATIONS: Skunk Creek is a major floodway. Do not use underpasses during heavy rains.

STARTING POINTS: West end of Arizona Canal, about 0.25 mile east of 75th Avenue; Sunset Park in Glendale (corner of 57th Avenue and Union Hills Drive); or 51st Avenue between Loop 101 and Union Hills Drive.

The Valley has several areas that are excellent spots to glimpse urban wildlife, and this route travels through one of them: Skunk Creek Linear Park. Skunk Creek is a major flood drainage and sanctuary for wildlife. You might see anything from cactus wrens to red-tailed hawks, cottontails to coyotes,

and javelina in between. Gambel's quail sound their primal calls all day long. This is a short path, but very sweet.

The route starts next to the Foothills Sk8 Court Plaza, where kids flaunt their skateboard skills. The park has restrooms and water.

The route dips under major roads and past sleepy communities as it travels westward along the shallow Skunk Creek drainage. During the spring, after a wet winter, the brittlebush congregated along the route bloom with lively yellow composite flowers.

Agave plants along Skunk Creek Bike Path.

About halfway you must meander northward up to 63rd Avenue to cross Union Hills Drive, then head south back to the route. (Signs will direct you.) Shortly afterward, you pass Sunset Vista Park, where you can get water and rest in the shade of a ramada. The park has many recreation facilities, as well, including volleyball and horseshoes.

The route ends on the western end of the Arizona Canal. You may return the way you came, or travel along the Arizona Canal bikeway (see Route 35, p. 96).

POLLUTION ADVISORY

While blue skies reign in the desert cities, a brown haze sometimes hangs heavy in the air. Made mostly of carbon dioxide and nitrogen dioxide gases mingled (unsafely on some days) with ozone, the mix will cause damage to your lungs when pollution levels rise. High-smog days, once an oddity, occur more often. When pollution reaches unsafe levels, limit activity to early morning or avoid riding completely on these days. For air pollution information, call 602-771-2367 in Phoenix, 520-882-4247 in Tucson, or log on to www.adeq.gov.

Route 38

SUMMIT ROAD
SOUTH MOUNTAIN PARK/PRESERVE

Difficult • Experienced

* Winds through a protected desert mountain environment
* Rich spreads of wildflowers after a wet winter
* Two lanes; no shoulder

DISTANCE: 6.5 miles one-way

PEAK CYCLING: November–April; early morning in warmer weather

ACCOMMODATIONS: Supplies, restaurants, and lodging in Phoenix

SPECIAL CONSIDERATIONS: Park opens at 5 a.m. and closes at 11 p.m. This road sees high vehicular traffic on the weekends. Be sure to park your vehicle in designated parking areas, not in obvious pulloffs along the road. The park rangers have been known to arbitrarily ticket vehicles parked along the road (a $50 fine).

STARTING POINT: Take Central Avenue south to the South Mountain Park/Preserve entrance; go 0.2 mile to the ranger station or follow signs to the recreation center and park. See map on page 93.

Phoenix residents know one of the best points to view a sunset is at the top of Dobbins Lookout in South Mountain Park/Preserve. Though not the tallest peak in the park, the lookout gives the best views of the Valley.

Cyclist starting a double S-curve on lower Summit road.

The road up to the lookout—one winding, twisting route with tight hairpin turns and muscle-building grades—makes an excellent workout.

The beginning of the route gives you a chance to warm up on a gentle grade, and speed bumps slow traffic. Once past the ranger station, the road starts snaking with short but bold rollers. At MP 1.5, veer left at a sign pointing to the Summit Road.

The grade switches from mild rollers to a consistent climb. After a long slog up the mountain, the route calms down a bit at MP 3, then picks up the angle again about 0.5 mile later. You get a reprieve at about mile 4.5 when the route descends into a saddle. At the signed turnoff, veer left for Dobbins Lookout. At MP 5, the route gets back into climbing mode again, this time with an austere tenor as the route ascends up to Dobbins Lookout.

Cyclists who cannot bear to stop at a lesser citadel should ignore the Dobbins Lookout turnoff and continue up the mountain. At about MP 6, you come to another fork in the road. Taking the Buena Vista turnoff gives you unabashed views south of the mountain, but it won't get you to the top. To continue to the road's end, veer right. The route doggedly climbs upward along a rocky and shrub-covered ridgetop, where bouldery outcroppings pop up among saguaro cacti.

At road's end, mile 6.5, television towers, microwave dishes, radio transmitters, and satellite receivers crowd along the road, sending all kinds of electronic signals. Because of the health controversies surrounding these electronics, you may want to avoid this area completely or immediately return the way you came.

On the whole, the climb up the mountain looks harder than you might find it and the ride down is more troublesome. The curves are hard to judge and easy to overshoot. But mastering the downhill is also part of hill work.

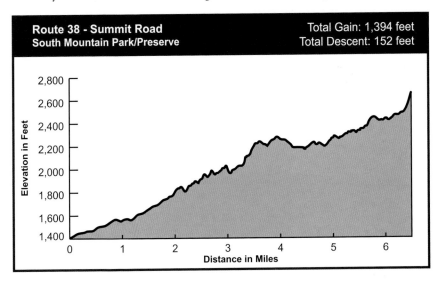

While most cyclists consider this route challenging enough on its own, some see it as the cherry on the top of the sundae and use it to finish off a long cycle ride. Tom Baker did just that back in 1979 when he and four other cyclists (Eric Prosnier, Doug Braly, Jim Stein, and Scott Trulson) decided they would embark on their own bicycle challenge inspired by the Big Ride Across America (which crossed the country from Seattle to Washington, D.C.). The cyclists charted a 325-mile route around Arizona that climbed a total of 17,000 vertical feet, with the intention of finishing in 24 hours or less. This private event, which they called Arizona Challenge, eventually evolved into the multiday road event called Answer to the Challenge, coordinated by Landis Cyclery. The current event covers 325 miles and 22,000 feet of climbing over three days instead of 24 hours.

All the cyclists finished that first Arizona Challenge. Eric Prosnier reports that he headed to a Dairy Queen, but it was not open at 5 a.m. Tom Baker headed to the top of South Mountain to finish his ride. With that in mind, you might consider this route an excellent one for a sunrise.

COOL TIPS FOR HOT WORKOUTS

- If you're not used to the heat, acclimatize slowly the first couple of weeks.

- Once you acclimatize, you reduce the amount of electrolytes released while sweating, but you also start to sweat earlier. The more in shape you become, the more water you will need. Trained athletes sweat more, and begin sweating sooner, than weekend warriors.

- Work out as early in the day as possible—when there's less heat and pollution—or late in the afternoon.

- Bring an electrolyte drink, and drink often. A general rule of thumb is to drink a quart of liquids every hour.

- During monsoon season, keep in mind that the extra humidity will hamper your body's system of cooling down through perspiration.

- Stop exercising if you feel dizzy, faint, and/or nauseous—all are possible signs of heat exhaustion. Head for shade and drink water until you recover, or you may face the risk of developing the more dangerous heatstroke.

Route 39

SAN JUAN ROAD
SOUTH MOUNTAIN PARK/PRESERVE

Moderate • Beginner

◆ Winds through a mountain preserve
◆ Rich spreads of wildflowers after a wet winter
◆ Two lanes; no shoulder

DISTANCE: 5.5 miles one-way

PEAK CYCLING: November–April; early morning in warmer weather

ACCOMMODATIONS: Supplies, restaurants, and lodging in Phoenix

SPECIAL CONSIDERATIONS: Park opens at 5 a.m. and closes at 11 p.m. This road sees a high amount of vehicular traffic on the weekends. If you bring your vehicle, try to park in designated parking areas, not in obvious pulloffs along the road. The park rangers have been known to arbitrarily ticket vehicles parked along the road, which gets a $50 fine.

STARTING POINT: Take Central Avenue south to its end at the South Mountain Park/ Preserve entrance. Drive 0.2 mile to the ranger station and park, or follow the signs to the recreation center parking lot. See map on page 93.

Summit Road in the distance behind a show of wildflowers in South Mountain Park.

S outh Mountain Park/Preserve, one of the country's largest city parks, has a reputation for its premier mountain bike routes. The park/preserve also has two excellent road bike routes. This one, San Juan Road, suits just about any level of cyclist.

The South Mountain system comprises three distinct ranges: Ma-Ha-Tauk Range to the north, Gila Mountain Range in the south, and Guadalupe Range in the east. In typical Sonoran Desert fashion, the ranges run diagonally across the desert floor. This route winds through San Juan Valley between the Ma-Ha-Tauk and Gila Mountain ranges to the western end of the park.

In this Lower Sonoran Desert vegetation zone, plants, bushes, and trees tend to gather where water does. The low-point roadsides, where much water eventually ends up, nurture a rich growth of flora: paloverde and ironwood trees; saguaro, cholla, and barrel cacti; and wolfberry and creosote bushes. Wildflowers color the desert floor after a wet winter. These wildflowers, particularly Mexican gold poppies and bladderpod, like to carpet the rumpled bajada fanning from the Gila Mountain Range. In the summer, heat-loving desert senna plants show yellow blossoms that fruit into pods.

With the road resurfaced in late 2004 and smooth as silk, the route feels like a genteel ride in the desert backcountry. Fun rollers get sandwiched between mild climbs that coast calmly on the downhill. These dips, heaves, and bends produce blind spots and demand your full attention while negotiating them.

The route ends with a final climb at San Juan parking area and ramada. A panoramic view to the north looks at downtown Phoenix, then reaches past distinctive Piestawa Peak to the Bradshaw Mountains on the far horizon. Return the way you came.

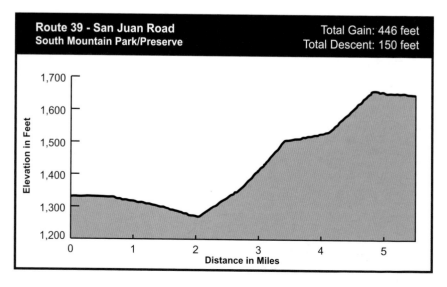

Route 39 - San Juan Road
South Mountain Park/Preserve

Total Gain: 446 feet
Total Descent: 150 feet

Route 40

PAPAGO SALADO LOOP
STREETS AND BIKEWAY AROUND PAPAGO PARK

Easy • Beginner

• Travels through three cities, passing through and around Papago Park
• Bike path and bike lanes

DISTANCE: 12-mile loop

PEAK CYCLING: November–April; early morning in warmer weather

ACCOMMODATIONS: Supplies, restaurants, and lodging in Phoenix and Tempe. Check out
Mucho Gusto Taqueria and Mexican Bistro (603 W. University Drive, 480-921-1850)
in Tempe for a different taste of Mexican fare that wins awards.

SPECIAL CONSIDERATIONS: A segment of this loop travels a busy street with a bike lane.

STARTING POINT: Osborn Road and 64th Street in Scottsdale.

Papago Salado, a route in the making, will form an 11-mile loop connecting segments from four 20th century canals through three cities: Phoenix,
Tempe, and Scottsdale. Until finished, this route will take you in the
general vicinity.

The route works for any level of cyclist, presenting a scenic, relaxing
route for experienced cyclists and a comfortable one for beginners. The first
leg starts in southern Scottsdale along the Crosscut Canal on 64th Street
at Osborn Road. The canal, built in the early 1900s for powering the
Crosscut Hydro Plant at Washington Street, now supplies power and drink-
ing water. A settlement of Yaqui Indians, who helped build and maintain the canal, once stood at this starting point.

Years ago, large trees shaded this and other canals. These were unlined, open-ditch canals, and the U.S. Army Corps of Engineers cut down the trees, thinking they slurped up too much canal water, lined the canals with con-

The lagoons in Papago Park near the bikeway bring an oasis atmosphere in the middle of the desert.

crete, and created the Salt River Project to manage the system. SRP closed the canals to the public for a while, perhaps because people used to water ski behind trucks along the pre-renovated canals. Nevertheless, Salt River Project has opened its arms to the non-motorized public in the past two decades.

At about mile 2, the route approaches the curious ruddy mounds called Papago Buttes. More curious is a pyramid, the tomb of Arizona's first governor, George Hunt, set at the buttes and seen from the bike trail. The route then passes through the Hunt Bass Fishery, a cottonwood-willow riparian area that gives a secluded feel. Arizona Game & Fish Department stocks this waterway. Watch for giant blue herons that wade in the shallows looking for aquatic life to munch. Urban fishing lagoons, located right next to the bike trail in the Papago Park system, present an oasislike place to break.

About 0.5 mile south of the lagoons, watch for a sharp right turn to another lagoon that will land you on College Avenue in Tempe (mile 3). Head south on College Avenue's superwide bike lane for about 1 mile to yet another waterway, Tempe Town Lake. A relatively new multiuse path takes you along the course of the Salt River. The city placed inflatable dams to pool the river for a developed river walk. When you get to Priest Drive, turn right (north). Cyclists not used to street traffic should use the sidewalk path for the next couple of miles, until the bike lane appears at Galvin Parkway.

Galvin Parkway presents a pleasant ride as it cuts right through the Papago Park system. Where the bikeway along Crosscut Canal took you on the eastern edge of the park, Galvin Parkway takes you through the heart. The Phoenix Zoo and Desert Botanical Gardens are located along this road. Just north of McDowell Road, watch for a spur path to take you back to the Crosscut Canal, or continue north on 64th Street to the start of this route on Osborn Road.

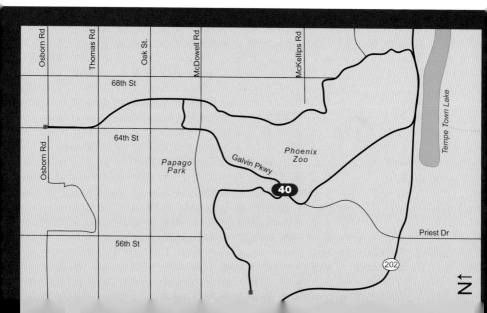

Route 41

PHOENIX SONORAN BIKEWAY
SOUTH MOUNTAIN PARK/PRESERVE TO CAVE CREEK

Easy to Moderate • Beginner to Intermediate

- Travels through several different neighborhoods in Phoenix
- Bike lanes and bikeways

DISTANCE: 38 miles one-way

PEAK CYCLING: November–April; early morning in hot weather

ACCOMMODATIONS: Supplies, restaurants, and lodging in Phoenix

SPECIAL CONSIDERATIONS: Parts of this route travel busy streets.

STARTING POINTS: South Mountain Park/Preserve (far southern end of Central Avenue); 3rd Avenue and Roosevelt Street in downtown Phoenix; or northern end of Cave Creek Road in Cave Creek. See map on page 93.

Called one of the best cycling secrets in Phoenix, the Phoenix Sonoran Bikeway takes you through several different neighborhoods to experience many of the Valley's different personalities: city streets to mountain parks, new downtown architecture to historic districts and western towns, barrios to bedroom communities. The route starts at South Mountain Park and stretches all the way to the town of Cave Creek. One of the best segments spans from Roosevelt Street to the end of the Dreamy Draw Bikeway in the Phoenix Mountains Preserve. This is a relaxing segment with easy cycling that appeals to every experience level.

Starting in South Mountain Park/Preserve and heading northward, watch for Mystery Castle located just outside the park. The three-story castle, made of stone, adobe, automobile parts, and petroglyphs, is held together by a quirky cement mixture that includes goat's milk.

South Entrance, Dreamy Draw Bikeway.

Continue north, following Central Avenue through the barrio. Some of the best Mexican restaurants lie on this southern segment. Keep that in mind when deciding where to start and stop your trip.

At about mile 6, you hit the edges of downtown Phoenix at Buckeye Road. The road becomes one-way around Lincoln Street where it ducks underneath a railroad viaduct. Watch for the route to jog left (west) on Jefferson Street to 3rd Avenue. Now you're in the heart of downtown Phoenix, where old buildings rub shoulders with high-rises.

Within 0.5 mile, the route enters the Roosevelt Historic District, Phoenix's first historic district. The neighborhood, settled in the late 1800s, was home to many prominent Phoenicians, including Congressman Carl Hayden and Baron M. Goldwater (father of Sen. Barry M. Goldwater). In Phoenix's rising-from-the-ashes style, the neighborhood has experienced a true renaissance. Old, dilapidated homes have been restored or remodeled, specialty restaurants and a bakery (stop at My Florist on McDowell near 6th Avenue for a bakery treat and coffee break) have opened, and art galleries have made it the heart of First Friday artwalks.

At McDowell Road, about mile 10.5, the route enters the Willo District, the neighborhood of choice for Phoenician artists and the art-minded. Detouring off the bike route into the residential section makes for a neat tour of the different architecture styles. At Virginia, a bike-route sign points in several different directions. This route keeps heading straight (north).

At about mile 13, the route crosses the Grand Canal bridge and enters another established neighborhood. The homes, especially 1 mile farther along, were built during a time when landscaping leaned toward cooling the area rather than conservation-oriented xeriscaping, which uses drought-tolerant plants. These homes get irrigation from a nearby canal to support the lush and mature landscaping, which cools the area by 10 degrees or more.

At Maryland Avenue, about mile 15.5, turn right (east). This segment of the route follows a bike lane all the way to the Squaw Peak Parkway at about mile 17.5. Follow the bike-route signs, turning left; just before Sierra Vista, turn right under the freeway and left out onto the street. Just before 20th Street, turn left (north) along the Arizona Canal, staying on the left side of the canal. After the underpass at Glendale Avenue (about 0.5 mile away), cross the bridge over the canal, continue across the right side of the canal, and enter a frontage route where you turn right (south), heading back toward Glendale Avenue. At Glendale, make a hairpin turn onto Dreamy Draw Drive—turn left (east) onto the sidewalk to get to Dreamy Draw.

This segment brings you into a quiet neighborhood lying right next to the Phoenix Mountains Preserve. It's an easy uphill climb for just over 1 mile to Dreamy Draw Park. About halfway, the route gets inundated with the smell of Mexican food wafting from Aunt Chilada's restaurant. By all means, do not resist the temptation to appease your appetite here, as it's one of the best Mexican restaurants on this side of town, with very popular happy hours and a wonderful breakfast buffet.

At the end of the street, turn right (east) onto a bridge that crosses the Squaw Peak Parkway, and then continue on a paved multiuse path in the mountain park. This 2-mile segment gives you an open-space experience in the city. After a wet winter, in March, wildflowers cover the desert floor. If you're cycling on a summer morning, yellow desert senna flowers bloom along the route.

The bike path ends at about mile 21.2, and the route travels bike lanes on neighborhood streets. Follow the Phoenix Sonoran Bikeway signs as the route jigs through the northeast side of Phoenix. At about mile 25, turn right (north) onto Cave Creek Road. Now on the edges of the city, the route heads into the open desert. In a few miles, a sign announces you're on the Desert Foothills Scenic Drive. The 10 miles you travel to Cave Creek's city limits take you through an enjoyable stretch of desert. A few miles farther, about mile 38, you reach the laid-back, Western-style downtown of Cave Creek. Definitely touristy, but with a good dose of class, the town has several neat venues to eat, grab a cup of coffee, or peruse shops and galleries.

Route 42
BARTLETT DAM ROAD
CAVE CREEK ROAD TO BARTLETT RESERVOIR

Difficult • Experienced

- Challenging ride through classic Sonoran Desert landscape to a desert lake
- Rollers, steep grades, and beautiful scenery
- Two lanes; no shoulder

DISTANCE: 14 miles one-way

PEAK CYCLING: November–February

ACCOMMODATIONS: Basic supplies, restaurants, and lodging in Cave Creek

SPECIAL CONSIDERATIONS: To avoid dangerous boater traffic, cycle in the winter. A summer ride can be hazardous—unless it's on a full-moon night, which Cave Creek resident Kaolin "Cosmo" Cummens recommends as his "actual favorite time to cycle in the desert."

STARTING POINT: From Cave Creek, go east 11 miles on Cave Creek Road to Bartlett Dam Road.

Kaolin "Cosmo" Cummens, owner of Cave Creek's Flat Tire Bike Shop, says this route has the most extreme climbing you can get in the area. He likes the excitement of the fast downhills into the Verde River drainage, and the endurance climb out.

"You don't have to brake on any of the hills," advises Cosmo. "I just circle the parking lot at the end of the road to slow down. Then I dip my front tire into Bartlett Reservoir. That's part of the whole trip, then riding back out."

Cosmo, who takes to the speed and reckless moments of mountain bike racing, says he hovers "in the 50s" on the route's downhills with his road bike twitching and feeling "like it's ready to come apart." Still, he wishes he had a "70 chain ring to pedal faster."

Once on Bartlett Dam Road, the easygoing stretch of the route ends and the fun begins. For the next 14 miles, starting at MP 0, the route twists around some rugged terrain as it screams down one ridge and struggles up the next. First the route snakes into Camp Creek drainage, showing you a beautiful desert landscape. In March, after a wet winter, wildflowers color the roadsides. In May, creamy clusters of flowers arc from shaggy yuccas, and funnel-shaped blossoms top off the arms of saguaro cacti.

The route struggles out of Camp Creek and tops out at about MP 5. Still winding with rollers, the route crosses a basin for several miles. At MP 7, you can see the Verde River canyon, but not the river. Another high-drama descent brings you to Indian Springs Wash and the climb out to MP 10. The azure waters of Bartlett Reservoir show up about this time, flowing at the feet of the Mazatzal Mountains. A sliver of a shoulder also shows up and leads you down to the reservoir.

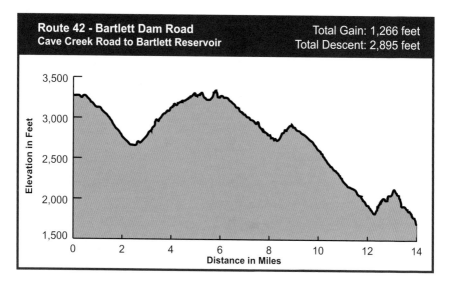

Route 42 - Bartlett Dam Road
Cave Creek Road to Bartlett Reservoir

Total Gain: 1,266 feet
Total Descent: 2,895 feet

Bartlett Dam Road to Bartlett Reservoir.

You don't have to pay anything to enter the recreation area at the reservoir. (Pay stations disburse parking passes, not admission passes, for $5.) Covered ramadas, restrooms, and cool Verde River water pooled in the midst of a wild desert landscape make this an unusual but beautiful place to rest before your climb out. Whether you return to the town of Cave Creek by way of bicycle or car shuttle, stop by cyclist-friendly Cave Creek Coffee Company (6033 E. Cave Creek Road, 480-488-0603) to remedy any weariness from this demanding route with coffee, sweet treats, and a relaxing atmosphere.

DRESSING FOR THE DESERT

Phoenix cyclist Eric Prosnier says, "There's never a bad time to ride in Arizona, just bad clothes." This statement holds especially true when temperatures rise and most people wear light-colored cotton or linen clothing that's loose-fitting to keep cool. This sane practice exempts cyclists, as black lycra shorts and synthetic materials that wick away moisture remain *de rigueur* for most cyclists. Wicking fabrics can work too well for your own good because you may not even know you are sweating. This means systematic hydration becomes imperative.

In the winter, when the weather cools to near freezing during the night and heats up to a sweet degree for a perfect ride, cyclists should simply layer, especially for long rides.

Most cyclists never stop riding in the high country, where daytime temps can span from the 80s to 90s in the summer to the 40s or 50s in the winter. That famous dry heat allows you to ride pretty much all day in the high desert, even during the highs. Just be sure to bring rain gear, especially in the summertime when storms stack up rather suddenly. Also, stuffing a long-sleeve top in your pack for a longer ride will make sense if a storm lets loose with the typical 20-plus-degree drop in temperature.

Finally, whatever the season, wherever you are: Always hydrate.

Route 43

BUSH HIGHWAY
EAST THOMAS ROAD TO AZ 87

Moderate • Beginner to Intermediate

◆ Travels a winding road with rollers in pristine desert

◆ Saguaro Lake makes a scenic destination

◆ Two lanes; bike lane first 6 miles, remainder has no shoulder

DISTANCE: 6 to 15 miles one-way

PEAK CYCLING: October–March

ACCOMMODATIONS: Supplies, restaurants, and lodging in Phoenix and Mesa

SPECIAL CONSIDERATIONS: This route has heavy traffic in warm weather, adding danger to the no-shoulder segment from Usery Road to Saguaro Lake and beyond. At the time of publication, a project to extend the shoulder to Saguaro Lake in 2007 was pending. The first six miles of this route are suitable for a beginner, with the remaining portion intermediate.

STARTING POINTS: Take the 202 Freeway towards its eastern end and turn left (north) on North Higley Road; go about 0.2 mile and turn right (east) onto East Thomas Road; go about 1 mile to Bush Highway. If you plan to do a loop or start from a point in the East Valley, take McDowell Road to Bush Highway. MP 21 is the first mile marker. See map on p. 93.

Bush Highway, named for Mesa businessman Harvey Bush, originated as the construction road from Apache Junction to the Stewart Mountain Dam, which forms the last, and most popular, reservoir along the Salt River,

Bush Highway starts out easy as it heads into the Goldfield Mountains.

Saguaro Lake. Bush championed the continuation of the road to AZ 87, also called the Beeline Highway, because he had a second home in Payson.

This route takes you all the way to the Beeline if you're ready for a good workout and grand panoramas of the Valley mountain ranges. But if it's lake-side scenery you're after, make Saguaro Lake your destination.

Right away, the route gets off to a scenic start as it heads north between Schlechts Butte and the Usery Mountains, dropping quickly into the lower Salt River Valley. A designated bike lane makes this user-friendly for cyclists. The smell of wet desert exudes from a sea of tamarisks, with glimmers of blue river water appearing in the breaches. Granite Reef Recreation Center gives you a chance to make a quick pit stop. Granite Reef Dam diverts water from the Salt River into canals running north and south of the river.

The road rolls with ease over the desert floor, surrounded by low-rising mountains, and with the almost 8,000-foot-high Four Peaks in the distant north, the scenery never stops. Watch for Mount McDowell, also called Red Mountain, rising 2,800 feet in the west. Wild horses roam in this area. In the movie *Man From Snowy River*, wild horses were called *brumbies*. With that in mind, area cyclists formed a group called the Red Mountain Brumbeys.

The route soon takes a more serious mien with dips and curves that require your full attention at MP 23, where a sign warns that these mountain characteristics continue for the next 10 miles. From now on, your ride is fast and fun, following the contours of the desert foothills that rise and fall.

The bike lane ends after the junction with Usery Pass Road at MP 27; this leaves you on your own on this two-lane highway for the rest of the route. Beginners may want to make this their turnaround point. As you wend your way toward Saguaro Lake, you pass some of best scenery of the ride along the Goldfield Mountains. The Great Western Trail, an off-highway route from Canada to Mexico, travels right through the area, and an access point entering

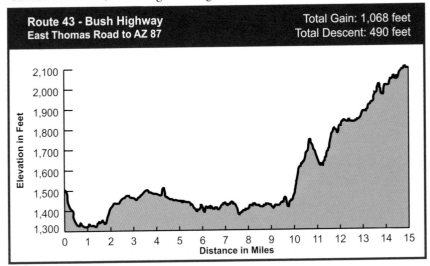

Bulldog Canyon in the Goldfields lies just before Sheep's Crossing (MP 29), where the road crosses the Salt River. The bend the road makes at this crossing seems to head you right into a volcanic tuff ridge of the Goldfields.

Stewart Mountain Dam (the dam's namesake mountain rises northwest of the highway) at MP 31 signals your arrival at Saguaro Lake. Detours on a couple of signed access points bring you to the lakeshore, the most popular and developed one being Saguaro del Norte near MP 33. By MP 34, you start one long ascent out of the river valley up to AZ 87. The route travels alongside The Rolls, a popular off-road-vehicle area known for its steep hills and treacherous technical moments.

Once at AZ 87, you can return the way you came or continue on a loop with a nice wide shoulder heading south on AZ 87 about 20 miles, left (south) on Gilbert Road about 2.5 miles, left (east) on McDowell Road about 10 miles, then left (north) on Power Road until it turns into Bush Highway and returns to your vehicle. If you plan to do a loop, be sure to take a moment at each hilltop after Saguaro Lake along Bush Highway to catch the gorgeous views behind you.

FREEWAY CYCLING

Cyclists are allowed on several of the major freeways in Arizona. You must use the shoulder at all times while on a freeway. Cyclists report seeing "all kinds of interesting things" along these shoulders, and you should pay attention to the pavement and what's upon it in order to avoid a problem.

Bicycles ARE allowed on the following freeways and segments:

- I-8: MP 0 (California border) to MP 174 (Trekell Road)
- I-10: MP 0 (California border) to MP 133 (99th Avenue); MP 267 (Valencia Road) to MP 391 (New Mexico border)
- I-15: Entire length in Arizona
- I-17: MP 217 (Pinnacle Peak Road) to MP 340 (Flagstaff)
- I-19: Kilometer 0 (Nogales) to kilometer 69 (Duval Mine Road)
- I-40: Entire length in Arizona
- Loop 303: Entire length

Bicycles are NOT allowed on the following freeways:

- Piestewa Peak Freeway (State Route 51)
- Loop 101
- Loop 202
- US 60: from MP 160 (Junction I-17 at Thomas Road) to MP 198 (Goldfield Road)
- State Route 143
- State Route 153
- State Route 210

Route 44

TORTILLA FLAT
APACHE TRAIL (AZ 88): APACHE JUNCTION TO END OF PAVEMENT

Difficult • Experienced

◆ Challenging route that twists through quintessential Sonoran Desert
  landscape with plenty of demanding rollers
◆ Popular training route
◆ Two lanes; no shoulder

DISTANCE: 16 miles (to Tortilla Flat) to 21 miles (to pavement's end) one-way

PEAK CYCLING: October–March

ACCOMMODATIONS: Supplies, restaurants, and lodging in Apache Junction
  and Phoenix; food at Tortilla Flat

SPECIAL CONSIDERATIONS: This route requires hill-climbing skills and experience
  handling a mountainous road without a shoulder. Do not cycle this route in the
  early morning from late spring to fall; the boating traffic is extremely dangerous.

STARTING POINT: In Apache Junction, go north on Idaho Road to AZ 88 and turn right
  (east); MP 199 is the first mile marker. See map on p. 93.

A favorite route with professional cyclists, the ride on the Apache Trail to
Tortilla Flat makes an excellent workout. Ironman triathlete Christian
Broadwell likes the intensity of the route to Tortilla Flat. Often going faster than
the cars, Christian flies around bends at 35 mph. While most cyclists turn around
at Tortilla Flat—a block-long clapboard town with a population of six and a
restaurant serving Killer Chili and half-pound hamburgers—Christian heads
up the road's final segment of pavement, a grueling climb of more than 5 miles.

"It tests all your strength," Christian says of the unrelenting climb. "It's
such a long hill, it makes the return ride seem easy."

For nonracers who don't mind a challenge as long as the route has lots
of scenery, this is one of the desert's best, winding between the Superstition
Mountains on the north and the gold-straked Goldfields to the south. Canyon
Lake makes an extravagant finale to this exceptional route.

Once an Indian trading and raiding route, the Apache Trail now links Phoenix
with the Roosevelt Dam. The state developed the route to haul equipment and
materials to build the dam. Heading east on Apache Trail, the route gets a
polite start as it travels the eastern edges of the Valley past remnants of civilization—scatterings of homes, last-chance markets and bait shops, a couple of
restaurants, and the ghost town of Goldfield. The landscape, rolling desert hills

covered with paloverde trees, several varieties of cholla cactus, and stunning saguaro cactus, gets a dose of drama from the powerful and pretty western ramparts of the Superstition Mountains. This segment of the Superstitions turns gold after a wet winter with one of the state's best displays of Mexican gold poppies. In May, the paloverde trees explode with yellow from thousands of flowers on each tree.

Needle Vista View Point, located near MP 204, gives you a safe pullout if you need it. The view of the Weavers Needle (whose shadow is supposed to fall upon the fabled Lost Dutchman Mine) deep in the Superstition Mountains comes up a little lackluster, however. If you want a good look at the formation, hike the Dutchman or Peralta trail.

If you don't need to stop at the vista, keep going to get momentum up for the first of many long, steep ascents up a ridge on this route—in this case, a mile-plus-long twisting climb. After a few dips and heaves, the road takes its time navigating a long, twisting descent. All these wriggling rollers and big climbs up and down ridgelines will keep pushing you, with little room for slack.

The route calms down at about MP 208 when it arrives at Canyon Lake. A steel trellis bridge crossing a canyon between MPs 209 and 210 allows only one vehicle at a time, so cross with caution. After you cycle a second bridge, which crosses Boulder Canyon between MPs 211 and 212, get ready for the climb out of the canyon and over and down another ridge to the town of Tortilla Flat. If you plan to end your ride at Tortilla Flat, stop in the Superstition Saloon for a beverage and soul-satisfying meal. Thousands of dollar bills and foreign currency deck the old wooden walls.

If you want to cycle to the pavement's end, about 5 miles farther, get ready for the longest climb of the route. Once you reach the turnaround just past MP 220, it's all downhill back to Tortilla Flat. Watch out during the route's decent for two sharp turns on particularly steep grades. Use your brakes or get ready for a long drop off the side of the mountain that will land you in the cactus.

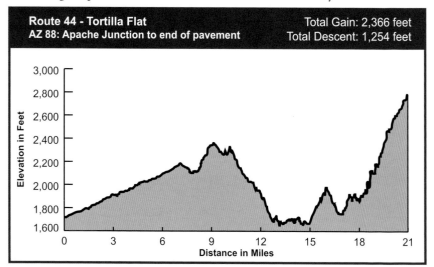

Route 44 - Tortilla Flat
AZ 88: Apache Junction to end of pavement
Total Gain: 2,366 feet
Total Descent: 1,254 feet

Route 45

RIO VERDE DRIVE
PIMA ROAD TO FOREST ROAD

Moderate • Intermediate

* Travels along the northern edge of the Valley downhill to the Verde River
* Two lanes; narrow shoulder

DISTANCE: 12 miles one-way

PEAK CYCLING: October–April; early morning in warmer weather

ACCOMMODATIONS: Supplies, restaurants, and lodging in Scottsdale

SPECIAL CONSIDERATIONS: This route sees less vehicle traffic on the weekend.

STARTING POINTS: West access: Pima Road, about 8.3 miles north of Loop 101. **East access:** north end of Forest Road (from Shea Boulevard, travel north on Fountain Hills Boulevard to McDowell Mountain Road, then continue on Forest Road to its end). See map on p. 121.

A fast, fun, and feisty route, Rio Verde heads right where its name implies: to the Verde River. While dropping about a thousand feet along the route to the river, you pass some of the most exclusive developments in the Valley. Landscaped as hybrid open space, the developments might remain invisible if their signs didn't announce them.

By about mile 5, you leave the developments behind and an imposing panorama of the rugged ridgelines of the Mazatzal Mountains looms ahead, including the distinctive Four Peaks. By mile 10, the Verde River's riparian cover comes into sight. Just under 2 miles farther, at the road's end, you can return the way you came or continue south on the McDowell Mountain Route (see Route 46, p. 120).

Route 46

McDOWELL MOUNTAIN ROUTE
FOREST ROAD, McDOWELL MOUNTAIN ROAD, AND FOUNTAIN HILLS BOULEVARD

Moderate • Intermediate

- ◆ Travels a diverse and beautiful desert landscape along a mountain park with stunning panoramas
- ◆ Two lanes; narrow shoulder

DISTANCE: 14 miles one-way

PEAK CYCLING: October–April; early morning in warmer weather

ACCOMMODATIONS: Supplies, restaurants, and lodging in Scottsdale and Phoenix

SPECIAL CONSIDERATIONS: This road sees less vehicle traffic on weekends.

STARTING POINTS: North access: From Pima Road, go east on Rio Verde Drive to Forest Road and turn right. **South access:** From Shea Boulevard in Fountain Hills, go north on Fountain Hills Blvd.

This route, part of a long training loop and a segment of the Tour de Phoenix perimeter ride in the spring, makes a great moderate ride on the northern edge of the Valley. The route has classic scenery, rollers, and a token shoulder—all the components of a great ride.

The route starts with gentle, pleasant rollers as it heads south from Rio Verde Drive on Forest Road. The Four Peaks rise in the east; in the southern distance Weavers Needle pokes up from the Superstition Mountains.

Cyclist hugging shoulder on McDowell Road with Four Peaks in the background.

A bike lane shows up along the Rio Verde development for a short distance. At about mile 3, turn right onto McDowell Mountain Road. This segment of the route starts with MP 11, leaving developed life behind as it travels alongside the McDowell Mountain Preserve. The route passes the park entrance between MPs 6 and 5, then crosses into Fountain Hills by MP 4. A bike lane takes you on Fountain Hills Road to Shea Boulevard and the end of this route. Experienced cyclists make a long loop of approximately 70 miles by turning right (west) onto Shea, then north onto Scottsdale Road, and east onto Rio Verde.

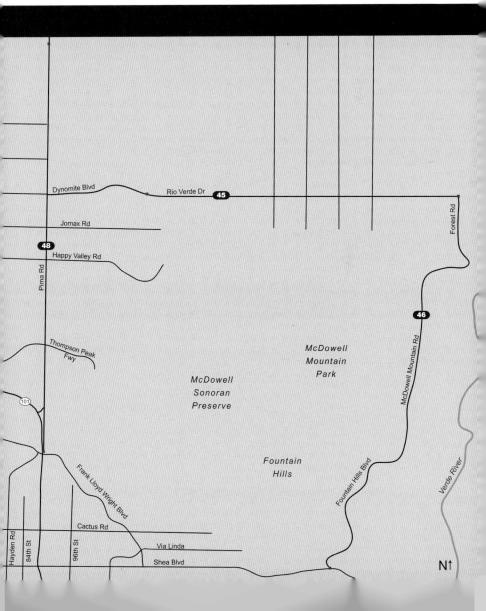

Route 47

PECOS ROAD
PECOS ROAD THROUGH AHWATUKEE

Easy • Beginner

- Travels a perimeter road just outside the southern end of the Valley
- A fast route with mountain scenery
- Four lanes; wide shoulder

DISTANCE: 7 miles one-way

PEAK CYCLING: November–April; early mornings in warmer weather

ACCOMMODATIONS: Supplies, restaurants, and lodging in Phoenix and Tempe. The Sheraton Wild Horse Pass Resort and Spa (602-225-0100), just south along I-10 on Wild Horse Pass Boulevard, keeps the local tribes' heritage alive. A beautiful lobby, water-feature wetlands, and extraordinary restaurants—Ko'Sin for breakfast, lunch, and dinner and Kai for a more formal dinner—make it a great stop after a ride.

SPECIAL CONSIDERATIONS: At the time of this writing, plans were pending to extend a freeway along this route. The final decision has gotten waylaid because of conflicting variables. With that in mind, we felt this popular route had a good chance of remaining open for a while.

STARTING POINTS: Just west of I-10, around 48th Street, on Pecos Road. From Chandler Boulevard, turn south onto 48th Street to Pecos Road.

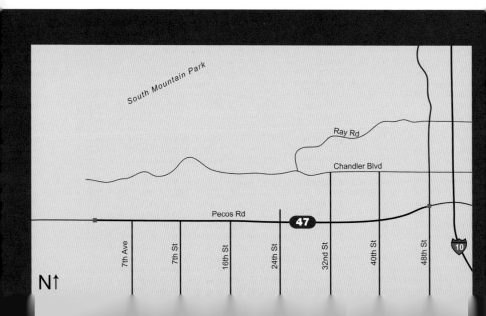

Without a doubt, Pecos Road is the route of choice for cyclists who live in the southeast Valley. Fast and moderate in length, with a w-i-d-e shoulder, this road has special appeal. Also, with South Mountain Park to the north and the Sierra Estrella to the southwest, the road has pleasing scenery with an out-of-town feel.

Starting from I-10, the road heads westward toward the Sierra Estrella, quickly parting company with the handful of businesses at the start of the route. The road passes residential pockets, which are throwing a monkey wrench into the proposed freeway route, and about midway intersects with Desert Foothills Parkway. You can add some hill work to your ride with a detour onto the winding and scenic roads of this mountainside community.

Continuing on Pecos Road, the route gets more acquainted with the Sierra Estrella and these mountains' rough-hewn topography. Wild horses roam around here, and you may spot one from the route. These mustangs gave the Sheraton Wild Horse Pass Resort, located just south on the Gila River Indian Community, its name.

This route ends when Pecos Road suddenly stops just past 7th Avenue with no connecting roads for an alternate route. Return the way you came.

Route 48

PIMA ROAD
FRANK LLOYD WRIGHT BOULEVARD TO END OF PIMA ROAD

Moderate • Beginner to Intermediate

- Travels the edge of the Valley in a patchwork of open space
- Excellent training route
- Two to three lanes; divided road with stretches of bike lane

DISTANCE: 18 miles one-way

PEAK CYCLING: Mid-October–April; early morning in warmer weather

ACCOMMODATIONS: Supplies, restaurants, and lodging in Scottsdale

SPECIAL CONSIDERATIONS: This route contains a several-mile stretch with high-use traffic. Less experienced cyclists should start the route at Thompson Peak Parkway, where a bicycle trail begins.

STARTING POINT: Northeast corner of Frank Lloyd Wright Boulevard and E. Shea Blvd. See map on p. 121.

Starting along a string of strip malls, this route takes you northward from the center of activity in south Scottsdale to the city's outer edges, where open space still stands. When the shopping area ends, a bike trail follows the road for cyclists that want less exposure to traffic. The imposing power lines along the very beginning of the route stretch all the way to the Grand Canyon.

About 2 miles into the route, near Cactus Road, the lanes increase to three. By about mile 4, at the intersection with the Loop 101 freeway, the sidewalk disappears, forcing all cyclists onto the road. Beginners might want to make this their turnaround point. Turn right as if heading onto the entrance ramp, but remain on the frontage road, which is Pima Road. Once again, an entrance sign for the Loop 101 appears, and you should hang to the right lane, which departs the freeway system once and for all. A bike lane wavers in and out of existence for the first mile, then stays the course from Thompson Peak Parkway (mile 8.4) to the road's end.

On weekends, this segment draws a number of cyclists. The persistent uphill grade makes a good strength-building workout. You can extend your ride by turning right at Dynamite Boulevard and cycling the Rio Verde route (see Route 45, p. 119) and even make a loop by continuing on the McDowell Mountain Route (see Route 46, p. 120), then heading west on Shea Boulevard back to Frank Lloyd Wright Boulevard. Shea Boulevard is a busy and fast highway with no shoulder.

Pima Road

REGION 5

CENTRAL ARIZONA (DESERT)

The lowlands in central Arizona, mostly ringing Phoenix, venture out into the desert where populations evanesce and scenery intensifies. Rollers and open space are the operative words here. Lying close to Phoenix's metropolitan area, some of these routes just might get swallowed up by development in the coming years. So go now, and enjoy them while you can.

ROUTES

The route to Wickenburg travels through dramatic desert mountains.

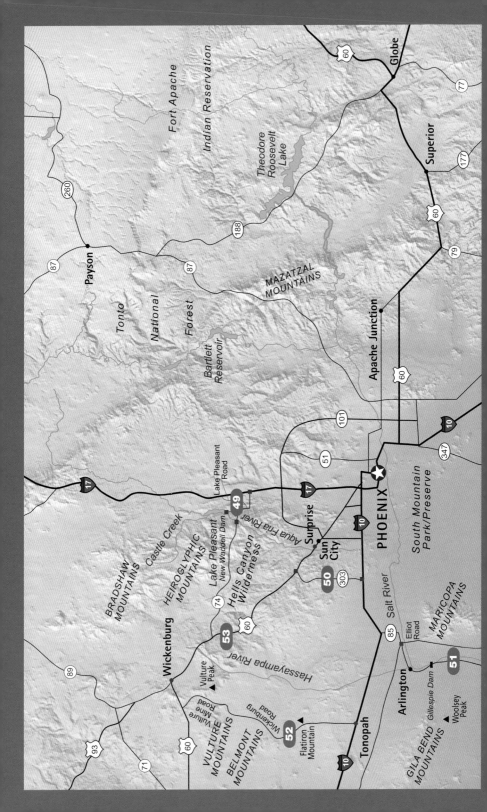

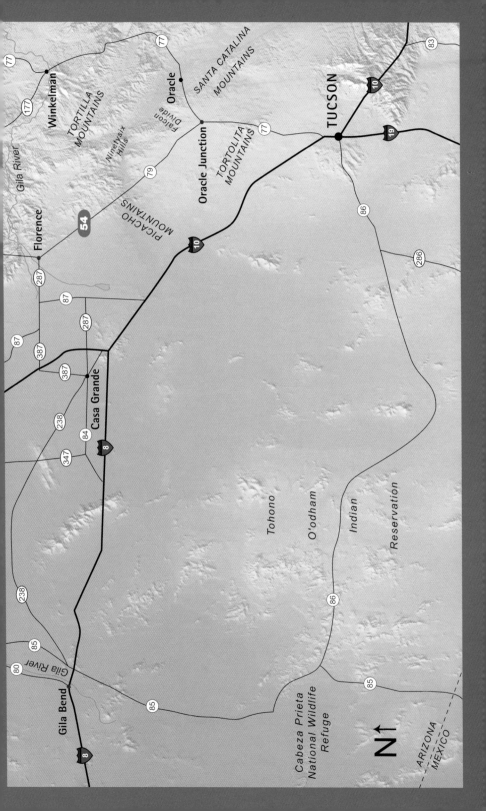

Route 49

LAKE PLEASANT
AZ 74 AND CASTLE HOT SPRINGS ROAD TO LAKE PLEASANT

Moderate • Intermediate

* Travels a diverse landscape from desert floor into low-rising mountains
* Dramatic lakeside scenery at Lake Pleasant
* Two lanes; wide shoulder (AZ 74) and soft shoulder (Castle Hot Springs Road)

DISTANCE: 16.5 miles (to end of pavement); 17 miles (to Lake Pleasant Park) one-way

PEAK CYCLING: October–April; early morning in warmer weather

ACCOMMODATIONS: Supplies, restaurants, and lodging in Phoenix and Wickenburg

SPECIAL CONSIDERATIONS: If you plan to cycle into the park, Maricopa County charges
    bicyclists a $1 admission fee.

STARTING POINT: From Phoenix, drive north on I-17 to AZ 74, the Carefree Highway
    (exit 223); MP 30 is the first mile marker.

One of Maricopa County's unique parks lies at the northern edge of the
county along the Agua Fria River. Centuries ago, Northern Yavapai and
Hohokam Indians lived along the river. Around the 1860s, prospectors picked
around the area, albeit unsuccessfully, for gold. Nowadays, the big draw to
the river is Lake Pleasant, pooled by the New Waddell Dam. Primarily a

After a wet winter, wildflowers spread along Lake Pleasant route.

storage reservoir for drinking water and irrigation purposes, the lake makes a cool destination in the sere Sonoran Desert.

There are several ways to cycle to Lake Pleasant. A decade ago, Lake Pleasant Road out of Sun City made a scenic route through undeveloped desert. Over the years, the area has experienced intense development and increased traffic without, at the time of this writing, more lanes on the road. Consequently, we currently do not advise that cyclists take this road.

AZ 74, while a well-traveled and fast road, has a wide shoulder and travels through some scenic country. The route starts out on a basin-flat desert landscape ringed by distant mountains. The open fields and mountains make for extraordinarily good thermal soaring. At Lake Pleasant Road (MP 24), you might catch sight of a glider plane or ultralight zooming around an airfield in the area.

You get your first taste of the many long, testy ascents along this highway at MP 21 near the Agua Fria River when the road climbs out of the river valley and up into the low-rising hills of the Hieroglyphic Mountains. Before you reach the top of this climb, you get a reprieve at the signed turnoff to Lake Pleasant at Castle Hot Springs Road around MP 19. The route turns right (north) toward Lake Pleasant.

This road is named for the old Castle Hot Springs Resort, located some 11 miles from AZ 74 in the middle of the desert wilderness. Though closed for a number of years, reports drift around about new owners reopening it. In its heyday, the resort had its share of Hollywood visitations.

Right away, you notice a difference in the countryside on Castle Hot Spring Road. While on AZ 74, you were cycling along the edge of the Hieroglyphic Mountains between a dichotomy of scenery: a series of mountain ranges congregated in the north with the low-rising ripples on the desert floor eventually

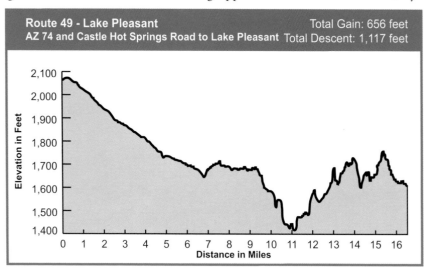

Route 49 - Lake Pleasant   Total Gain: 656 feet
AZ 74 and Castle Hot Springs Road to Lake Pleasant Total Descent: 1,117 feet

flattening out to the south. Now you are heading right into the precipitous sea of mountain ridges, with the 7,000-foot-plus Bradshaw Mountains rising in the rear.

Thick forests of saguaro cactus cover the Hieroglyphics' slopes. The sanguine slopes add warmth to the scene. After a wet winter, brittlebush further colors the landscape with bright yellow composite flowers interspersed with pools of pink owl clover.

When you pass Lake Pleasant ACC Road, about 2 miles from AZ 74 (there are no MPs on this road), you top off your first ascent. The Bradshaw Mountains rise boldly in the background, and they may have a snowcap if you're cycling in the winter.

You cross the county line at mile 4.5, then come to the pavement's end in another mile. The hardpack road is inviting to continue upon (over 30 miles, bending around the Hells Canyon Wilderness back to AZ 74), and we highly recommend it if you have a tour bike. If you do travel farther, be advised that the road travels in washes and experiences some rough spots around Castle Creek at about mile 15, then it gets into fat-tire country on the west side of the wilderness area.

Route 50

SUN VALLEY PARKWAY
SUN VALLEY PARKWAY: SURPRISE TO I-10

Easy • Beginner

- Travels a lonely desert highway on the outskirts of the western Valley
- Great shows of wildflowers after a wet winter
- Wide shoulder along the whole route

DISTANCE: 28.5 miles one-way

PEAK CYCLING: October–March; early morning in warmer weather

ACCOMMODATIONS: Supplies, restaurants, and lodging in Surprise and Phoenix

SPECIAL CONSIDERATIONS: This road travels isolated land. Be sure you are well-equipped and take plenty of water.

STARTING POINTS: North access: the end of Bell Road (east of 303 Loop) just west of Surprise. South access: exit 109 on I-10 (about 35 miles west of central Phoenix); MP 133 is the first mile marker.

When you start this route on the western edge of the city of Surprise, a sign reads, "No services next 38 miles." With no stoplights or signs, no paved intersections, and light traffic, this perimeter route provides a non-stop roadway on which to train or to just plain enjoy. Just keep your eye out for snakes and lizards that like to soak in the heat thermals on the side of the road.

The 4,000-foot-high, freestanding White Tank Mountains rise between the Phoenix Basin on the east and the Hassayampa Plain to the west. The mountains get their name from a process involving flash floods scouring out depressions (or tanks) in the white granite rock. These tanks played an important role in attracting the Hohokam Indians, who inhabited the mountains from A.D. 500 to A.D. 1100, especially near canyon mouths on the east and north sides of the range.

The highway's wide shoulders brush up against classic lower Sonoran Desert vegetation. Wire-thin branches from mesquite trees sometimes reach into your space. You can smell the pungent resin waft from creosote bushes. Brittlebush gathers in rows that glow golden with flowers in the springtime.

The route starts out heading west on a gradual climb that doesn't relent until about MP 122. From there, it's practically all downhill, in the same gradual increments. By MP 120, the route bends southward and travels the west side of the White Tanks. A few shallow rollers give a little resistance.

By MP 107, the route sees some housing development—your signal the route ends in 2 miles, just past MP 105. This route will be part of a new bike event (debuting in 2006) called New Year's Revolution and sponsored by Bike-2-Bike Inc. The two-day event starts with a cycle ride on this route on New Year's Eve and then continues New Year's Day on a route in the southern Valley.

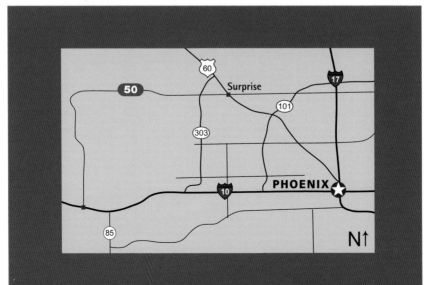

Route 51

OLD HIGHWAY 80
OLD AZ 80: ELLIOT ROAD TO GILA BEND

Easy • Beginner

◆ Travels through rural farmland
◆ Diverse birdlife along the Gila Bend Canal below Gillespie Dam
◆ Two lanes; medium shoulder

DISTANCE: 39 miles one-way

PEAK CYCLING: November–April; early morning in warmer weather

ACCOMMODATIONS: Supplies, restaurants, and lodging in Phoenix

SPECIAL CONSIDERATIONS: This route travels lonely country. Be sure you are well-equipped.

STARTING POINTS: North access: AZ 85 and Elliot Road (MP 39).
    South access: Gila Bend, exit 119 on I-8 (MP 1).

Old Highway 80 gives you a look at Phoenix countryside-past, when the four "C's" aptly described Arizona's resources: cotton, citrus, cattle, and copper. Farms of all types spread from this two-lane highway that sees little traffic, from cotton to citrus to olives. Copper mines speckle the hills of the

The steel trellis bridge at Gillespie Dam.

Gila Mountains, rising to the west of the highway. As for cattle, you may smell a little of the bovine by-product on a just-fertilized farm.

The landscape on this countrified road vacillates between creosote flats flecked with lava cobbles (the route lies near the Sentinel Plain Lava Flow, the largest lava flow in the state, measuring five to 15 feet thick) and verdant farms. Starting at MP 39, the route separates itself slowly from civilization, passing homes and a few businesses. By MP 30, it dips into the town of Arlington. The Desert Rose Café, just before MP 26, gives you a chance to make a pit stop. After that, the route takes off into the country and doesn't look back as it winds, bends, dips, and climbs around lava-rock hills.

After crossing a steel trestle bridge at Gillespie Dam (MP 22), the route follows a flat course on floodplain sandwiched between the Maricopa Mountains to the east and the Gila Bend Mountains to the west. At about MP 18, you're due east of Woolsey Peak, the high point of the low-rising Gila Bend Mountains. The mountains' lava-dark ridgeline poses a striking backdrop to the emerald farm fields.

The Gila Bend Canal, following right along the road, attracts some interesting avian life. While flocks of sparrows and finches feed upon the seeds remaining on plants in the fields, American kestrels hover for their next meal, and red-tailed hawks rest atop telephone poles or peruse fields from on high. Along the canal, you might spot a green heron gracefully taking wing or hear the raspy chatter of a belted kingfisher in the winter.

The landscape turns scrappy by MP 4 when the creosote bushes return. Watermelon Road signals the end of the route, with I-8 about 1 mile away. Return the way you came.

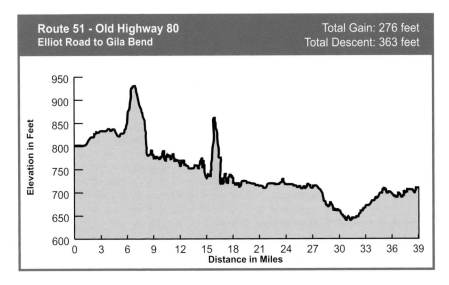

Route 51 - Old Highway 80
Elliot Road to Gila Bend

Total Gain: 276 feet
Total Descent: 363 feet

Route 52

WICKENBURG TO TONOPAH
VULTURE MINE AND WICKENBURG ROADS

Moderate • Intermediate

* Travels a diverse desert landscape, from low, rolling mountains to river plain
* Beautiful cover of wildflowers in March after a wet winter
* Two lanes; narrow shoulder

DISTANCE: 10 miles (to Vulture Mine) to 42 miles (to Tonopah) one-way

PEAK CYCLING: October–April; early morning in warmer weather

ACCOMMODATIONS: Supplies, restaurants, and lodging in Wickenburg; basic supplies, restaurant, and camping in Tonopah. In Wickenburg, check out the scrumptious Chaparral (45 N. Tegner St., 928-684-3252) for homemade ice cream, pastries, and bread for breakfast, lunch, or a treat.

SPECIAL CONSIDERATIONS: There are no services along the route.

STARTING POINTS: From Wickenburg, drive west on US 60 to Vulture Mine Road, and turn left (south); MP 25 is the first mile marker. From Phoenix, drive about 40 miles west on I-10 to exit 94; head east on Indian School Road to the left, turn (north) onto Wickenburg Road, reversing the route.

Back in the late 1860s, when gold fever started spreading eastward from California, prospectors started trickling into Arizona. Some of the biggest claims showed up in the Wickenburg area. A few miles south of Wickenburg,

The sun lights up Vulture Peak along Vulture Mine Road

along the Hassayampa River, the Vulture Mine produced the richest gold strike in the history of the West.

This route begins on Vulture Mine Road, which leads to the Vulture Mine. According to hearsay, the mine got its name from Henry Wickenburg, who discovered the bonanza. Wickenburg saw a vulture just before he found the mine. You might see vultures soaring on the thermals conjured up by the sun over the Vulture Mountains. Don't take them as an omen for gold, but rather a reminder to take enough water.

The road wends its way through some pretty country, rich in scenery and open space, to get to the famous Vulture Mine. Within the first mile, a sign cautions "Dips–Winding Road Next 18 Miles" as the road begins to wend through the Vulture Mountains. The distinctive peak to the southeast is Vulture Peak. Rollers and bends mean a fast, fun ride. Watch out, though, right after a heavy rain. The road dips into a number of washes that fill with flash floods. Sand and gravel sometimes gather in the roadway at these dips, and you may have to walk your bicycle through the thick debris that collects after heavy rains. During March, after a wet winter, wildflowers cover the desert floor, and they especially congregate around the network of washes.

Saguaro and cholla cacti and paloverde and ironwood trees dominate the landscape. If you're lucky, during a quiet moment between the sparse traffic, you may spot a phainopepla perched on the crown of a paloverde tree and hear its *querp*-sounding chirp. The shiny black bird with the elegant crest loves the berries from the mistletoe that grows on the trees.

The old buildings situated right alongside the road around MP 15 are the remains of the Vulture Mine. The mine makes a good turnaround point for a shorter ride.

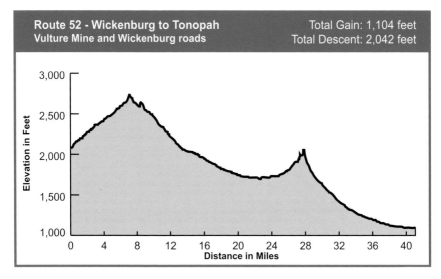

Route 52 - Wickenburg to Tonopah
Vulture Mine and Wickenburg roads

Total Gain: 1,104 feet
Total Descent: 2,042 feet

Once past the mine, at about MP 14, the road drops into the Hassayampa Plain and smoothes out. The saguaro cacti stay behind, and a cover of creosote bushes dominates.

Just past MP 7, turn left onto Wickenburg Road, which heads south-southeast. The next marked mile starts with MP 27, and the saguaro cacti and trees return at about MP 22 when some substantial washes cut through the plain. Then watch for the Belmont Mountains to saddle up to the road. Low-rising and precipitous, the ridges look like islands in a desert sea. The prominent Flatiron Mountain, at the south end of the range, comes in view around MP 18, just before the aqueduct.

You are in the backcountry and several miles from any town, so the appearance of a street sign for 355th Avenue is incongruous. Turn onto 355th Avenue, cycle about 3.5 miles to Indian School Road, and turn right (west); then cycle another 7 miles to Tonopah.

Tonopah, exit 94 on I-10, looks insignificant on a map. However, from a bicycle it can equate to Nirvana, particularly at the corner of 411th Avenue and Indian School Road, where Alice's Restaurant serves big, delicious, home-cooked meals. A bit farther west on Indian School lies El Dorado Hot Springs, where you can soak off the rigors of the ride in a tub containing mineral hot springs. Just be sure you have a ride home or are planning to spend the night in the adjacent campgrounds. Wet noodles (how your muscles will feel after a soak) don't make for good cycling.

A POUND OF FLESH, A CUP OF SWEAT

Cyclists, especially those looking to stay healthy by bicycling, know how many miles it takes to melt a pound of flesh. But they often don't know how many cups of sweat they shed. To hydrate enough, you must know how much fluid you lose on a ride.

To get your correct sweat rate, weigh yourself naked before and after your ride. Each pound lost equals 2 cups (16 ounces) of fluid lost to sweat. Add the amount of liquids you drank during the ride, and divide the total by the number of hours you rode. The final tally equals your hourly sweat rate. You should drink this amount of fluids each hour you cycle.

Here's an example:

- Say you weighed 165 pounds before and 162 pounds after your two-hour ride.
- 3 pounds lost equals 6 cups of fluid lost to sweat.
- Say you drank 2 cups of water during the ride—add that to the total fluid lost and you get 8 cups of fluid.
- 8 cups of fluid divided by 2 hours equal 4 cups per hour. Optimally, you want to drink 1 cup of liquid every 15 minutes.

Route 53

WICKENBURG
AZ 74 AND US 60 TO WICKENBURG

Moderate • Intermediate

◆ Travels a diverse landscape from desert floor into low-rising mountains
   and then a classic Western town
◆ Great two-day cycle ride
◆ Two (AZ 74) and four lanes (US 60); wide shoulders

DISTANCE: 47 miles one-way

PEAK CYCLING: Mid-October–April; early morning in warmer weather

ACCOMMODATIONS: Supplies, restaurants, and lodging in Wickenburg. Check out genteel
   Rancho de los Caballeros resort (1551 S. Vulture Mine Road, 928-684-5484) in
   Wickenburg. You can make reservations to eat there, too. It is some of the best
   food in town.

SPECIAL CONSIDERATIONS: Both highways are well-traveled and require your continued
   attention to the traffic around you.

STARTING POINT: From Phoenix, drive north on I-17 to AZ 74, the Carefree Road (exit
223) and head west; MP 30 is the first mile
marker.

Mike Shapiro and Robin Szekeres have a
roadside chat about their maiden road bike
trip to Wickenburg.

Most Arizona cyclists with any years
behind them have made a trip to
Wickenburg. Though the route travels
on high-traffic highways, it passes
through some wild open spaces with
mountainous terrain. This makes for a
very appealing trip.

Even beginners embark on this classic
route. Mike Shapiro and Robin Szekeres,
both budding road cyclists from Phoenix,
chose this route as their maiden voyage
together, both riding on used Bianchi
bicycles. Mike got his for $50 at, "of all
places," he says, a used shoe store. Robin,
measuring a tad over 5 feet tall, got hers
at a raffle for $10. Amazingly, the bike
fit her frame perfectly. The couple, who

plan to tour around the country eventually, camped in Wickenburg after a steak dinner. Though they considered the route fun, they admit, "The route has hairy moments when there's lots of traffic and the shoulder gets bumpy."

The route starts out on AZ 74, tackling steep-graded rollers right away. Traveling through undeveloped desert that dips and heaves through extraordinarily scenic land, the route retains an untamed feeling as it travels to US 60. The Hieroglyphic Mountains parallel the highway for several miles, with their jagged ridgelines cutting a wild but beautiful panorama. The shoulder gets a bit jagged, too, and may require you to interlope into the highway at times. Do so with caution, and signal your intentions to traffic well before your maneuver by pointing your finger where you intend to go.

At US 60, turn right and breathe easier because of its four lanes and wide shoulder. The rolling foothills reaching down from the Bradshaw Mountains add character to the road. Within a few miles, a string of cottonwood trees following the road shows where the Hassayampa River flows. Legend says if you drink from the Hassayampa, you will never tell the truth again. Just before you reach the town of Wickenburg, the highway crosses the Hassayampa River, which flows underground at this point. A sign on the bridge exhorts "No Fishing From Bridge." Intelligently, you didn't bring a fishing pole, but you do have an appetite. Head for Screamers drive-in for the best hamburgers around or Anita's Cocina for Mexican fare.

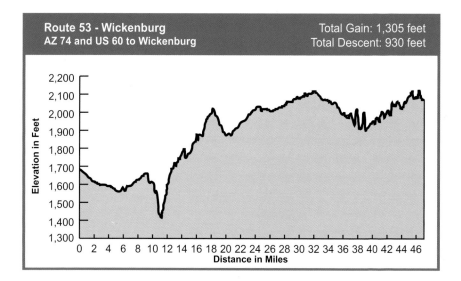

Route 53 - Wickenburg
AZ 74 and US 60 to Wickenburg

Total Gain: 1,305 feet
Total Descent: 930 feet

Route 54

PINAL PIONEER PARKWAY
AZ 79: FLORENCE TO ORACLE JUNCTION

Moderate • Experienced

◆ Travels a scenic desert landscape
◆ Two lanes; wide, then narrow, shoulder

DISTANCE: 42 miles one-way

PEAK CYCLING: October–April; early morning in warmer weather

ACCOMMODATIONS: Supplies, restaurants, and lodging in Phoenix and Tucson

SPECIAL CONSIDERATIONS: This highway is remote but can have high traffic.
    Cyclists planning a shuttle might want to start on the southern end and
    head north—it's all downhill.

STARTING POINTS: From Florence Junction on US 60, go south on AZ 79 about 16 miles
    to Florence; MP 135 is the first mile marker. If you're planning a cycle ride from
    Phoenix to Tucson, head south on AZ 87 (Gilbert Road), and then, near Coolidge, go
    east on AZ 287 to Florence.

After a wet winter, a springtime ride along the Pinal Pioneer Parkway showcases some of the state's best desert scenery.

Once the main highway between Florence and Tucson, the road was downgraded to secondary status when I-10 came on the scene. The highway passes through a pristine Sonoran Desert landscape. During March, the desert floor fills with wildflowers, especially after a wet winter.

Arizona's fifth-oldest city started as a mining town. Over the years, it has acquired a passel of prisons, including private, county, and state institutions. Nevertheless, the town has an aesthetic air, with a large number of buildings that appear on the National Register of Historic Places.

Once you're past Florence, the shoulder narrows and you're on the Pinal Pioneer Parkway. This road has an impressive assemblage of desert vegetation, with signs identifying specific cacti, plants, and trees. Roadside tables at about MP 122 and just past MP 115 give you a chance to pull off the highway safely. The second table memorializes the spot where the cowboy movie star Tom Mix fatally crashed his roadster.

Continuing southward, you enter a nice slice of desert that gets voluptuously green after a wet winter. Globemallow, lupine, and Mexican gold poppies splatter color along the roadsides. At about MP 113, the ascent picks up until you top off on the Falcon Divide at about MP 95. From there, you get to coast down to the route's end at Oracle Junction, with the Falcon Valley to the east and the Tortolita Mountains out west. You can either continue into Tucson (see Route 77, p. 198) or return the way you came.

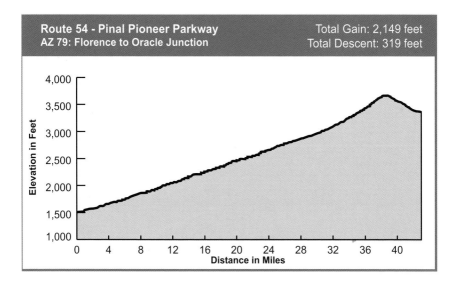

Route 54 - Pinal Pioneer Parkway
AZ 79: Florence to Oracle Junction

Total Gain: 2,149 feet
Total Descent: 319 feet

REGION 6

CENTRAL ARIZONA (MOUNTAINS)

When you cycle into central Arizona, make sure you have hill-climbing techniques you can rely upon to get you up and down its rugged mountains. Some of the state's most challenging routes traverse these ranges, and they lie in isolated countryside. This remoteness creates an added cachet for those who like to feel the wild element in an area, but it also demands that you travel fully prepared.

ROUTES

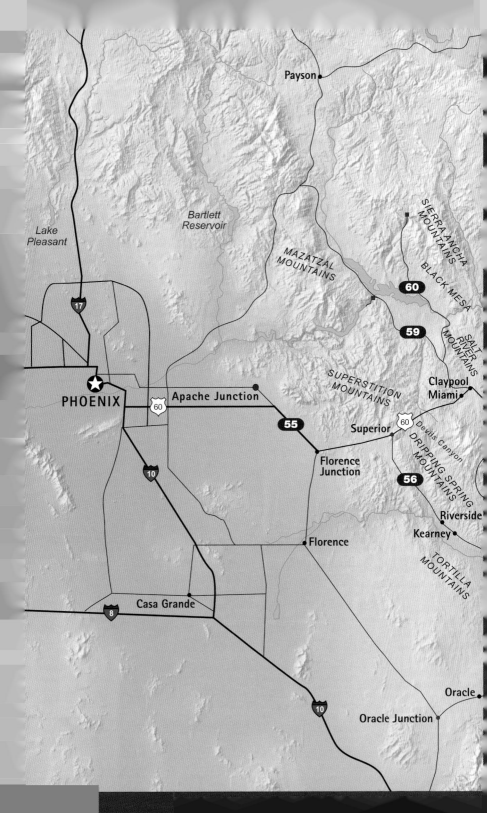

Route 55

ROAD TO GLOBE
US 60: APACHE JUNCTION TO GLOBE

Moderate to Difficult • Intermediate to Experienced

* Crosses scenic and well-traveled but remote desert country
* Two lanes; shoulder most of the time

DISTANCE: 32 miles (to Superior) to 55 miles one-way

PEAK CYCLING: October–April; early morning during warmer weather

ACCOMMODATIONS: Supplies, restaurants, and lodging in Phoenix, Apache Junction, Superior, Miami, and Globe. If you're looking for some good Mexican food in Superior, check out Café Piedra Roja in the Old Town section. In Miami, watch for Burger House Cocina de Casillas. In Globe, turn left onto Broad Street and head for El Ranchero.

SPECIAL CONSIDERATIONS: This route requires hill-climbing skills. The segment between Superior and Globe passes through a mountainous landscape difficult to cycle, with no shoulder in several segments and a tunnel. This stretch is popular with experienced cyclists, but it can be dangerous. Consult a land-management map if you intend to park a vehicle along US 60; the area contains segments of State Trust Land, where a permit is required.

STARTING POINT: Mountain View Road and US 60 in Apache Junction; MP 200 is the first mile marker.

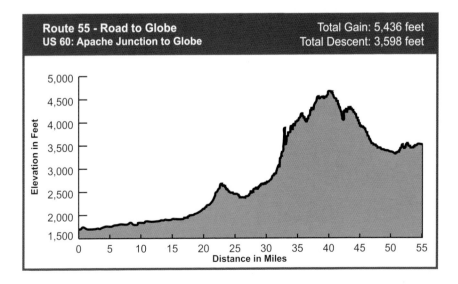

Route 55 - Road to Globe
US 60: Apache Junction to Globe
Total Gain: 5,436 feet
Total Descent: 3,598 feet

Though this route gets plenty of traffic, it crosses one of the most remote areas in central Arizona. Skirting the southern end of the Superstition Mountains, the road crosses some lonely segments of desert where civilization can hardly be found except in the form of a passing car—or fellow cyclist.

Len Covert, who lives in the tiny community of Queen Valley several miles north of US 60, rides the road to Superior because "it's the only road around." Yup, the area's that isolated. Len warns "you have to time your ride when traffic is light (the earlier the better) because the cars don't slow down" where the route loses the shoulder a couple of times and passing lanes force cyclists onto the highway.

After you cycle past the traffic lights in Apache Junction and Gold Canyon and leave the developed areas behind, this ride takes you past stunning scenery signature to the Sonoran Desert. All this happens past MP 204 until a possible interruption at about MP 207: During February and March weekends, when the Arizona Renaissance Festival takes place, you encounter lines of traffic waiting to access the festival grounds.

After that, and a last possible pit stop (service station at MP 209) before Superior, you're on your own. Saguaro and cholla cacti become your faithful companions. In February and March, after a wet winter, the desert floor will have incredible spreads of color from blankets of wildflowers, such as Mexican gold poppies, owl clover, and Coulter's lupine. The jagged ridgelines of the Superstition Mountains, once a cauldron of volcanic activity, come into view, and by MP 212 you start to understand just how much in the middle of nowhere you really are when the mountains come closer and the cactus get thicker.

The gradual grade the route has flirted with starts to steepen by MP 218. The road loses its shoulder because of a passing lane during the climb, then whittles down because of a passing lane in the other direction on the descent. By MP 220, the road gets its shoulder back and reverts to four lanes. About that time, massive Picketpost Mountain, which stands south of the highway, looms in front of you and shows off its fabulous volcanic geology. Arizona State Parks' Boyce Thompson Arboretum, the oldest arboretum in the Southwest and a great spot to stop for a picnic lunch, spreads at the mountain's feet.

At MP 225, civilization comes into view at the town of Superior. You can turn on the signed road to Old Town Superior before MP 226 to take a look at the historic section of town, founded in 1900. If Globe is your destination, continue on US 60. The highway starts a long climb up to Oak Flat past the eastern end of the Superstition Mountains. Around MP 232, the route enters its most scenic segment as it winds through Devils Canyon. Ruddy-hued pinnacles, hoodoos, and spires stack wonderfully along the canyon walls. You'll get a thrilling moment cycling over the Pinto Creek bridge and ducking under a long tunnel, and then the route settles down as it coasts into a string of mining towns, starting with Miami, then Claypool, and finally Globe.

Route 56

MINING COUNTRY ROUTE
AZ 177: SUPERIOR TO WINKELMAN

Difficult • Experienced

* Travels a challenging mountain landscape rich in minerals and scenery
* Two lanes; varying shoulders

DISTANCE: 32 miles one-way

PEAK CYCLING: October–April; early morning in warmer weather

ACCOMMODATIONS: Supplies, restaurants, and lodging in Superior and Kearny; basic supplies and restaurants in Winkelman. If you're looking for a meal to load up on before or after the ride, check out Los Hermanos on US 60 in Superior; don't leave without ordering a piece of homemade "pie" (fruit turnovers).

SPECIAL CONSIDERATIONS: Well-developed hill-climbing skills will make your ride more manageable.

STARTING POINT: From Superior, head south on AZ 177; MP 167 is the first mile marker.

Delving into midsized mountains rich in history and minerals, this route starts in the mining town of Superior, where Billy the Kid, Wyatt Earp, and Doc Holliday all made appearances. As usual, minerals brought out the

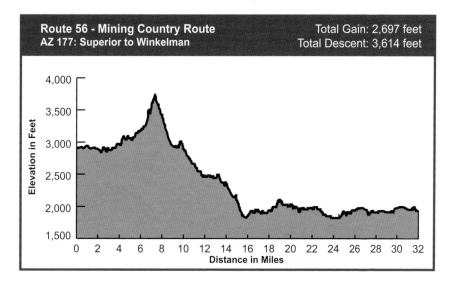

Route 56 - Mining Country Route
AZ 177: Superior to Winkelman
Total Gain: 2,697 feet
Total Descent: 3,614 feet

wild side of this area. When prospectors came through, the Apaches took great umbrage. After several years of bloody warfare, the Indians were subdued, but not the land. Its wild and untamed nature remains, and this route writhes through some rough-and-tumble countryside without any signs of civilization.

Once you're on the highway the cycling gets as serious as the characters that colored the area. What you see in the beginning of the ride—curves, swerves, dips, and climbs—is what you get for the whole ride. The extreme topography presents a great opportunity to challenge cyclists, and with that in mind the annual Mining Country Challenge metric century was created. The challenge starts slowly with a consistent uphill grade, then tackles a climb nicknamed "End of World." This route follows part of the springtime event.

Forests of saguaro cactus add character to the desert landscape. Shortly south of Superior, you pass a side road marked with a sign that reads "Apache Leap." Here, legend says, Apache warriors leapt to their death from a cliffside in order to evade capture. The story of Apache tears, or translucent pieces of obsidian, comes from this legend.

The austere Mining Country route gets a sweet touch from spring wildflowers.

By MP 165 the road narrows, letting go of the wide shoulder it began with, and at MP 162 the End of World climb tests your mettle. A 10 percent grade lifts you into the Tortilla Mountains, and then drops you into a rough-hewn canyon with the same pitch. Repeat: These long, hard heaves and plunges come practically back-to-back. This climb represents the hardest part of the annual Mining Country Challenge, and equals the cyclist's version of the Boston Marathon's Heartbreak Hill.

"After you've done 80 miles with fierce climbs, you've got this last nasty one waiting," explains Jack Graham of the Phoenix Saturday Cycling Group; he manned the 2005 Mining Country Challenge SAG located just south of the climb.

Once you get past the "nasty" climb, at MP 158, the road relaxes out into a dream with relatively new pavement as it drops toward a low point at Mineral Creek. The Ray Mine Overlook (MP 156) explains why this route is called Mining Country. This huge open-pit mining operation supplies thousands of tons of what the Apaches called *besh*, or "lightning metal." The highly conductive copper ore gets shipped via the local Copper Basin Railway to a concentrator in nearby Hayden. The route also passes through the relatively new town of Kearny at MP 146. Founded in 1958, Kearny replaced the towns of Ray, Sonora, and Barcelona, which the mine pit consumed. Outside of Kearny, the route tames into gentle rollers as it follows the Copper Basin Railway to the town of Hayden at MP 138.

Located on the confluence of the San Pedro and Gila rivers, Hayden's outskirts have a scenic appeal, including camping for touring cyclists. The route ends next-door at Winkelman (MP 137).

Route 57

EL CAPITAN
AZ 77: GLOBE TO WINKELMAN

Difficult • Experienced

* Travels through remote and rugged mountains with challenging grades
* Two lanes; narrow shoulder

DISTANCE: 36 miles one-way

PEAK CYCLING: October–April; early morning in hot weather

ACCOMMODATIONS: Supplies, restaurants, and lodging in Globe. The Noftsger Hill Inn (928-425-2260, 425 North St.) was once a schoolhouse. It is a unique place to stay and has huge rooms (and gracious host Rosalie cooks up a wonderful breakfast!).

SPECIAL CONSIDERATIONS: This route is known for its challenging terrain. Do your hill work before you try this one.

STARTING POINT: From Globe, head 2 miles east on US 70, and then turn right (south) onto AZ 77.

The rugged country through which this route travels hosts some challenging backcountry adventures, from technical canyoneering routes to hair-raising backroads. This cycle route is known around the world for its demanding terrain. Though taxing, the route is extraordinarily scenic.

This route starts in Tonto National Forest with twisting rollers wending through an Upper Sonoran Desert landscape. Deeply carved gullies snake their way to the road from the Pinal Mountains rising in the west. Thick stands of saguaro cactus cover volcanic slopes that turn ruddy in early and late sunlight. In the spring, after a wet winter, the ground glories in wildflowers.

What starts out nonchalantly with gradually ascending rollers turns austere with demanding hill climbs. By MP 163, you're climbing an 8 percent grade, then topping off at a roadside table with a view of El Capitan Mountain. A plaque memorializes the route as the one Kit Carson took when he led "Kearny's Army of the West" (100 mule-mounted troops) to California. This route bypassed the "unpassable canyon" of the Gila River, a problem remedied by Coolidge Dam (see Route 61, p. 158).

The road holds roughly level for the next mile before it starts its scream into El Capitan Canyon. The Mescal Mountains, as wild as the reputation of the potent liquor made from the agave plant for which the mountains were named, present some beautiful panoramas in the east. Enjoy the mountains now, because by MP 158 the route drops fast into stunning El Capitan Canyon, twitching down 7 percent and 8 percent grades.

After this Wild Mouse rollercoaster ride, you enter a continuous coast toward the Gila River starting around MP 153. Rollers kick in around MP 150. Watch for the Christmas Mine at about MP 146. This mine, started on Christmas Day at the turn of the 20th century, produced more than 55 million pounds of copper, along with substantial amounts of gold and silver. In 1986, the mine shut down, and the last three families living in the ghost town finally left. The pavement has gotten beat up here from landslides pouring down the precipitous cliffs along the roadway near the mine.

If you look to the east, you can see the Gila River. The road starts its downward coast again to the waterway and its end at the town of Winkelman, a nice wrap-up for this wild ride.

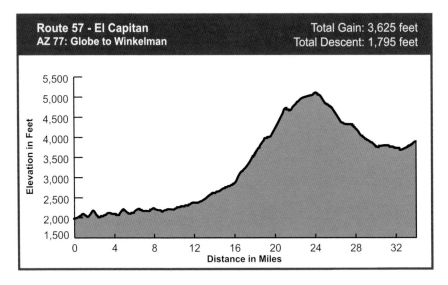

Route 57 - El Capitan
AZ 77: Globe to Winkelman
Total Gain: 3,625 feet
Total Descent: 1,795 feet

Route 58

BLACK HILLS RUN
AZ 77: WINKELMAN TO ORACLE JUNCTION

Moderate • Intermediate

◆ Travels from the Upper San Pedro River Valley up into the Black Hills
   near the Santa Catalina Mountains
◆ Two lanes; rough shoulder

DISTANCE: 43 miles one-way

ACCOMMODATIONS: Supplies, restaurants, and lodging in Tucson;
   supplies and restaurants in Mammoth

SPECIAL CONSIDERATIONS: The segment through the Black Hills
   requires hill-climbing experience.

STARTING POINTS: North access: From Winkelman, head south on AZ 77;
   MP 134 is the first mile marker. South access: From Tucson, go north
   on AZ 77 to Oracle Junction and veer right (northeast).

Rising sharply out of the San Pedro River Valley, this route gives a good
workout. The route starts on a relatively flat course, climbs several thousand feet into the hills, and then descends slowly toward the Tucson basin.

The first segment of the route lolls around farm country along the San
Pedro River. A medley of cholla cacti mixed with paloverde and mesquite

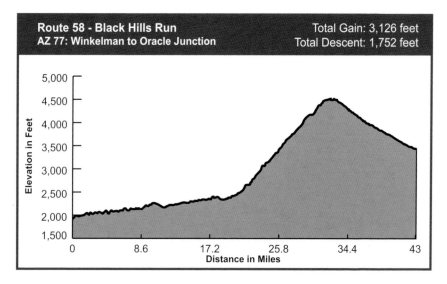

Route 58 - Black Hills Run — Total Gain: 3,126 feet
AZ 77: Winkelman to Oracle Junction — Total Descent: 1,752 feet

trees covers the landscape. A ribbon of cottonwood trees follows the path of the San Pedro River. By mile 122, the route elevates enough to attract forests of saguaro cacti.

After a bend in the road that crosses the river at the town of Mammoth (MP 115), get ready to climb into the foothills of the Santa Catalina Mountains. With the Black Hills to the north and the rounded ridgeline of the Santa Catalina Mountains in the south, the route gradually ascends into piñon-juniper country via rolling grasslands. The climb relents by MP 101, and you get to coast back down to the desert. Very cool.

AZ 77 rises into the Black Hills at an argentine moment nearing twilight.

ELECTROLYTES—DON'T LEAVE HOME WITHOUT THEM

When humidity hovers in the single digits and temperatures in triple figures, your body requires large amounts of liquids. The only means your body has to cool itself when the temps break 95 degrees is sweating. Because the dry desert air evaporates perspiration so quickly, dehydration happens. As soon as you feel thirsty, you've already stepped into the weary world of dehydration, characterized by fatigue, loss of energy, foggy thinking, dry mouth, and irritability.

Biking in the desert requires thoroughly hydrating before you start, methodical hydration during the workout, and often drinking extra liquids at the end of the workout to replace any deficiency. Water, however, is not enough.

Plain water can actually turn off your thirst response before your body gets thoroughly hydrated. Research consistently shows a well-formulated electrolyte drink (correct balance of electrolytes and carbohydrates) keeps athletes hydrated and performing better than water only.

Route 59

ROOSEVELT DAM
AZ 88: Globe to Roosevelt Dam

Moderate to Difficult • Beginner to Experienced

◆ Travels through saguaro-studded mountains
◆ Follows the southern shore of Roosevelt Lake
◆ Two to four lanes; medium shoulder

DISTANCE: 35 miles one-way

PEAK CYCLING: October–April

ACCOMMODATIONS: Supplies, restaurants, and lodging in Globe and Roosevelt Lake

SPECIAL CONSIDERATIONS: Segments of this route require hill-climbing experience. The ride is difficult from Globe to MP 234, but moderate from MP 234 to Roosevelt Dam.

STARTING POINT: AZ 88 just west of Globe and north of US 60, near MP 215. Nearby Guayo's El Rey Mexican Restaurant makes a very effective talisman on the return trip.

Before the Bureau of Reclamation built Roosevelt Dam (1903–1911), the Salt River ran amuck when rains and snowmelt caused major flooding. The dam gave more predictability and allowed for successful farming. President Teddy Roosevelt believed harnessing water was the key to developing the still-wild West. In the late afternoon of March 18, 1911, Roosevelt pushed

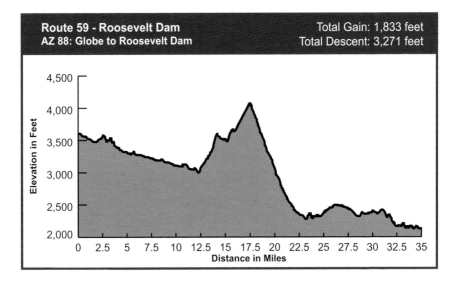

the button that released water from the brand-new dam named in his honor. Salt River Project now operates and maintains the dam.

AZ 88 takes you through some lonely desert backcountry to get to this marvelous feat of engineering. The first half of the route presents a challenge, with grueling hill climbing and tightly twisting turns on the downhill. Once you get to Roosevelt Lake, one of several reservoirs on the Salt River, the ride becomes a breeze.

The first few miles of the route present many reminders that you're still in copper country. Mines, tailing ponds, and piles stay in sight, and tiny towns with names like Radium pop up. The two-lane highway's narrow shoulder grows to a comfortable width.

By MP 220, the route enters the Tonto National Forest with a string of rollers as it begins its climb into the Salt River Mountains. During this transition zone, the vegetation mixes with ancient saguaro cactus forests on the south-facing slopes, with columnar cacti over a century old. Juniper trees dot the north faces. The big ascent comes at MP 222 with a 9 percent grade that doesn't let up, save for a few minor downhills where you can catch your breath, until you top off at The Summit, just past MP 227. Then the road zooms

down at the same steep grade it climbed up, passing AZ 288 between MPs 229 and 230, and enters the Salt River Valley.

By MP 234, the road has gained back its composure and has taken to negotiating pleasant rollers. If you're looking for a pit stop, watch for a gas station and Quail's Nest market nearby.

Roosevelt Lake comes into view at MP 240, right

A cyclist peers at Roosevelt Bridge at the end of the Roosevelt Dam route.

across from the entrance to the Tonto National Monument. The monument presents well-preserved cliff dwellings occupied by the Salado culture during the 13th to early 15th centuries. These Indians farmed in the Salt River Valley. The river's unpredictable flow, vacillating between scouring floods during snowmelt and muddy sludge in the dry seasons, added a devastating edge to the agrarian life for the Indians and pioneers that followed. Roosevelt Dam tamed the river into a farming tool and energy source.

The arched, cyclopean-masonry dam, a Greco-Roman style of building that uses huge, irregular blocks, has seen many renovations and currently wears a cover of concrete. The dam spans a narrow gorge once called "The Crossing," just below the confluence of the Salt River and Tonto Creek, where Indians, farmers, and ranchers would ford the river.

You can cycle across the one-lane bridge that spans the dam, then head for the dam viewpoint just past MP 223. From there, the road turns into the Apache Trail, traveling 24 unpaved, mountain miles to the next sign of pavement, 5 miles east of Tortilla Flat. If you have a touring bike, you can continue all the way to Apache Junction, 46 miles away. Another option is to cross Roosevelt Bridge to AZ 188 and cycle 35 miles across the Tonto Basin to AZ 87. Otherwise, return the way you came, keeping Guayo's El Rey Mexican Restaurant in the back of your mind.

Route 60

YOUNG HIGHWAY
AZ 88 AND AZ 288: GLOBE TO PAVEMENT'S END ON AZ 288

Difficult • Experienced

* Travels down to the Salt River and beyond
* Excellent route for hill training
* Two lanes; shoulder most of the way on AZ 88; no shoulder on AZ 288

DISTANCE: 27 miles one-way

PEAK CYCLING: October–April; early morning in hot weather

ACCOMMODATIONS: Supplies, restaurants, and lodging in Globe

SPECIAL CONSIDERATIONS: This route requires experience with hill climbing.

STARTING POINT: Go about 2 miles west of Globe on US 60, and turn right (north) onto AZ 88.

This route gives you plenty to sweat over as you make your up-and-down way to the floor of the Salt River Valley and back. The 9 percent grade up The Summit in the Salt River Mountains gets you on the way in, and the climb out of the Salt River Valley has you going on the way out. Still, it's one beautiful ride that's lots of fun.

The route starts on AZ 88 for the first 15 miles (see Roosevelt Dam, Route 59, p. 154). During the descent in the Salt River Mountains, be sure you don't miss the right-hand turnoff for AZ 288 as the scenery passes on this downhill screamer. AZ 288 also goes by the name of Young Highway. The century-old road's scenic byway designation, From the Desert to the Tall Pines National

Scenic Byway, gives you a clue to the many vegetation zones through which the 67-mile road passes as it climbs from a low elevation of 2,100 feet to 7,600 feet atop the Mogollon Rim. This route only travels 12 of these miles, to the end of the pavement.

AZ 288 takes you down to the Salt River.

As soon as you turn off AZ 88, the two-lane road makes a big drop. Twists and turns take you in and out of Poison Springs Wash, down to the Upper Salt River Recreation Site, and over the one-lane steel trellis bridge that crosses the Salt River around MP 262.

By MP 264, the road has you climbing as if it were following the path of a thrilling roller coaster on its first slow ascent. Continuing in roller-coaster fashion, the road drops and curves wildly until the next slo-mo climb. The descent this time gives way to gentle swerves that land you back in the desert floodplain at MP 266. This gaping plain gives you an idea of the monumental flow of water that drains from the surrounding mountains into the Salt River and how flooding could wreak havoc in the area.

After settling into a nice series of rollers, the road starts its climb into the Sierra Ancha Mountains at MP 270. This route ends shortly when the pavement ends. A tour bike can continue on this graded mountain road; otherwise return the way you came.

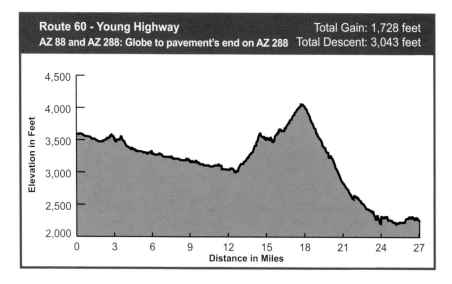

Route 60 - Young Highway Total Gain: 1,728 feet
AZ 88 and AZ 288: Globe to pavement's end on AZ 288 Total Descent: 3,043 feet

Route 61

COOLIDGE DAM
CALVA ROAD/INDIAN ROUTE 3: US 70 TO COOLIDGE DAM

Moderate • Beginner

* Travels through a diverse landscape, from low, rolling mountains to river plain
* Two lanes; no shoulder or fog line

DISTANCE: 13 miles one-way

PEAK CYCLING: October–April; early morning in warmer weather

ACCOMMODATIONS: Supplies, restaurants, and lodging at Apache Gold Casino on San Carlos Indian Reservation; basic supplies and food in San Carlos; beverages and snacks near Coolidge Dam

SPECIAL CONSIDERATIONS: You need a permit to travel on the San Carlos Apache Reservation. You can purchase one ($10) at Circle K Store and Express Stop in Globe on Ash Street, or Apache Gold Convenience Store, Basha's grocery store, or San Carlos Recreation Center on the reservation along US 70.

STARTING POINT: From Globe, drive 19 miles east on US 70, and turn right (south) onto Calva Road (Indian Route 3).

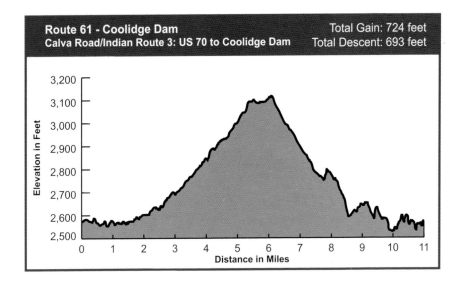

Route 61 - Coolidge Dam
Calva Road/Indian Route 3: US 70 to Coolidge Dam
Total Gain: 724 feet
Total Descent: 693 feet

Remote and with low traffic, this route takes you through Gila River country to Coolidge Dam, which pools the river into San Carlos Reservoir. One of Arizona's major waterways, the Gila rarely sees a good flow, except for snowmelt and occasional flooding from heavy summer storms.

The road starts in Sonoran Desert landscape on the San Carlos Apache Reservation and winds slowly into the Gila drainage. By MP 3, the route wrangles free of the reservation's residential area and enters a segment of pristine desert that colors nicely with wildflowers after a wet winter. The road, full of rollers, takes you into the foothill of the Mescal Mountains.

Coolidge Dam pools San Carlos Lake.

San Carlos Reservoir comes into view at about MP 5. The ridges rising behind it belong to the Santa Teresa Mountains. You get a chance for a pit stop at a general store located near MP 10, right before the route makes a final climb up a long hill. Finally, the route plunges down to the river and Coolidge Dam.

This old-fashioned dam was named for America's 30th president, Calvin Coolidge, who dedicated it in 1930. The road continues around the lake and back to US 70. This eastern segment has rough and sandy segments. If you are not riding a tour or mountain bike, return the way you came.

DON'T LOOK BACK

The immortal words of baseball's Satchel Page, "Don't look back, something might be gaining on you," don't necessarily apply to road biking as well as they do to stealing bases. Richard Corbett, who teaches bicycle safety classes in Tucson, says many cyclists don't know where the real risks lie.

"Most cyclists fear the traffic behind them," Richard says. "But it's what's in front that's going to get you."

Drivers sometimes just don't see cyclists or they don't realize how fast a cyclist is traveling. Richard advises cyclists to make eye contact with drivers and hold it with a nonaggressive, friendly wave of the hand that says, "Hey, I'm here!"

"It works," he says of the wave. "It holds drivers' attention longer and they get a better assessment of your speed."

Route 62

POINT OF PINES
SAN CARLOS INDIAN ROUTE 8: US 70 TO POINT OF PINES

Difficult • Experienced

◆ Climbs from the desert into ponderosa pines through a long segment of incredible open space

◆ Two lanes; no shoulder

DISTANCE: 50 miles one-way

PEAK CYCLING: April–October; early morning during warmer weather

ACCOMMODATIONS: Supplies, restaurants, and lodging at San Carlos Indian Reservation Apache Gold Casino or Globe; primitive camping along the route

SPECIAL CONSIDERATIONS: You need a permit to travel within the San Carlos Apache Reservation. You can purchase one ($10) at Circle K Store and Express Stop in Globe on Ash Street or Apache Gold Convenience Store, Basha's grocery store, or San Carlos Recreation Center on the reservation along US 70. There are no services along the route or at its end. Plan to have a shuttle and sag wagon for an ideal cycle ride.

STARTING POINT: From Globe, drive 22 miles east on US 70, and turn left (north) at a signed turnoff for Point of Pines; MP 1 is the first mile marker.

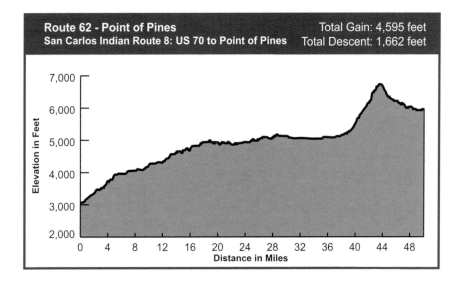

Route 62 - Point of Pines
San Carlos Indian Route 8: US 70 to Point of Pines
Total Gain: 4,595 feet
Total Descent: 1,662 feet

Often overlooked because of its tucked-away location on the San Carlos Indian Reservation, the road to Point of Pines presents an incredibly beautiful ride. Traveling through isolated open space that emanates an attractive mystique, you almost feel like you've passed into another world. The reservation is known for its wildlife, and this route will bring you right into antelope and then elk country.

The highway starts on the rough side with no fog lines. Right away, too, the route sees plenty of rollers as it travels through the foothills of the Gila Mountains. The landscape holds saguaro cactus forests brushy with creosote and jojoba bushes. After a wet winter, lupine, owl's clover, and Mexican gold poppies color the roadsides. The three-peaked landmark, Mount Triplet, rises to the west. By MP 5, the road climbs into the junipers, then starts showing off panoramas when it reaches Antelope Flats (MP 6).

Cycling along the grassy basin lifting rhythmically with rollers, you can see for miles ahead and watch the ribbon of road you're following climb up a distant hill. The scene epitomizes open space: no power lines, few adjacent roads, and fewer homes. Herds of pronghorn antelope frequent the grasslands.

In stair-step fashion, the road makes its way into the mountains. Rocky knolls and gullies appear as it climbs with more frequency around MP 14. Soon afterward, at about MP 15, the road surface improves tremendously and turns practically smooth as silk.

At Ash Flats (MP 17) the route enters an elegant landscape carved with rivulets and packed with one panorama after another. A couple of roadside tables give you an opportunity to take a break and check out this special landscape.

The tribe has closed off certain areas of the reservation to nonmembers, and one area starts at about MP 25 and extends to about MP 43. You may stay on the road while cycling this segment, but may not travel off it. Midway, about MP 37,

Point of Pines has a little of everything, from Sonoran Desert to grasslands and pine forests.

the route bends northeast and starts a steep climb up the Natanes Plateau. Precipitous cliffs start to articulate into strange, erosion-carved hoodoos. At Barlow Pass, you reach the end of the closed area and top off the climb. From there you drop into a pine-oak landscape and stay in the pines until MP 48, when expansive meadows span the area. The pavement ends at the ranger station at MP 50. Unless you have a tour bike, return the way you came.

Route 63

SALT RIVER CANYON–SOUTH ROUTE
AZ 77: GLOBE TO THE SALT RIVER

Difficult • Experienced

* Travels through the high desert and down into the scenic Salt River Canyon
* Two lanes; with and without shoulder

DISTANCE: 29 miles one-way

PEAK CYCLING: March–November

ACCOMMODATIONS: Supplies, restaurants, and lodging in Globe and Show Low; camping at Jones Water Campground

SPECIAL CONSIDERATIONS: There are no services along the route. Trucks travel this route. Early morning, when traffic is lowest, presents the safest cycling.

STARTING POINT: From Globe, drive east a short distance to AZ 77, and turn left (north); MP 252 is the first mile marker.

One of the most challenging routes in the state, this is also one of the most scenic. Cyclists able to negotiate steep grades, hairpin turns on the downhill, and fast-traveling traffic will revel in this difficult route. Negotiating these variables may not even be the hardest part of the route—rather, it's keeping your eyes off the high-drama scenery and on the road.

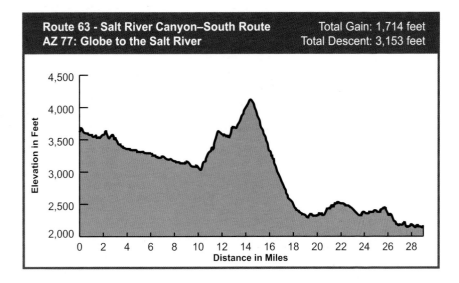

Route 63 - Salt River Canyon–South Route
AZ 77: Globe to the Salt River
Total Gain: 1,714 feet
Total Descent: 3,153 feet

Starting in the desert, this route has you climbing up into high country where big rollers give you big views. The Salt River Mountains through which you are traveling rise and fall in powerful waves. Juniper trees dot the slopes, and strings of cottonwood trees line drainages that twist at the base of the mountains. A passing lane at MP 260 takes away the shoulder for 2 miles, as does another at Jones Water Campground (MP 268). The shoulder fades in and out, but the dramatic scenery and terrain are nonstop. The climb up to MP 279 will leave you breathless and in pine country—junipers mix with ponderosas. The next climb, at MP 282, finishes the uphill grunt. Then it's a coast down to rolling grasslands until MP 287, where the route levels out for a breather while passing through the community of Seneca. A mile later, the road starts its corkscrew decent into the canyon. This is a fast drop with a 6 percent grade.

You get a good look at the Grand Canyon–like gorge at about MP 289. But watch yourself. This road is so full of curves and hairpin turns on a relentless 6 percent grade that staring a moment too long could have you heading off the road, especially starting at MP 290. If you need to gawk, stop at a scenic pullout. Also, watch for gravel around these curves. One high-profile cyclist wiped out on this route while screaming too fast on the downhill. He sheepishly conceded he should have braked on the curve that got him. When you finally do reach the river, you can continue northward out of the canyon to Show Low or return the way you came.

Hairpin turns zig-zag down to the Salt River.

Route 64

SALT RIVER CANYON—NORTH ROUTE
AZ 77: Show Low to Salt River

Difficult • Experienced

◆ Travels from the high country on the Mogollon Rim down to
   the scenic Salt River Canyon
◆ Two lanes; shoulder

DISTANCE: 48 miles one-way

PEAK CYCLING: March–November

ACCOMMODATIONS: Supplies, restaurants, and lodging in Show Low

SPECIAL CONSIDERATIONS: Trucks travel this route. Early morning, when traffic
   is lowest, presents the safest time to travel.

STARTING POINT: From Show Low, head south on AZ 77.

No matter which direction you head for the Salt River Canyon, it's a challenging route and definitely full of thrills and spills if you don't watch where you're going. Just as the southern route experiences distinctive and scenic countryside, so does this northern segment—only in a saner fashion.

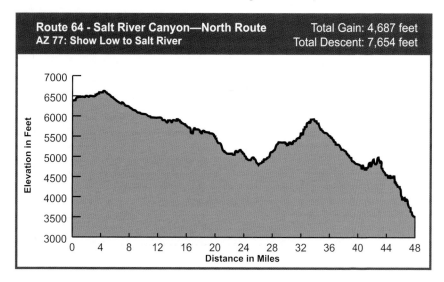

Route 64 - Salt River Canyon—North Route
AZ 77: Show Low to Salt River
Total Gain: 4,687 feet
Total Descent: 7,654 feet

As the route heads southwest from Show Low, the town thins out and Sitgreaves National Forest takes over and melds with the Fort Apache Indian Reservation at MP 337. A pristine land with a nice atmosphere, the landscape has a remote but comfortable feel to it, even during the hairier moments of the route nearer the Salt River. Ponderosa forestland and meadows carry you several miles into comfortable waves of rollers. You hit the route's first screamer around MP 322. This drops you below the red-rock walls of Corduroy Canyon.

The route stays in scenic Corduroy Canyon for several miles, hovering just above the floor. If you need a pit stop, watch for a store around MP 318. Then get ready for another drop into the Carrizo River Canyon. Not nearly as dramatic as the Salt River Canyon, but certainly notable, the climb out of this canyon gives you a taste of what awaits on your climb out of the Salt River Canyon as you grind almost 3 miles up and out of the gorge to MP 313.

The route now rolls around red-earth mountains before it drops once again, around MP 305, into Flying Canyon via a run that's more of a cruise than a scream. The route saves the real screamer until MP 298 when, after teetering on the rim of the canyon momentarily, it takes the final plunge toward the Salt, a good 5 miles away. When you finally do reach the river, you can continue southward out of the canyon to Globe or return the way you came.

The Salt River Canyon.

REGION 7

EASTERN ARIZONA

Like most of Arizona, the eastern reaches have a variety of landscapes. The Four Corners country in the northern end colors with red-rock Navajo sandstone. Volcanic cones form sexy slopes covered with grasslands heading toward the Mogollon Rim. The White Mountains throw in alpine forests. If you plan to cycle this neck of the woods, make sure you like open space because you'll find lots of it here, along with small towns and beautiful scenery.

ROUTES

The hairpin turns, steep grades, and striking scenery make a grand finale on the Coronado Trail.

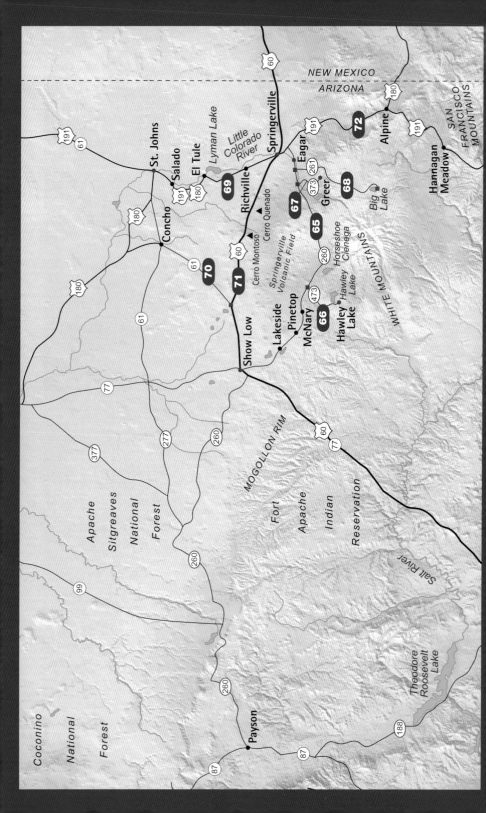

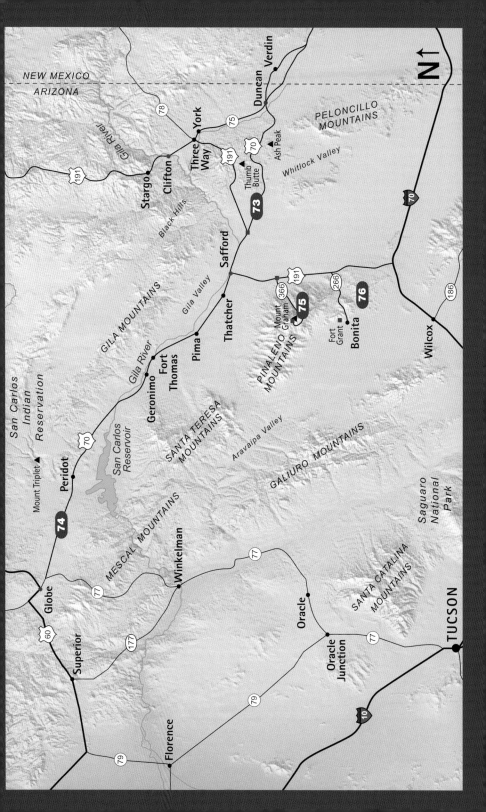

MOGOLLON RIM EAST
AZ 260: SHOW LOW TO EAGAR

Moderate • Experienced

◆ Travels the high country of a 2,000-foot-high wooded escarpment across Arizona
◆ Two to four lanes; no shoulder to wide shoulder

DISTANCE: 56 miles one-way

PEAK CYCLING: April–October

ACCOMMODATIONS: Supplies and restaurants in Show Low, Pinetop-Lakeside, and Eagar

SPECIAL CONSIDERATIONS: Parts of this route travel in remote areas. Bring a repair kit, food, and enough water.

STARTING POINT: US 60 and AZ 260 on the east side of Show Low, at MP 341.

Many people think the White Mountains start at Show Low. Unless you're looking for an extreme ride in the mountains, you'll be happy to know you're still on the Mogollon Rim with much of this route; healthy rollers are the extent of its challenge.

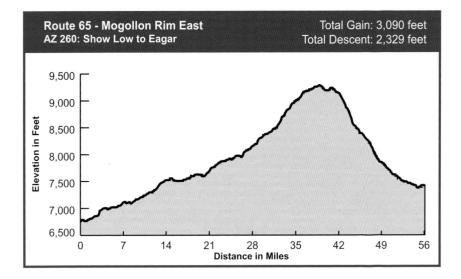

Route 65 - Mogollon Rim East
AZ 260: Show Low to Eagar

Total Gain: 3,090 feet
Total Descent: 2,329 feet

Shortly after MP 341, watch for a sign directing a right turn for AZ 260. The road becomes a bit countrified as the businesses wane and mix with the pines for the next several miles. At the town of Pinetop-Lakeside, another business district gives you a chance for a decent pit stop. The route finally wrangles free of the communities by MP 355. Within another mile, you enter the Fort Apache Indian Reservation. After the turnoff for the Hon-Dah Resort Casino at AZ 73 and the town of McNary 1 mile farther, the route parts company with civilization.

Cycling the eastern Mogollon Rim is a pleasant ride with rollers and pine forests.

From here, the roller-filled route travels a beautiful landscape where large meadows separate forests of tall pines. By the Hawley Lake turnoff, between MPs 368 and 369, the route climbs high enough for forests of aspens to congregate. They make a stunning scene with their argentine bark mingling with the old-growth orange of the ponderosa pines. Watch for Horseshoe Cienega at MP 372.

When the route exits the reservation and enters Apache-Sitgreaves National Forest, the landscape leans toward prairies rather than forest. At the AZ 373 turnoff (MP 386), which leads to the town of Greer, the route heads back into the forest momentarily, and then an 8 percent grade drops it back into a meadow big enough to swallow you up. This is the kind of open countryside you cycle during the route to Big Lake (see Route 68, p. 175), whose turnoff lies at MP 393.

Continuing on AZ 260, attractive ranchland leads you to the end of the route in the town of Eagar at MP 396. You may continue north into Springerville on US 191 or south along US 191 into the White Mountains (see Route 72, p. 183).

Route 66

HAWLEY LAKE
AZ 473: From AZ 260 to Hawley Lake

Moderate • Intermediate

◆ Travels an isolated road to a mountain lake

◆ Two lanes; no shoulder

DISTANCE: 9.5 miles one-way

PEAK CYCLING: May–October

ACCOMMODATIONS: Supplies and restaurants in McNary and Eagar; grocery store, cabins, campsites, and laundry facilities available at Hawley Lake

SPECIAL CONSIDERATIONS: This route travels in a remote area. Bring a repair kit, food, and enough water. This high-elevation area gets cold at night. Freezing temperatures have been recorded even during the summer.

STARTING POINT: About 12 miles east of McNary, between MPs 368 and 369 on AZ 260.

A striking forest of aspen and mixed conifers starts you out on this winding road of rollers. The route only gets more scenic as it snakes through a narrow chasm between miles 2 and 3. Beyond, the loose-knit forests make excellent habitat for wildlife. Don't be surprised if you see deer, elk, or even bear.

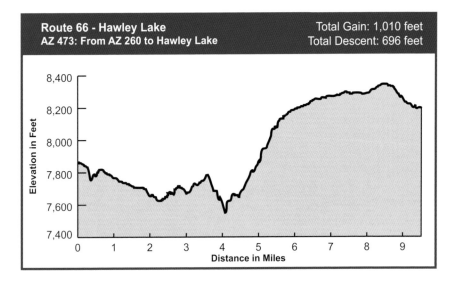

Route 66 - Hawley Lake
AZ 473: From AZ 260 to Hawley Lake
Total Gain: 1,010 feet
Total Descent: 696 feet

Hawley Lake is one of the coolest spots in the White Mountains—a great summer destination.

At the road's midpoint, you pass through an aspen-fir forest. In late September and early October, the aspens form a matrix of gold in this dark forest. In the summer, the forest cools like a cavern.

AZ 473 officially ends at MP 9, but the pavement continues another 0.5 mile to Hawley Lake. The lakeshore, pretty and peaceful, has picnic benches, washrooms, and drinking water.

CLIMBING ARIZONA'S HILLS AND MOUNTAINS

Like anything you end up doing well, hill climbing takes practice. It's how you build your strength, establish endurance, master your gears, and develop timing.

Before you tackle a difficult climb, get yourself into a positive mental state where you know you can match the challenge. During the climb, breathe deeply and watch your posture. The straighter you sit (hands out of the well), the more oxygen fills your lungs. On shorter climbs of less than an hour, don't waste your energy on digesting food by eating. But do eat lightly during a several-hour ascent. Standing gives you more pedal power, but takes more energy.

When the going gets rough, break your progress down into segments. For instance, say you want to climb one of Arizona's largest peaks. You can encourage your progress by tracking vegetation zones—for example, you might rest for two minutes (or take an extra gulp of liquids) once you leave the saguaro cactus forest, then again when the junipers start, and later when you see the first ponderosa pine. During exceptionally grueling grades, you can further break down these goals by celebrating (preferably later) when you reach a sign, landmark, or pavement tread a few hundred feet away. Remember, too, that when you get to the top, it's downhill all the way back.

Route 67

ROAD TO GREER
AZ 373: From AZ 260 to Greer

Easy • Beginner

◆ Travels an isolated road to a historic mountain village

◆ Two lanes; no shoulder

DISTANCE: 5 miles one-way

PEAK CYCLING: May–October

ACCOMMODATIONS: Restaurants and lodging in Greer. Molly Butler Lodge (928-735-7226) has been around about as long as the town, and its bar is a big draw. The restaurant is known for its aged prime rib. The Red Setter Inn and Cottages (928-735-7441) at the end of the road cloisters guests in luxury and peace, with memorable meals. The Amberian Peaks Lodge and Restaurant (928-735-9977) offers all the comforts of home sans phones, plus it delivers pizza anywhere in Greer.

SPECIAL CONSIDERATIONS: Greer is the only town in the area, and this road gets lots of traffic in the summer.

STARTING POINT: About 10 miles west of Eagar at MP 386 on AZ 260.

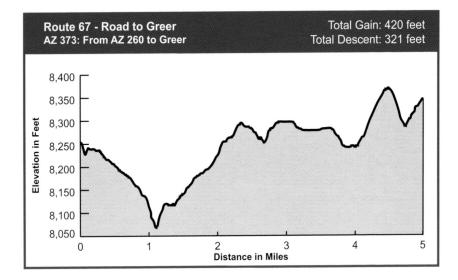

Route 67 - Road to Greer
AZ 373: From AZ 260 to Greer
Total Gain: 420 feet
Total Descent: 321 feet

Greer has some of the coolest temperatures in the state during the summer. It also has some good food and great lodging. With that in mind, the little mountain village makes a great base for some great road-biking routes.

If you just want to visit this town, located in a mountain valley, take this short and sweet road that travels between mountain ridges and follows along the crystal-clear Little Colorado River.

A mixed conifer forest shows fall color on the way to Greer.

Route 68

BIG LAKE
AZ 261 AND AZ 273: FROM AZ 260 TO BIG LAKE

Moderate • Intermediate

* Travels to a mountain lake surrounded by alpine meadows
* Tour bikes can explore unpaved roads heading in several different directions from Big Lake
* Two lanes; no shoulder

DISTANCE: 23 miles one-way

PEAK CYCLING: May–October

ACCOMMODATIONS: Supplies and restaurants in Greer and Eagar; general store with basic provisions and camping available at Big Lake

SPECIAL CONSIDERATIONS: This route travels in a remote area. Bring a repair kit, food, and enough water.

STARTING POINT: About 3 miles west of Eager at MP 393 on AZ 260; MP 413 is the first mile marker.

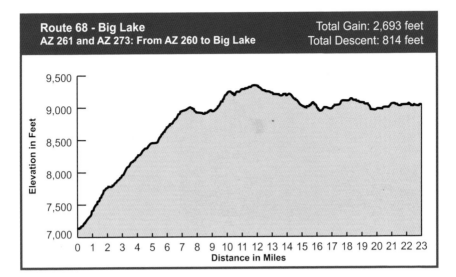

Route 68 - Big Lake
AZ 261 and AZ 273: From AZ 260 to Big Lake

Total Gain: 2,693 feet
Total Descent: 814 feet

This scenic two-lane road starts you on a climb and keeps you there for a good portion of the route to an isolated mountain lake. The ascent relents here and there to entertain segments of rollers, but it always returns to its climb. The landscape is big country here—loose-knit mixed conifer forests and expansive prairies undulating like kettles and moraines in post-glacier country.

By MP 405, aspen forests appear. Shortly after, the route tops off in a meadow, dimpled with cienegas, that stretches almost to the horizon in every direction. Finally, the route gives you some downhill thrills for a couple of miles starting at MP 398. This is a particularly scenic area where the road snakes around hillocks sprinkled with conifers.

At the end of AZ 261, turn left onto signed AZ 273. The route follows along the lake for 3 miles past a visitor center, and it ends at Big Lake General Store. If you have a tour bike, you can explore the unpaved roads that take off in several directions from the Big Lake hub. Otherwise, there is no alternate paved road at Big Lake. If you've got skinny tires, return the way you came.

Big Lake route starts at its low point on the South Fork of the Colorado River

Route 69

LYMAN LAKE
US 191: Springerville to St. Johns

Easy • Intermediate

- Travels in the midst of endless prairies dotted with cinder cones rising from the grasses like waves on a roiling sea
- Offers a shorter variation that leads to a reservoir lake
- Two lanes; medium shoulder

DISTANCE: 17 miles (to Lyman Lake) to 29 miles (St. Johns) one-way

PEAK CYCLING: March–November

ACCOMMODATIONS: Supplies, restaurants, and lodging in Springerville and St. Johns. Lyman Lake State Park has a developed campground and yurts.

SPECIAL CONSIDERATIONS: This route travels in a remote area. Bring a repair kit, food, and enough water.

STARTING POINT: From Springerville, head northwest on US 60 to US 191; MP 402 is the first mile marker.

This route travels on a mostly straight course across the high desert past some interesting volcanic geology. Raspy ridges of lava break out of the grasses like the edges of a serrated knife. The effect is like a grassy moonscape,

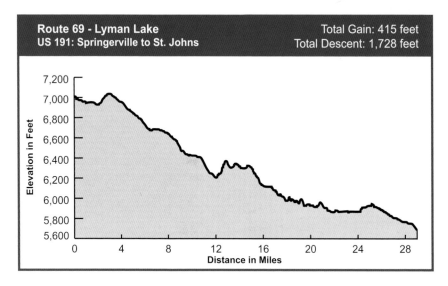

a scene of simple beauty, and the views of this natural landscape have an endless reach.

About 3 miles from the route's start at Springerville, US 60 veers left (west) and US 180/191 continues straight. Stay on US 180/191. The Little

Colorado River drainage follows along the highway to the east, but you won't notice it until MP 383 when mesalike hills rise with basalt walls. You can see Lyman Lake, pooled from the river, in the near distance to the east. The land takes a salmon tinge here, adding a pretty contrast to the green grasses and junipers. The entrance for Lyman Lake between MPs 381 and 380 takes you to the pleasant lakeshore. One of eastern Arizona's best-kept secrets, Lyman Lake has more wildlife than it does people who know the lake exists. You can rent a yurt here or set up a tent for an overnight stay.

The sandstone scenery follows faithfully along the road for several more miles. By MP 374, Navajo sandstone

Lyman Lake route travels rolling grasslands peppered with lava cones.

formations start to grow into cliffs, showing hints of what lies ahead in the Navajo Nation, about 55 miles due north.

St. Johns' city limits lie at MP 372, and the business district starts 2 miles later. This route ends 1 mile past town, at AZ 61, and you have several choices: If you continue north on US 191/AZ 61, the route crosses extremely remote land with no accommodations until the town of Chinle (about 140 miles away). AZ 61 travels west 45 miles to Show Low (see Route 70, opposite). Finally, you may return the way you came.

Route 70

CONCHO ROUTE
AZ 61: St. Johns to US 60

Moderate • Intermediate

◆ Travels hilly and remote high-desert countryside

◆ Two lanes; medium shoulder

Distance: 34 miles (to US 60) to 45 miles (to Show Low) one-way

Peak Cycling: March–November

Accommodations: Supplies, restaurants, and lodging in Show Low and St. Johns

Special Considerations: This route travels in a remote area. Bring a repair kit, food, and enough water.

Starting Point: From St. Johns, head west on US 180.

The aura of this route wobbles between the homespun demeanor of its Mormon communities and the sensual nature of its landscape. The landscape has the sexy slopes of a championship golf course—scenic and, in this case, natural. The highway, too, has plenty of character, with loads of rollers and serpentine curves you can view from a distance.

The route starts on US 180 heading west from St. Johns. At MP 364, US 180 veers to the north. To continue on this route, cycle straight ahead

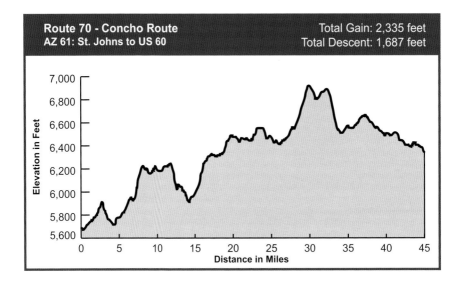

An Americana scene along the Concho route.

on AZ 61. At MP 373, watch for bentonite cones (purple-colored hills) like you see in the Painted Desert, located about 50 miles north of here as the crow flies. A mile later, the route enters the community of Concho.

For a small town in the middle of nowhere, Concho covers a lot of ground; it stretches for about 4 miles. Expect the bare minimum in the way of provisions at a gas station in town. Even though this area is intensely remote, homes pop up often enough in case an emergency should arise.

Rollers take on a rigorous stance around MP 358, as the landscape, now nubby with juniper trees, turns roller-coaster-like. This route ends at the intersection with US 60, at MP 354. You may return the way you came or take US 60 west to Show Low or east to Springerville (see Route 71, opposite). If you have the experience, you can do a near century by taking US 60 east to Springerville and US 191 north to St. Johns (see Route 69, p. 177).

SUNRISE-SUNSET CHART

MONTH	SUNRISE	SUNSET
January 1	7:33 a.m.	5:32 p.m.
February 1	7:24 a.m.	6:00 p.m.
March 1	6:56 a.m.	6:25 p.m.
April 1	6:16 a.m.	6:49 p.m.
May 1	5:40 a.m.	7:11 p.m.
June 1	5:19 a.m.	7:33 p.m.
July 1	5:22 a.m.	7:42 p.m.
August 1	5:41 a.m.	7:28 p.m.
September 1	6:02 a.m.	6:53 p.m.
October 1	6:23 a.m.	6:12 p.m.
November 1	6:47 a.m.	5:36 p.m.
December 1	7:15 a.m.	5:21 p.m.

You must display a white light on the front of your bicycle and a red reflector on the back if you travel before sunrise or after sunset. Arizona does not practice daylight-saving time (except for the Navajo Nation).

Route 71

CERRO MONTOSO
US 60: Show Low to Springerville

Difficult • Intermediate

◆ Travels hilly and remote countryside past mountainous cinder cones
◆ Two lanes; medium to wide shoulder

DISTANCE: 45 miles one-way

PEAK CYCLING: April–October

ACCOMMODATIONS: Supplies, restaurants, and lodging in Show Low and Springerville

SPECIAL CONSIDERATIONS: This route travels in a remote area. Bring a repair kit, food, and enough water.

STARTING POINT: From Show Low head east on US 60; MP 352 is the first mile marker.

Nonstop rollers. Wide shoulders. Smooth road surface. Miles of scenic open space. The hillsides along this route have a sensual appeal, especially with a cover of green after a wet winter or summer rains.

We could end the description there and you'd understand what a great route this one is. However, we have to add that if the crosswinds in this big

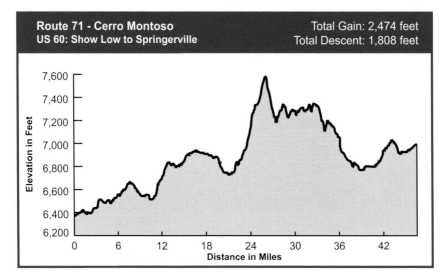

Route 71 - Cerro Montoso
US 60: Show Low to Springerville
Total Gain: 2,474 feet
Total Descent: 1,808 feet

Cerro Montoso has just what its Spanish name says—hills and mountains.

country don't slow you down on some days, the big hills will. *Cerro* means "hill" and *montoso* means "hilly" or "mountainous," and just as the name of this roadside peak implies, you get to climb a double portion of mountainous rollers after MP 365. Two big ones—Cerro Montoso and Cerro Quemado—make bold statements just south of the road, topping 8,000 feet. You get a respite from intense climbs at MP 378—though the rollers don't stop, the unforgiving grades do.

You'll reach Springerville's city limits at MP 384. A left (north) turn will take you into the city; continuing another mile on US 60 connects you with US 191. You may return the way you came, head back to Show Low on US 260 (see Route 65, p. 170), or head south into the White Mountains (see Route 72, opposite).

Route 72

CORONADO TRAIL
US 191: SPRINGERVILLE TO CLIFTON

Moderate to Difficult • Intermediate to Experienced

- Travels through remote, undeveloped national forest land
- Abundant wildlife
- Autumn color in late September and early October
- Excellent touring route (two days) or challenging single day
- Two lanes; no shoulder

DISTANCE: 123 miles one-way

PEAK CYCLING: April–October

ACCOMMODATIONS: Supplies, restaurants, and lodging in Eagar; basic supplies, lodging, restaurant, and campground in Hannagan Meadow; several campgrounds and primitive camping along highway

SPECIAL CONSIDERATIONS: This route travels in a remote area. Bring a repair kit, food, and enough water. Steep grades and hairpin turns require excellent skills and experience from Alpine to Clifton, while the Eagar to Alpine route is more moderate. At the time of publication, the MPs did not always follow in sequence.

STARTING POINT: From Springerville, head south on US 191, jogging east then south (and briefly joining AZ 260); MP 402 is the first mile marker.

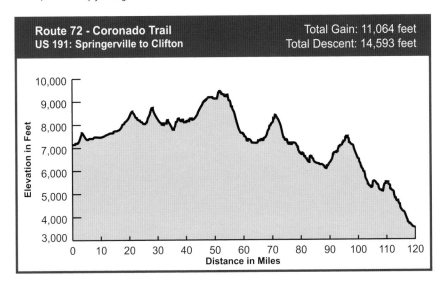

Route 72 - Coronado Trail
US 191: Springerville to Clifton
Total Gain: 11,064 feet
Total Descent: 14,593 feet

This route's dramatic ride does not exactly follow the historic route that its namesake, Francisco Vásquez de Coronado, took during his 16-day pass through the White Mountains. But the road gets close. Looking for the gilded city of Cibola, the Spaniard led a flamboyant entourage over a precipitous route just west of the highway in A.D. 1540 The route left them bedraggled, and the Coronado Trail will do the same to cyclists who don't have experience and endurance.

Watch for bighorn sheep around the Phelps Dodge Mine near Morenci.

As beautiful as this route is—one of the most scenic in the state—it travels a demanding course full of hairpin turns (570 according to one source) and steely grades. Basically, you're either climbing uphill or screaming down. The route ascends 2,000 feet in the first 60 miles and then descends almost 5,000 feet through several vegetative zones in its second half, starting near KP Cienega Campground. This range in life zones compares to traveling from Mexico to Canada. Climate fluctuates from subalpine to desert. Landscapes change from aspen-fir forest to barren desert scrub. Tempestuous thunderstorms brew in the summer. Snow comes by November, stays into May, and sometimes visits in the summer.

The route warms up on long, languorous rollers between Springerville and Nutrioso, rising about 500 feet. Nelson Reservoir (MP 407), a favorite fishing hole with the locals, will give you a chance to pull off the road if you need to fine-tune anything. It's a popular spot for birding, especially for waterfowl, including giant blue herons, cinnamon teals, killdeer, and coots. From late October to March, bald eagles hunt over the lake.

After the town of Nutrioso (MP 416), named for the marmotlike rodents called nutria that populated the area, the road starts some serious climbing that will take you from prairie lands to aspen-fir forests. Sprawling meadows lure elk in the early morning and evening hours. Twists and dips hide traffic and call for your full attention.

By hamletlike Alpine (MP 425), you've climbed over 1,000 feet and have 1,000 more to go to the route's high point near KP Campground. Along the way, you can rent a cabin or a room, pick up bare essentials at the general store, or sit down to a meal in Hannagan Meadow at MP 232, the only opportunity for accommodations for the next 83 miles. Now you're in Mexican gray wolf country, where wildlife sightings outnumber human encounters.

In summer, this area mirrors a coastal rainforest. Mixed conifer forests, swaddled in a sweet pine redolence and dripping with lichen, nurture stands of aspen that form an argentine matrix through the dark green timberland. Meadows separate forests of aspen, pines, and fir trees. All this beauty comes from daily precipitation in the form of thunderstorms with high winds, dousing rain, lightning, and hail. Plan to take a couple hours of downtime between early and late afternoon, in the shelter of a rest area if possible, to avoid getting caught in one of these storms.

In the fall, this area lights up with aspens that knit a pattern of gold in the evergreens. Elk start bugling in late August, building in frequency and intensity to the height of the rut around October 1.

The turnoff for KP Cienega Campground (MP 224) marks the route's high point and the start of one wild ride that requires negotiating challenging double S-curves dropping several thousand feet down the ridge. If you want to stay in the high country, make this your turnaround point. Within only a of couple miles, you're down in the ponderosa pines. Watch for wildlife here, as bears, deer, wolf, and elk make regular appearances. Several rest areas give you a chance to take a break if you need it.

A rest area at MP 221 will give you a chance to recover from this first high-drama

Autumn color starts in late September along the higher reaches of the Coronado Trail.

drop. The road settles down some from here, but soon starts a steep climb that squeezes the energy out of muscles spoiled from the long downhills. You get a glimpse of the grasslands the route is heading for at a beautiful panorama at MP 207. The mountains you see to the east lie in New Mexico.

After a tiring string of rollers, you get a long screamer. This is repeated until you hit Four Bar Mesa at MP 194, where you get a flatland breather for a moment and then continue on the downward coast. After the Granville Campground at MP 180, the route tightens its turns on deeper descents in stair-step fashion down to the Phelps Dodge Mine.

The route continues to coil down its final miles toward Clifton, where you can get supplies and limited accommodations. Turn left at MP 168 if you need provisions. Otherwise continue down to the town of Clifton at MP 165. Your next chance for food and accommodations comes 43 miles away in Safford.

Route 73

THREE WAY NEAR-CENTURY LOOP
US 70 NEAR SAFFORD TO US 191 TO AZ 75 TO US 70

Moderate to Difficult • Intermediate to Experienced

- Travels a variety of desert landscapes with small towns and interesting geology
- Offers a near-century ride for experienced riders or separate shorter rides
- Two lanes; narrow to wide shoulders

DISTANCE: 93-mile loop

PEAK CYCLING: October–April

ACCOMMODATIONS: Supplies and restaurants in Safford and Duncan; very basic supplies at Three Way

SPECIAL CONSIDERATIONS: This route travels in a remote area with full sun. Avoid traveling during the daytime hours in the summer. Bring a repair kit, food, and enough water.

STARTING POINT: From Safford, head east on US 70; MP 340 is the first mile marker.

You don't have to do this whole route; each of its three segments makes a great day route by itself. However, road cyclists with century experience will like this one full of hill climbing, rollers, scenery, and history.

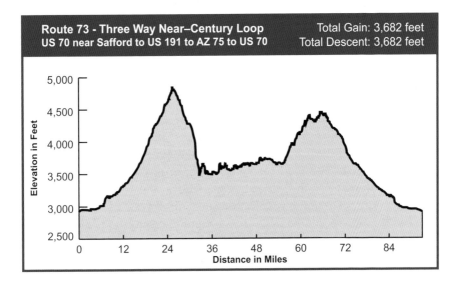

Route 73 - Three Way Near–Century Loop
US 70 near Safford to US 191 to AZ 75 to US 70
Total Gain: 3,682 feet
Total Descent: 3,682 feet

The route starts out from Safford, heading east on US 70/US 191 (see Route 74, p. 188). When you get to the intersection where US 191 forks left (around MP 349), you have two choices: (1) If you want to get the challenging hill climb done early, or if you're planning to make Three Way a turnaround point, then continue on US 191; or (2) if you plan to cycle to Duncan and back, continue on US 70. This route continues onto US 191.

Starting at MP 131 heading northeast on US 191, this segment of the route begins with a series of rollers that continuously climb into the Peloncillo Mountains. At MP 134, you start a sleeper of a climb that doesn't look like much but will knock the wind out of unprepared

The segment along AZ 75 has several interesting detours; this one is on Cosper Loop.

cyclists. This unpretentious-looking climb doesn't let up until MP 139; then the steep part begins. The killer climb lets up for a breather around Thumb Butte (MP 142), then quickly resumes for several more miles. A couple of passing lanes give you a nice wide shoulder and a little leeway from traffic during this tough slog.

At about MP 151, the route falls like a rock down to the Gila River. The climb out of the drainage and up to Three Way is easy compared to the last 20 miles you've just climbed.

Three Way, a point on the map rather than a town, has a convenience store. If you're looking for a restaurant, turn right (south) onto AZ 75 or go back to Safford.

Once you're on AZ 75 (MP 398), the route heads into a homespun countryside with old homesteads and farmland. The road travels along the Gila River and presents scenic sculpted bluffs. A number of interesting side roads loop from the highway; each makes a great diversion that adds only a mile or two to the route but offers loads of history and character.

At MP 395, watch for the Cosper Loop that diverts to the community of York. The 1.5-mile-long loop travels through cotton fields and past interesting old buildings, such as the York Community Clubhouse and the Homemakers Club. At MP 389, Burma Road, walk your bicycle across the gravelly riverbed to a shady lane of walnut trees for a cool break. Around MP 384, Stevens Loop dips closer to the Gila River, showing chalky cliffs and galleries of cottonwood trees along old farmland. Finally, the Virden Loop, toward the end of this segment near the town of Duncan, takes you a few decades back in time. The road travels a few miles past an interesting mix of quiet money and Jeff Foxworthy joke material to an old town with gravel streets and a variety of building styles, from adobe to modern. This route continues to Duncan and turns right onto US 70 (see Route 74, below); it's 39 miles back to Safford from here.

Route 74

OLD WEST HIGHWAY
US 70: GLOBE TO DUNCAN

Moderate • Intermediate

- Travels a variety of desert landscapes with small towns and interesting geology
- Links with two other roads for a near-century (see Route 73, p. 186)
- Two lanes; narrow to wide shoulders

DISTANCE: 118 miles one-way

PEAK CYCLING: October–April

ACCOMMODATIONS: Supplies and restaurants in Globe, Safford, and Duncan. In Globe, check out the Noftsger Hill Inn (928-425-2260), a bed and breakfast with huge rooms that were once classrooms in an old school building. La Paloma Mexican Restaurant (5183 E. Clifton St., 928-428-2094) in Solomon serves great food and daily specials.

SPECIAL CONSIDERATIONS: This route travels in a remote area with full sun. Avoid traveling during the daytime hours in the summer. Bring a repair kit, food, and enough water.

STARTING POINT: From Globe, head east on US 70; MP 340 is the first mile marker.

This route doesn't have any famous destination, but it does present a rich aura of the Old West—small towns and high-desert scenery in some big country. The route starts in Globe and heads east to the New Mexico border.

Within a few miles of Globe, the route enters the San Carlos Apache Indian Reservation. A few miles farther, it passes the Apache Gold Casino. From there, you're basically on your own for the next few dozen miles. At the turnoff for San Carlos Reservoir (right turn) and Peridot (left turn), around MP 270, Peridot Mesa rises to the north. The basalt hill contains gem-quality deposits of its namesake light-green gemstone. Farther north, look for Mount Triplet.

As the countryside gets more remote, the rollers get more intense. Around MP 279, the landscape turns chalky white—limestone deposits from an ancient lake—and the hills become a challenge to climb. Flatter land returns by MP 289 near the small town of Bylas. This will be your first chance for a roadside pit stop; supplies are sparing.

At MP 300, the route exits the reservation and continues in backcountry-like surroundings, with the Gila Mountains to the north and Santa Teresa Mountains in the south. Soon, the route enters an emerald valley fed by the Gila River and full of cotton farms—not just any cotton but the famous Pima cotton, which produces a fine grade of material. These farms accompany you through the towns of Geronimo, Fort Thomas, Pima, and Thatcher. Don't count on much in the way of provisions until you hit Safford at MP 329. There is, however, a Tastee-Freez in Thatcher.

Much like the landscape coming into Safford, the farms follow you out of town for quite a ways. Edging on the northern tip of the San Simon Valley, the landscape seems to take a low profile, but you are actually starting a long-term climb up a moderate grade. By MP 357, the route shows some character as it heads into the Peloncillo Mountains. This rough-hewn range makes a stunning panorama from the road. Inside the volcanic ridges lies a labyrinthine maze of canyons. Watch for some distinctive peaks around MPs 360 to 362. Later, the landscape colors with purple hues, which contrast nicely with summertime spreads of grasslands and carpets of yellow snakeweed.

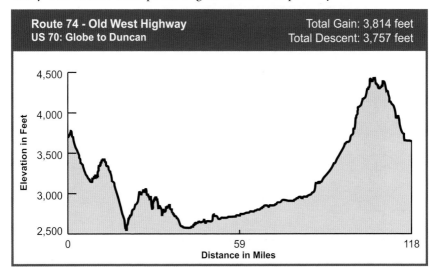

Route 74 - Old West Highway
US 70: Globe to Duncan
Total Gain: 3,814 feet
Total Descent: 3,757 feet

Though the land has a gentle demeanor, it has an edgy past filled with Anglo/Indian battles memorialized by roadside monuments. Ash Peak, the area's high point, rises to the south around MP 373.

As the route pulls away from the mountains, elegant foothill slopes appear and dissolve into hardscrabble creosote flats. A ripple of rollers carries you into the town of Duncan (MP 379). The town has a quirky edge and the personality of a colorful character. If you're hungry, you have some decent choices, such as Old Jo's Café or Angie's Cocina. For an even stronger blast from the past, head 6 miles east, a short distance into New Mexico, to the town of Verdin. Take the Verdin Highway on the east end of Duncan and enter old-time, rural Americana, then come back to Duncan for refreshments and food or continue in New Mexico for 29 miles to Lordsburg.

The Peloncillo Mountains show elegant folds along US 70.

Route 75

SWIFT TRAIL
AZ 366 up Mount Graham

Very Difficult • Experienced

* Travels up one of Arizona's highest mountains through several vegetation zones
* Two lanes; no shoulder

DISTANCE: 21 miles one-way

PEAK CYCLING: May–October

ACCOMMODATIONS: Supplies, restaurants, and lodging in Safford. The Olney House bed and breakfast (928-428-5118) is a change of pace from franchise lodging. The innkeeper has unusual antiques that liken the inn to a museum. Check out the Essence of Tranquility mineral hot springs (6074 Lebanon Loop, 928-428-9312) in Safford. Laid-back, bohemian, and utterly comforting, the resort offers camping and tepee lodging in addition to a soothing soak.

SPECIAL CONSIDERATIONS: This route requires expert hill-climbing skills. Start your ride in the early morning to avoid getting soaked in a summer thunderstorm.

The Swift Trail starts in the Sonoran Desert where cactus and succulents reign.

STARTING POINT: From Safford, go south on US 191 about 7 miles and turn right (west) onto AZ 366.

The Pinaleno Mountains once went by the name Sierra Bonita, Spanish for "beautiful mountain." As this route travels up the highest peak in the Pinaleno Mountains, you can see how the name fits. A ride up the Swift Trail will not be quick. It's a long, slow pull toward the top of Mount Graham, one of Arizona's highest mountains. Phoenix cyclist Reed Kempton, who has cycled almost half of Arizona's paved highways, ranks this route with Arizona's most difficult.

"Climbing Mount Graham is difficult because it's so steep," Reed says. "But it's a great climb."

This route will take you from the desert floor to the peak's upper reaches, climbing all the way from 3,400 feet to 9,000 feet (10,720 feet if you have a tour bike). Start this ride early, before the desert temperatures climb into the triple digits (shortly after dawn on some summer days). The mountaintop's high temperature usually runs lower than the desert's summertime low, rarely topping 80 degrees.

The route starts you climbing almost from the start at MP 115 on a persistent but low-grade, straight-as-an-arrow ascent. Once you hit the foothills at MP 117, the road goes up like an airplane, so get ready for the climb. By MP 120, a sign warns, "Curves and Mountain Grades Next 23 Miles."

This road has several recreation areas at which you can stop for a few minutes to catch your breath, make a pit stop, or take some nourishment. The first, Noon Creek, appears around MP 121. A bit farther, the pine-oak habitat past the recreation area shows where the 2004 Heliograph fire scorched the slopes. After a couple more miles, around the 6,000-foot elevation marker, the plant life gets schizophrenic, wobbling between high-desert vegetation on the south face and mixed-conifer high country when the road bends to the north face.

The Arcadia Campground at MP 125.5 gives you a shady respite from the climb. You may need it, as the road climbs 1,000 feet just about every 3 miles and you have more than 2,000 feet to go. Much of the way travels in the shadows of a thick forest of mixed conifers. The mountain has some beautiful old-growth Douglas fir stands on it. One tree, listed on a database of the world's oldest trees, dates to A.D. 1257. Some of the animals that live in these ancient forests, the Mount Graham red squirrel and Mexican spotted owl, have made the mountain an intense point of interest for environmentalists.

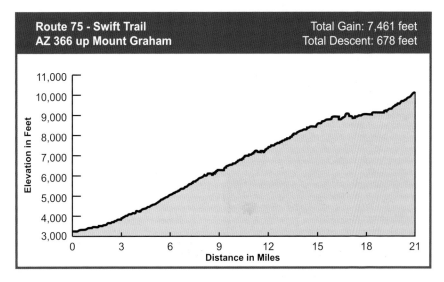

Route 75 - Swift Trail
AZ 366 up Mount Graham

Total Gain: 7,461 feet
Total Descent: 678 feet

You hit one of the hardest pulls at MP 130 when you climb 500 feet in just under 1 mile. A scenic panorama of the valley below from Lady Bug Saddle will give you a good excuse to catch your breath. The grade relents and the route takes its time climbing the next 500 feet into the aspen forests that crown the ridgetops. Shannon Campground, located near MP 136, marks the end of this route if you do not have a tour bike.

What goes up the mountain must come down, and the descent on the Swift Trail gets as intense as the climb. As tempting as the urge may be to zoom down the mountain, you can't do it safely. The hairpin turns and gravel patches will wipe you out, not to mention the slower-moving vehicles. Wait for the last 2 miles (MP 118) to pull out all the stops and go as fast as your bicycle will let you.

Hairpin turns define the upper reaches of the Swift Trail.

Route 76

ROAD TO FORT GRANT
AZ 266: SAFFORD TO FORT GRANT

Difficult • Intermediate

* Travels a mountain pass with distinct geology
* Offers a midway turnaround point for an easier ride
* Two lanes; no shoulder

DISTANCE: 10 miles (to rest stop) to 28 miles one-way

PEAK CYCLING: October–April

ACCOMMODATIONS: Supplies, lodging, and restaurants in Safford

SPECIAL CONSIDERATIONS: This route travels in a remote area with full sun. Avoid traveling during the daytime hours in the summer. Bring a repair kit, food, and enough water.

STARTING POINT: From Safford, head south on US 191 about 10 miles to AZ 266, and turn right (west); MP 105 is the first mile marker.

Much less strenuous a climb into the Pinaleno Mountains than the Swift Trail, this route takes you across Stockton Pass toward Fort Grant, an old military outpost turned prison. The soldiers used to called it Stockton's Gap after a cattle rancher in the area. The pass also goes by the name Eagle Pass because it lies near Eagle Rock Peak. The ride across the pass makes a scenic adventure through a field of balanced rocks and weathered boulders colored with chartreuse lichen.

Starting out with moderate rollers, the route's first climb doesn't come until MP 110, but then you keep climbing for several miles. By MP 112, you're on a more concerted pull up the pass. By MP 114, the landscape has entered a piñon-juniper forest thick enough to give the distant slopes a carpeted look.

A roadside table between MPs 115 and 116 gives you a chance to catch your breath if you need a break and a good turnaround point for a shorter, easier ride. It also makes a great lunch stop on the way back. If you can use a breather, you'll get a break from the climb a couple of miles farther along at MP 118, when a swift downhill starts you on one long screamer. The route hits the desert floor around MP 121 and is still coasting a couple of miles later at the turnoff for Fort Grant. If you're ready for another challenge—3 miles with a several-hundred-foot climb to the prison—take the turnoff. If not, the pavement ends just ahead and you can return the way you came.

The road to Fort Grant travels though a pass in the Pinaleno Mountains.

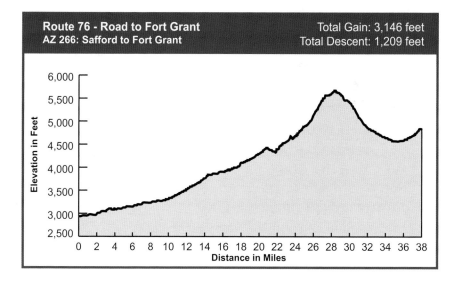

Route 76 - Road to Fort Grant
AZ 266: Safford to Fort Grant

Total Gain: 3,146 feet
Total Descent: 1,209 feet

REGION 8

TUCSON BASIN AND BEYOND

The Tucson Basin has drawn cyclists from around the world to its Sonoran Desert landscape. Pancake-flat in its midsection, the basin ripples around its edges with rolling hillsides as it melds with the several mountain ranges that surround it. This landscape makes for some excellent routes, as cyclists can get a little of every type of terrain if they ride long and far enough in this university city that knows the value of holding onto its cultural heritage.

ROUTES

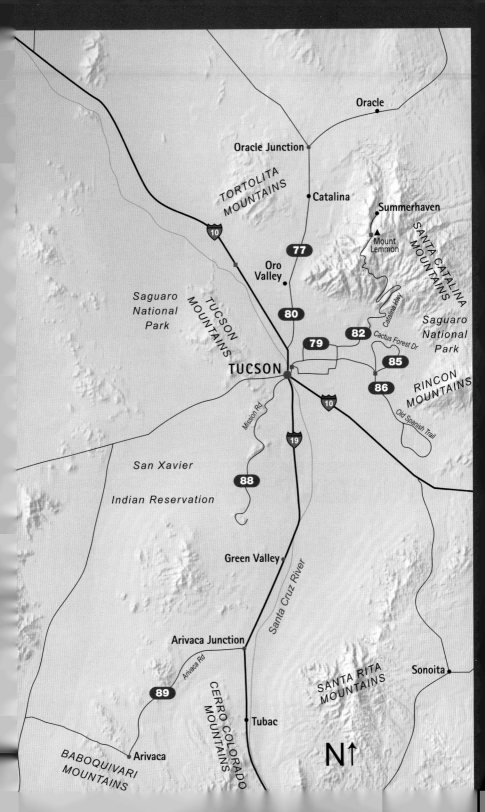

Route 77

ORACLE JUNCTION
AZ 77: TUCSON TO ORACLE JUNCTION

Moderate • Intermediate

- ◆ Travels the outskirts of Tucson
- ◆ Excellent midlength cycle ride with steady hill climbing
- ◆ Four- to six-lane road; wide shoulder

DISTANCE: 25 miles one-way

PEAK CYCLING: October–April; early morning in warmer weather

ACCOMMODATIONS: Supplies and restaurants in Catalina; lodging in Oro Valley and
Tucson. Check out Westward Look Resort (245 E. Ina Road, 520-297-1151), a
Tucson classic for the last century, with great specials. Special extras: homemade
ice cream and other culinary greats created by Chef Jamie West in The Gold Room
or one of the area's best sport massages at the Sonoran Spa.

SPECIAL CONSIDERATIONS: This segment of highway gets rush-hour traffic.

STARTING POINT: From the intersection of River and Oracle roads, head north
on Oracle Road; MP 72 is the first mile marker.

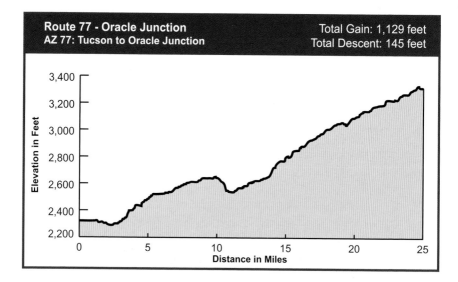

Route 77 - Oracle Junction
AZ 77: Tucson to Oracle Junction
Total Gain: 1,129 feet
Total Descent: 145 feet

This route, popular with local cyclists, will take you northward from Tucson city limits, climbing out of the Tucson Basin into the rolling hills along the Santa Catalina Mountains. The steady climb provides a moderate challenge on the way out of town and becomes a carrot for the downhill coast on the way back.

It takes a few miles for this route to get loose from the city's hold, but it travels next to the massive rock faces of the Santa Catalina Mountains, which makes for some nice scenery. Suburbia enters the scene by MP 84 at Oro Valley. Watch for the little Espresso To Go shop in the next town of Catalina (east side of the highway near MP 87) if you need a shot of caffeine to finish off the few more miles to go. These miles travel mostly undeveloped desert. The route ends at Oracle Junction (MP 91), at the junction of AZ 79 and AZ 77. You may continue in either direction (see Route 54, p. 141, to follow AZ 79 or Route 58, p. 152, for AZ 77). Or, return the way you came.

Route 78

VENTANA CANYON LOOP
FOOTHILLS OF SANTA CATALINA MOUNTAINS

Moderate • Intermediate

* Travels through residential foothills
* Mostly two lanes; bike lane on segments

DISTANCE: 14-mile loop

PEAK CYCLING: October–March; early morning in warmer weather

ACCOMMODATIONS: Supplies, restaurants, and lodging in Tucson. Check out Lowes Ventana Canyon Resort (7000 N. Resort Drive, 520-299-2020), coined the nation's first ecologically planned resort and rated as one of the best to stay at.

SPECIAL CONSIDERATIONS: This route is short but steep.

STARTING POINT: Fort Lowell Park, at the southeast corner of Craycroft and Fort Lowell roads, on the northern edge of Tucson.

This route travels the best of both worlds—residential and wilderness—in the Santa Catalina foothills. Besides the twists and turns in the residential segment of the route, you also get a chance at some hill work while cycling along the mountains.

Heading north on Craycroft Road, the route crosses the Rillito River just before mile 1. The bridge spans the drainage just upriver from its junction

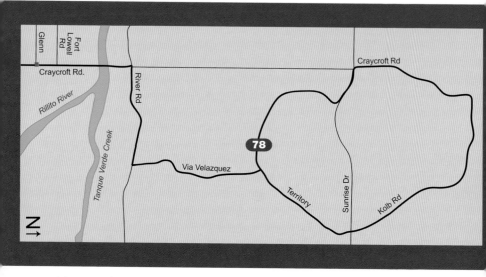

with two other major drainages—Tanque Verde Creek and Pantano Wash—in the Tucson Basin. You won't see water in these drainages until a heavy downpour, when it comes rushing off the nearby mountains. At River Road, which follows the north side of the Rillito River across northern Tucson, turn right (east). At about mile 2, turn left (north) onto Tanuri Drive.

This segment of the route meanders with dips and bends on intimate roads through quiet residential areas in the foothills. The narrow roadway does not have a bike lane, but traffic is minimal and travels at low speeds. At mile 3, veer right onto Via Velazquez, then right again at mile 3.5 onto Territory. Now the route opens up in a shallow canyon with a soft shoulder along the road.

At Kolb Road, about mile 4.6, turn left (north); cross Sunrise Drive and

Ventana Canyon route takes you close enough to the Santa Catalina Mountains to feel their foothills and scenic moments.

continue north on Kolb Road, climbing up to the feet of the Santa Catalina Mountains. The long ascent up Kolb to Ventana Canyon doesn't make big demands, but the top-out point near its meld with Craycroft Road, about mile 6.5, starts you on a series of rollers as the route bends to the south.

Rather then an easy coast back down to Sunrise Drive, the road takes some serious plunges, one quick-and-steep descent at a time. Once back at Sunrise Drive (mile 8.5) turn left (east); this busy street has a nice, wide bike lane. At about mile 9, turn right (south) onto Paseo Sonoyta, which brings you back into the residential neighborhoods.

The route twists and dips through a sleepy neighborhood, then turns left (east) onto Via Velazquez at mile 9.7. You get to negotiate up and down one last steep hill just before the route veers right (south) to continue on Via Velazquez at about mile 10.6. With the loop closed, the route returns to Tanuri Drive at mile 11.1 and River Road at mile 12.1. After a right (west) turn onto River Road and a left (south) turn onto Craycroft Road at mile 13.1, you return to Fort Lowell Park in another mile.

Route 79

BEAR CANYON
LOOP THROUGH NORTHEAST TUCSON

Easy • Intermediate

- Travels the undeveloped edges of northeast Tucson
- A colorful spread of wildflowers blooms after a wet winter along outer roads
- Outer roads have two lanes, no shoulder; city streets have four lanes, medium to no shoulder

DISTANCE: 20-mile loop

PEAK CYCLING: October–March; early morning in hot weather

ACCOMMODATIONS: Supplies, restaurants, and lodging in Tucson

SPECIAL CONSIDERATIONS: Take extra care on heavily traveled Tanque Verde Road.

STARTING POINT: From Swan and Grant roads in Tucson, drive east on Grant Road; just past Wilmot Road, veer east onto Tanque Verde Road; just past Kolb Road, watch for Udall Park on the south side of the road.

Like all the roads that border the Tucson Basin as it merges with the foothills of the surrounding mountains, the ones in this route contain rollers and hills as they travel along a pristine Sonoran Desert landscape. Getting to the scenic edge requires a few miles' cycle on busy Tanque Verde Road; be careful to stay in the correct lane just after starting the route, heading east on Tanque Verde. The road forks right into Wrightstown Road. Straight ahead, Tanque Verde Road climbs a bridge over Pantano Road. Don't let a left-turn lane about 0.1 mile before the overpass confuse you. You want to stay on Tanque Verde as it climbs the overpass and heads northeast. Also, watch for incoming traffic from a feeder road on the right as Tanque Verde descends from the overpass.

Once you get past these junctions, the route settles down into a pleasant ride and gets nearer to undeveloped desert. Around mile 4, turn left (north) onto Bear Canyon Road. This road heads toward the Santa Catalina Mountains past homes on large-acreage lots. A bikeway becomes available for a short distance, providing a safe route for children to commute to a school. Then the route continues without a shoulder toward the mountains.

At mile 6.5, turn right (east) onto Snyder Road. Fast and shoulderless, this two-lane road travels close enough to the Santa Catalina Mountains that you can see the thick saguaro cactus forest that covers their south faces. East of Harrison Road, just past mile 7, the route takes on a more remote feel. By Houghton Road, at mile 8, the landscape becomes pristine. Keep in mind when crossing the Catalina Highway, around mile 9, that traffic on that highway does not stop, even though the route you're following has a stop sign. Catalina Highway will take you to the top of Mount Lemmon in the Catalina Mountains (see Route 82, p. 207).

Near Snyder Road's end, turn right (south) onto Soldier Trail. The route starts a downhill glide that takes you a few miles to Tanque Verde Road. Turn right (west) onto Tanque Verde, and then turn left (south) near mile 14 onto Tanque Verde Loop. This altogether pleasant part of the route enters a cloistered neighborhood composed of ranches and large spreads along Tanque Verde Creek. At Speedway Boulevard (mile 15), the route turns right (west) and heads back into town. After cycling about 4 miles on Speedway, turn right (north) onto Grady Avenue (just past Pantano Road). Follow the bike-route signs, turning left (west) onto Pima Street, right (north) onto Camino Pio Decimo, and left (west) onto Tanque Verde Road. At this point, you might want to stay on the sidewalk on the south side of Tanque Verde Road to travel the 0.5 mile back to the park and the end of this loop.

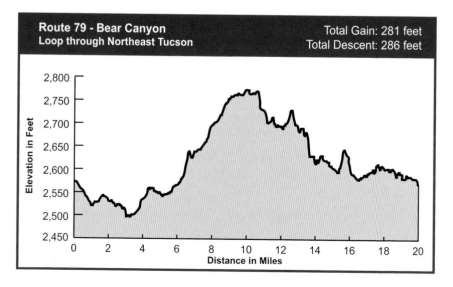

Route 79 - Bear Canyon
Loop through Northeast Tucson

Total Gain: 281 feet
Total Descent: 286 feet

Route 80

CHRISTIE HILLS LOOP
SANTA CATALINA FOOTHILLS

Moderate • Beginner

◆ Travels the undeveloped edge of the Santa Catalina foothills
◆ Good for a quick workout or beginner hill climbing and training
◆ Residential area is two lanes, no shoulder; Ina Road has a bike lane

DISTANCE: 4.7-mile loop

PEAK CYCLING: October–March or early morning

ACCOMMODATIONS: Supplies, restaurants, and lodging in Tucson

SPECIAL CONSIDERATIONS: This route has short but tough hills.

STARTING POINT: Southeast corner of Oracle and Magee roads

This route passes right by the trailhead for Pima Canyon, a popular hiking route that climbs several thousand feet from the desert floor to a ridgetop. Like the hiking trail, this cycling route makes a tidy little workout. Located in the foothills of the Santa Catalina Mountains near Pima Canyon, the roads in the route dip and climb up and down some feisty little hills. This makes a nice quickie workout or good place for beginner to get some hill work.

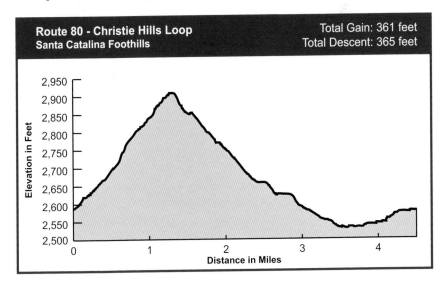

Route 80 - Christie Hills Loop
Santa Catalina Foothills
Total Gain: 361 feet
Total Descent: 365 feet

Tucsonan Craig Kafura rides the route after work. Craig likes the concentration hill climbing requires and compares climbing hills on his Specialized bicycle to rock climbing, another favorite activity.

"Hills take more focus," Craig says, "like rock climbing does."

Tucsonan Craig Kafura working out on the Christie Hills route.

Start the route heading east on Magee Road. Within moments the route leaves behind the commercial traffic on Oracle Road, one of Tucson's main drags, and enters into the soulful Sonoran Desert atmosphere. The hills come quickly.

At mile 1.4, the road bends right (south) into Christie Drive. The turnoff for the Pima Canyon Trailhead comes up on your left shortly. Speed bumps and traffic islands on Magee Road and Christie Drive make this route too tedious for most vehicle traffic, so you will have the road pretty much to yourself. On the other hand, you have to finesse the speed bumps on the downhills.

When you get to Ina Road, at mile 2.7, turn right (west) and cycle 1 mile to Oracle Road, then turn right (north) and cycle 1 mile back to the route's start at Magee Road. Or you can return the way you came for a double dose of the Christie Hills.

DO YOU NEED FEET TO STOP?

When Jack Sieder, a veteran cyclist who taught bicycle workshops and led rides with a group connected with the American Youth Hostel, stopped at a stop sign by balancing on his bicycle without putting his feet on the ground, a police officer tried to ticket him. Jack talked his way out of the ticket, but says he has witnessed police arbitrarily ticket cyclists based upon how many feet they place on the ground at a stop sign.

A police officer may try to judge your stop by the number of feet you have on the ground, but you only have to cease motion. If you need feet to do that, by all means use them. If you have the ability to balance on your bicycle without putting one or both feet on the ground after stopping, go ahead.

A legal stop requires three steps (with or without one or both feet on the ground): First you must cease motion for at least three seconds; the second step requires you to yield to any traffic; you may proceed when safe to do so.

Route 81

RILLITO RIVER PARK
BIKEWAY ALONG RILLITO RIVER

Easy • Beginner

- A paved, multiuse bikeway that travels along a contained riverbed
- An easy route that presents scenic panoramas and glimpses of wildlife

DISTANCE: 7.5 miles one-way

PEAK CYCLING: October–April; early morning in warmer weather.

ACCOMMODATIONS: Supplies, restaurants, and lodging in Tucson.

SPECIAL CONSIDERATIONS: Do not park in adjacent business parking lots; see Starting
   Point below. An unpaved stretch on the eastern end of the bikeway, from Hacienda
   del Sol to Alvernon, requires a tour or mountain bike.

STARTING POINT: Parking area at Campbell and River roads, on the southeast bank of
   the river, across from Trader Joe's.

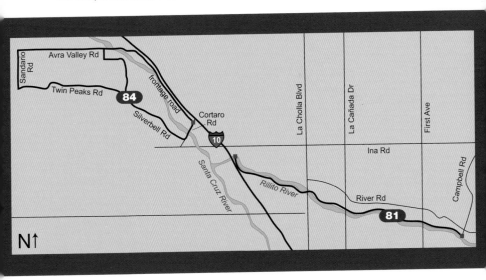

Like many Arizona rivers, the Rillito normally doesn't flow except during heavy rains. A perfect example of the term "drainage" to describe rivers and creeks, the river flows when water drains from the mountains surrounding the city. The city built the Rillito River Park as a means of flood control after major flooding occurred in 1983.

Steep soil and cement walls along each side of the river hold the promise of protection from future flooding. The walls also isolate the riverbed to form a protected greenway for wildlife. You might see a coyote trotting along the sandy bed or quail fluttering at the edge of the steep embankments.

The trail, part of a planned network that eventually will connect all the major waterways in Tucson, runs westward from Craycroft Road to just short of I-10. At the time of this writing, segments of the bikeway remain unpaved.

Cocooned between a line of mesquite, paloverde, and desert willow trees, this route gets smatterings of shade as it follows the narrow park plotted along the Rillito River. Picnic benches, parks, and restrooms along the route give opportunities for pit stops and rests.

During late fall and winter, when the temperatures hover around 70 degrees, the route gets high daytime use. Springtime sees a beautiful spread of wildflowers after a wet winter. In the late spring and summer, desert willow flowers exude a sweet scent.

The paved segment of this route runs nonstop from Campbell to the bikeway's end. At La Cholla Boulevard (mile 5), the pavement ends on the north side of the river. Cyclists will have to switch to the south side here. After another mile, the path ends at the Union Pacific Railroad tracks just shy of I-10. Return the way you came.

EL TOUR DE TUCSON—MORE THAN A CENTURY

Tucson cyclist Dave Peashock describes the start of the annual El Tour de Tucson, a cycle event compassing the Tucson Basin, as awesome. Thousands of cyclists pedal en masse in front of the Tucson Convention Center to the tune of high-energy rock music. The event, renowned as one of the country's best-organized, is the largest perimeter bicycling tour in the country.

Dave has ridden in the annual event, always occurring on the Saturday before Thanksgiving, six out the last eight years. In the years he doesn't ride, he volunteers assistance. The event has four starting points for 109-, 80-, 66-, and 35-mile rides. The 2005 ride hosted about 7,700 cyclists with a winning time of 4:21:23. The winner, Tucsonan Curtis Gunn, came across the finish line all by himself with the runners-up trailing by more than half a minute.

Route 82

SKY ISLAND SCENIC BYWAY
CATALINA HIGHWAY UP MOUNT LEMMON

Very Difficult • Experienced

- ◆ A scenic byway that travels through seven life zones up Mount Lemmon in the Coronado National Forest
- ◆ The longest climb in the state and a favorite of hardcore cyclists

DISTANCE: 30 miles (to Summerhaven) one-way

PEAK CYCLING: April–November

ACCOMMODATIONS: Supplies, restaurants, and lodging in Tucson. Restaurants in Summerhaven and at Mount Lemmon Ski Resort. When you finish the ride, check out Hacienda del Sol Guest Ranch Resort (520-299-1501). This inn presents a true taste of Tucson with hacienda-style lodging and gorgeous views. Its restaurant, The Grill, stays on the best-of lists in Tucson.

SPECIAL CONSIDERATIONS: Most of this route is a 5 percent climb. Temperatures vary up to 30 degrees cooler in the heights compared to the desert floor. Summer storms (a daily occurrence in the higher reaches during the monsoon season of mid-July to mid-September) can quickly drop temperatures 20 to 30 degrees.

STARTING POINT: Tanque Verde Road and Catalina Highway. MP 1 starts 5 miles into this route at the national forest boundary.

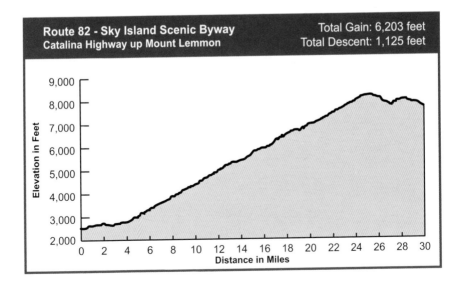

When it comes to hill climbing," says Phoenix cyclist and hill-climbing champion Scott Price, "there are two kinds of people: Either you're scared of the climb, or you love it and attack it."

Scott has raced with Landis Trek VW and has held several hill-climbing records. He now coaches athletes. Scott held the record climb up Mount Lemmon until recently, with an average speed of around 16.2 mph. Fuel and pacing play a big part, he says of hill climbing, and the psychological aspect is just as important. Cyclists should strive for a state of nothingness, or no mind, where they don't listen to the doubts and let the best flow out.

Mount Lemmon has always drawn the hard-core cyclists. Chef Craig Dibbern at Hacienda del Sol Guest Ranch Resort's restaurant, The Grill, has cycled up Mount Lemmon in 2.5 hours (and only 37 minutes for the descent), and then repeated the climb two more times right afterward. Lance Armstrong trained for a Tour de France on Mount Lemmon at the turn of the century. Whatever your experience when cycling the Sky Island Parkway up Mount Lemmon, keep an open mind and know that when you finish you will have cycled a route preferred by some of the world's best cyclists.

Starting from Tanque Verde Road, the route travels a gradual grade on a new surface that feels like silk. When you hit the national forest and a sign that reads Sky Island Scenic Byway, you pedal right into a saguaro forest on a road that wastes no time in settling into a mettle-testing climb—an ascent that winds upward through the seven life zones you would see if you cycled north to Canada.

By MP 3, you leave the saguaros behind and enter high-desert grasslands. A couple of pullouts near MPs 8 and 9 give you a chance to safely pull off the road if you need to. By MP 10, the route enters a fantasia of rock walls and boulders chiseled by the environment into formations that run the gamut from dramatic to quirky. The show starts out slowly, but by MP 12 you're right in the middle of some fantastic formations. Most are hoodoos and balanced rocks, but you'll see a few curiously carved features and animal look-alikes. Watch for pedestrians crossing the road around Windy Point.

Ponderosa pines appear around MP 17, and the route ducks into pine-forest shade a couple of miles later. If you need help, watch for the Palisades ranger station at MP 20.

The road gets its first downhill around MP 21, but resumes the climb quickly, hitting aspen forests by MP 23. A fork in the road at 7,851 feet veers right for Mount Lemmon Ski Resort, a stiff climb of a couple of miles, or left and down to the mountain hamlet of Summerhaven. Both destinations have food and restrooms. The Mount Lemmon Highway continues climbing to 9,157 feet, and the road to Summerhaven drops into Sabino Canyon and ends at 7,410 feet. With this route starting at an elevation of about 2,700 feet (2,950 feet at the national forest boundary), no matter which direction you choose you'll have climbed a long way.

Route 83

ORO VALLEY LOOP
ORO VALLEY, NORTHWEST OF TUCSON

Moderate • Beginner

- Travels segments of El Tour de Tucson route in the outskirts of Tucson
- Excellent workout if cycled counterclockwise
- Two to four lanes; wide shoulders

DISTANCE: 18-mile loop

PEAK CYCLING: October–March; early morning in warmer weather

ACCOMMODATIONS: Supplies, restaurants, and lodging in Tucson. Check out the Hilton
El Conquistador Golf & Tennis Resort (520-544-5000). It's got a great location,
a handful of miles from the starting point of the 35-mile course of El Tour de
Tucson, nestled in the Santa Catalina Mountains. Its restaurant Dos Locos serves
large portions of delicious Latin-inspired meals. Also located near the El Tour route,
all-inclusive Miraval Resort (800-232-3969) will ease your recovery after a strenuous bike ride with the world's best body treatments. Or better yet, stay there the
night before your workout and get an acupuncture session. The resort's acupuncture therapist has the magic touch that will get your meridians wide open and
full of energy for the day of the race.

SPECIAL CONSIDERATIONS: Parts of this route travel roads with heavy traffic.

STARTING POINT: From Ina and Oracle roads, go north on Oracle to Calle Concordia in
Oro Valley; turn left (west), and go 0.2 mile to Weaver Park on the north side of
the street.

You see several different sides of life and stages of land development on
this route around Oro Valley, a small city just northwest of Tucson. The
route follows a clockwise direction. If you ride it counterclockwise, you get
an excellent workout on two several-mile-long grades.

The route starts in a quiet neighborhood heading west from Weaver Park
on Calle Concordia. Horse properties give the narrow road a pastoral feel.
Most of Calle Concordia has a bike lane, except for a short 0.5-mile segment,
and the traffic is slow and low. In fact, the whole network of side streets south
of Calle Concordia, between Oracle Road and La Cañada Drive, makes for
easy, peaceful riding and is worth exploring at the end of this route as a
scenic way of winding down.

At La Cañada Drive (mile 1.5), turn right (north). One of the busier streets
on the northwest side, La Cañada has fast traffic and a bike lane. After

La Cañada climbs to Lambert Lane at mile 3, turn right (east). From here to First Avenue (mile 5.2), you can cycle the street or a bike path that follows right along the road. At the time of this writing, Lambert has only two lanes. Less experienced cyclists should take the bike path. At First Avenue, turn left (north).

With undeveloped desert between you and the Pusch Ridge Wilderness in the Santa Catalina Mountains to the east, this segment gives a wild touch to the route. At Tangerine Road (mile 6.5), First Avenue becomes Rancho Vistoso Boulevard. Here the landscape starts to show signs of development. By the time the road bends eastward at about mile 9, the land has an every-hair-in-place look, courtesy of the Rancho Vistoso master-planned community. Here, the boulevard starts a pleasant downhill coast, with a powerful panorama of the Santa Catalina Mountains that lasts all the way to Oracle Road (mile 12.5), where you turn right (south).

A favorite route for cyclists, Oracle Road has a nice, wide shoulder on which to ride. It's a busy artery, however, so pay attention to the activity around you, which may include a faster cyclist wanting to pass you. This 5.2-mile-long segment of the route continues with the downhill grade and picturesque scenery of the Santa Catalinas that started on Rancho Vistoso, and the miles pass fast. At Calle Concordia (mile 17.7), turn right (west). When you get back to Weaver Park, you can return to your vehicle or check out the neighborhood streets mentioned earlier.

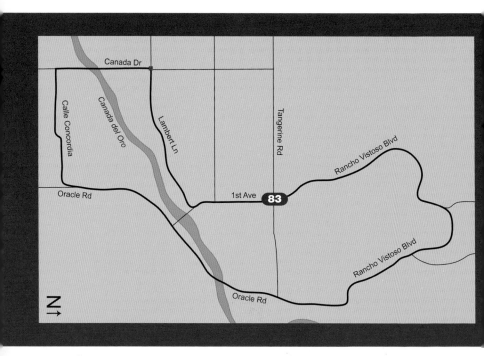

Route 84

AVRA VALLEY LOOP
NORTHWEST TUCSON

Easy • Beginner

- Travels through the northwest end of the Tucson Basin
- Two lanes; occasional bike lane

DISTANCE: 19.5-mile loop

PEAK CYCLING: October–March; early morning in warmer weather

ACCOMMODATIONS: Supplies, restaurants, and lodging in Tucson

SPECIAL CONSIDERATIONS: Segments of dips and curves cause blind spots.

STARTING POINT: From I-10, take exit 246 (Cortaro Road); park and cycle south on
Frontage Road (one-way at this point) to Cortaro Road. See map on p. 205

This route is relatively easy, travels through scenic saguaro cactus country, passes pristine farmland, and begins and ends in a shopping area with comfort-food restaurants. A few congested areas might make some beginners nervous, but this route will suit most cyclists.

The route starts along the Frontage Road, heading south. After a few blocks on the one-way road, turn right (southwest) on Cortaro Road. This segment is in the midst of a busy shopping area. Pay special attention to vehicles turning in and out of the parking lots. At Silverbell Road, turn right (northwest).

For the next few miles, you get a marked bike lane. With the Santa Catalina Mountains behind you and the Tucson Mountains rising to the left, the route leaves the edge of Tucson's development. By the time the route hits Twin Peaks Road, about mile 4, you get a taste of what the land was like a few decades ago,

Avra Valley Loop, flat and fast, throws in some sexy curves and rollers to round out the route.

when Tucson's outskirts were several miles south. You actually feel a sense of solitude in this pretty desert landscape.

A couple of S-curves twist the route onto Twin Peaks Road, and you head deeper into wild desert covered with creosote. At about mile 9, turn right (north) onto Sendario Road. With no shoulder and little traffic, this ribbon of a road cuts straight through farm country and creosote flats. When you come to Avra Valley Road, turn right (east). Now traveling the outer reaches of Tucson, the route skirts around the Tucson Mountains for a while. The Santa Cruz River at about mile 14.5 signals the route's reentry into civilization. By mile 15.5 you come to the Frontage Road, where you turn right (south). This is a fast segment that passes an industrial area of the valley as you cycle back to the start of this route.

Route 85

CACTUS FOREST DRIVE
LOOP ROAD IN SAGUARO NATIONAL PARK–EAST

Moderate • Beginner

* Travels a saguaro cactus forest in Saguaro National Park–East
* Colorful show of herbaceous wildflowers after a wet winter, from late February to mid-March, and cactus flowers and paloverde trees in early- to mid-May
* Two lanes; no shoulder

DISTANCE: 8-mile loop

PEAK CYCLING: October–March; early morning in warmer weather

ACCOMMODATIONS: Supplies, restaurants, and lodging in Tucson. The park's visitor center has restrooms and water.

SPECIAL CONSIDERATIONS: The national park opens daily from 7 a.m. until sunset and charges cyclists $3 to enter. This route has a steep downhill that can be dangerous at high speeds.

STARTING POINT: Saguaro National Park–East visitor center. From East Broadway in Tucson, head southeast on Old Spanish Trail for 4 miles to the park entrance.

Saguaro National Park–East harbors more than 600 species of plants. The park's namesake cacti fill the foothill slopes of the Rincon Mountains so densely they create a forest. In the springtime, after a wet winter, dozens of species of wildflowers color the desert floor. In May, cacti and trees bloom.

Tucson cyclist Dave Peashock rates Cactus Forest Drive as one of the prettiest cycle routes around Tucson. Sitting just outside the edge of the city in the foothills of the Rincon Mountains, Cactus Forest Drive travels through a pristine Sonoran Desert landscape undulating with hills.

"One of the characteristics of cycling Tucson is its hills," Dave says. "If you do short rides in the city, you can stay on a pretty flat course. Once you start racking up miles, you always encounter hills on Tucson's outskirts."

He warns the first downhill on the drive has a treacherous side with its double S-curve. Also, he says, the steep climb toward the end of the loop can discourage beginner cyclists.

"It's just over a mile long," Dave says, "but it seems to go forever."

No question: This is a fun ride on a bicycle; you just don't want to miscalculate any of the route's ultra-sharp hairpin turns and end up in the cacti The road didn't get named Cactus Forest for nothing; it has prickly pear, several different species of cholla cactus, and saguaro cactus. In addition to this prickly mélange, the mesquite trees have thorns.

The narrow road starts out as a one-way drive. As Dave Peashock advises, the route begins in a frenzy, with twists, turns, and deep plunges like a Wild Mouse rollercoaster ride; then it settles down on the desert floor for a while. Within a couple of miles, the saguaro cacti get thick and start to take on the interesting shapes that typify them. In yet another couple miles, the route is back to thrills, chills, and, if you take your eyes off the road to gawk at the cacti, spills. The infamous hill rises midway on the loop and doesn't stop climbing for well past 1 mile.

Watch for a sign that points to "Loop Drive," which you will follow. The road turns two-way and finishes in another mile back at the visitor center.

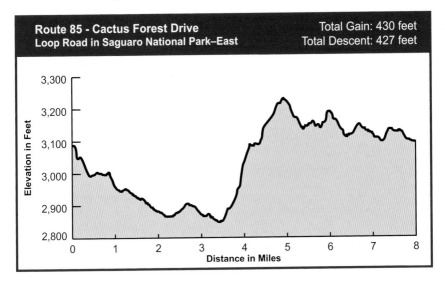

Route 86

OLD SPANISH TRAIL LOOP
SOUTHEAST TUCSON

Easy • Intermediate

◆ Travels along the foothills of the Rincon Mountains

◆ A bikeway travels between Broadway and Saguaro National Park

◆ Sees colorful spreads of wildflowers after a wet winter along outer roads

◆ Two lanes; medium shoulder and some segments without a shoulder

DISTANCE: 35-mile loop

PEAK CYCLING: October–March; early morning in warmer weather

ACCOMMODATIONS: Supplies, restaurants, and lodging in Tucson

SPECIAL CONSIDERATIONS: Beginners not yet comfortable with hills and fast roads should keep to the bikeway.

STARTING POINT: Old Spanish Trail at Broadway. Park in the dirt lot next to the Japanese Kitchen, immediately south of Broadway.

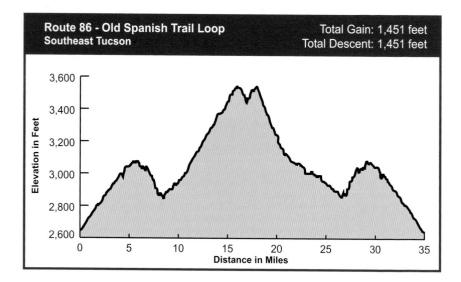

Route 86 - Old Spanish Trail Loop
Southeast Tucson
Total Gain: 1,451 feet
Total Descent: 1,451 feet

The historic Old Spanish Trail traversed several southwestern states to link Santa Fe with Los Angeles. The segment that spanned Arizona arced across its northern edge, and travelers from landlocked territories traveled the pack-mule trail to the coast between 1829 and 1848.

Tucson's Old Spanish Trail, connected only in name with the historic trail, takes you several miles outside the city and into the desert boonies. Starting at Broadway, the bike-laned route leaves the city limits at Melpomene Way (mile 2) and enters undeveloped desertlands near Saguaro National Park–East, at mile 4. From there, the rollers begin. When the route starts its drop into the Rincon Valley, look for Mica Mountain—the Rincon Mountains' citadel—in the east.

The route crosses the usually dry Rincon Creek bed near mile 7.5; this runs into Pantano Wash, a major drainage on the east side of Tucson. Flash flooding is possible here during wet weather, which may preclude your crossing the wash. The Rincon Country Store almost 1 mile farther makes a good pit stop. The roadside store has just about every sweet and salty form of carbohydrates possible and provides a few picnic benches to enjoy them.

The route starts to climb slowly out of the Rincon Valley around mile 13. The road turns ragged here, compared to the fairly smooth surface up to this point. The route turns right (south) at about mile 15 onto Pistol Hill Road and begins a nonstop climb until it tops off just over 1 mile later on the namesake hill. Around mile 17, turn right (west) onto Colossal Cave Road, then 1 mile further turn right again (north) onto Camino Loma Alta.

After cruising through a development for a few miles, the route travels on a series of shallow rollers back toward Tucson. When you reach Old Spanish Trail at around mile 21, turn left (northwest) and repeat the 12-mile-long segment back to Broadway and the route's end.

Route 87

GATES PASS LOOP
SAGUARO NATIONAL PARK–WEST

Difficult • Experienced

◆ Travels through thick saguaro forests in a national park
◆ Two lanes; some segments with shoulder

DISTANCE: 34-mile loop

PEAK CYCLING: October–March; early morning in warmer weather

ACCOMMODATIONS: Supplies, restaurants, and lodging in Tucson

SPECIAL CONSIDERATIONS: Some segments of this road are steep and have blind curves. Less experienced cyclists can start at the Red Hills Visitor Center and cycle the more moderate segments of this route.

STARTING POINT: From I-10, take exit 248 (Ina Road), park, and head west.

The narrow, winding road in the national park offers the thrill of a roller coaster as it dips and heaves across the desert floor, climbs steeply to one of the top scenic viewpoints in Tucson, then drops into the lap of development where the route crosses the boundary of Tucson Mountain Park at the city limits.

Heading west on Ina Road from I-10, the start of this route takes you across the northwest edge of the city toward the Tucson Mountains. At Wade Road, about mile 2.5, turn left (south). At about mile 3.1, the road bends west into Picture Rocks Road, and in another 0.5 mile you enter Saguaro

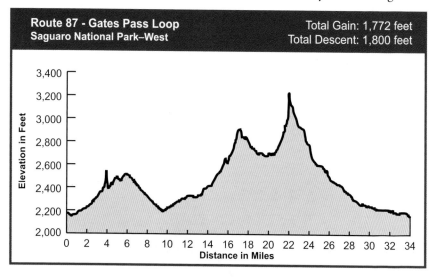

Route 87 - Gates Pass Loop
Saguaro National Park–West
Total Gain: 1,772 feet
Total Descent: 1,800 feet

National Monument. You're now in the low-lying desert mountains, and you start to feel it with short but steep climbs.

It doesn't take long for the route to get to the forest of saguaros, and when it does (about mile 4) it enters one of the world's rare natural features. This beautiful stretch of Sonoran Desert has quintessential vegetation: saguaro cacti, paloverde and ironwood trees, bursage bushes, and ocotillo. After a wet winter, the ground colors with dozens of species of wildflowers. This section of road is fun with all of its bends, dips, and rises.

The road traffic thins out at about mile 7 as the route heads outside the national park briefly. At Sandario Road, about mile 9.5, turn left (south). This fast segment of the route presents a mass of rollers that deepen when the road reenters the national park at about mile 10.5 and starts climbing into the heights of the Tucson Mountains. Veer left at Kinny Road, about mile 13.

This cozy segment of the route cuts right into the forest of giant saguaros that gather thickly around the road and dwarf all that travel it. The cacti bloom around May and June, producing the creamy-white blossoms designated as Arizona's state flower. The process of blooming takes a long time. A saguaro doesn't bloom until it is about

The start of the climb up Gates Pass.

30 years old, and it doesn't bud an arm until around 70 years old. When you cycle this section, you are in the company of centurions.

At almost mile 15, you pass the Red Hills Visitor Center, which has water and washrooms. Almost 1 mile further, turn left toward Old Tucson. For the next 4.5 miles, the road twists along over mild rollers. Turn left at the signed intersection for Gates Pass. Immediately, a sign warns "Steep Grades, Narrow Road." The friendly rollers soon turn into demanding grades, and within less than 1 mile you're climbing a relentless slope to the top of one of the most celebrated passes in the state. The saguaros, once towering giants along the monument road, now look like so many little green sticks on the surrounding mountainsides. The 8 percent grade tops out at about mile 22.2, with the city of Tucson spreading across its namesake basin.

The route gives you a chance to catch your breath before it starts its hair-raising descent along an 8 percent grade filled with hairpin turns.

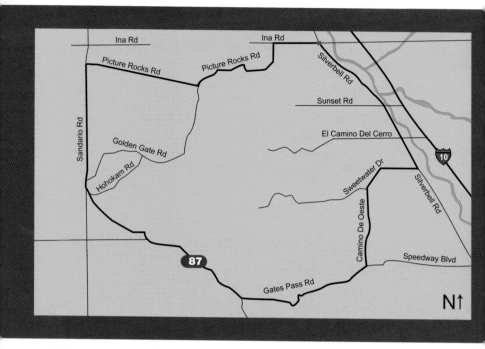

Within 1 mile after the route leaves the park boundary (about mile 25), turn left (north) on Camino de Oeste. This fast road has plenty of rollers that are fun but edgy as they run close together to form deep dips. The road descends gradually to the flatlands. At about mile 27, the route bends right (eastward) into Sweetwater Drive, giving an impressive view of the Santa Catalina Mountains. The route continues with lots of bends and rollers. The engineers laid this road out like a ribbon on the desert floor, with minimal grading and maximum effect from its corrugated contours.

At Silverbell Road (about mile 29), turn left (north). The shouldered road travels through a dichotomy of foothill homes on one side and industrial parks on the other. At mile 34, turn right (east) onto Ina Road. Follow this nicely shouldered segment back to your vehicle.

Route 88

ANZA TRAIL
MISSION ROAD: MENLO PARK TO GREEN VALLEY

Easy • Intermediate

- Travels from downtown Tucson deep into the desert on the
  Juan Bautista de Anza National Historic Trail
- Passes San Xavier Mission
- Four lanes with bike lane in city; then two lanes with and without shoulder

DISTANCE: 9 miles (to mission) to 35 miles one-way

PEAK CYCLING: October–April; early morning in warmer weather

ACCOMMODATIONS: Supplies, restaurants, and lodging in Tucson. Check out Catalina
Park Inn Bed & Breakfast (520-792-4541) or the Arizona Inn (520-325-1541), both
in downtown Tucson. Catalina Park innkeepers present a truly civilized stay in this
desert city, with a gourmet breakfast; the Arizona Inn has kept its tasteful and
historic design and quality service since opening in 1930. Its restaurant, though
formal, serves award-winning food and has a cozy atmosphere.

SPECIAL CONSIDERATIONS: Several sections of this route travel in isolated desert,
in the San Xavier Indian Reservation. Bring a repair kit, food, and enough water.

STARTING POINT: Menlo Park. From Congress Street and Granada in downtown Tucson,
go north on Granada to St. Mary's Rd., and turn left (west); watch for Menlo Park
on the south side of the street. Turn left at Menlo Park, on N. Grande Ave., which
becomes S. Mission Road.

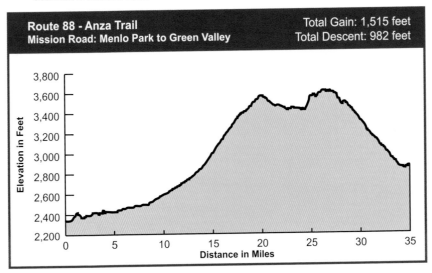

Route 88 - Anza Trail
Mission Road: Menlo Park to Green Valley
Total Gain: 1,515 feet
Total Descent: 982 feet

This route will take you from downtown Tucson to remote reaches of the Sonoran Desert. As the route travels southward via bike lanes in the city, it passes under Sentinel Peak, aka "A" Mountain. The Spaniards' lookout mountain turned collegiate in 1915 when University of Arizona students whitewashed a giant A upon the peak to celebrate a victory over Cal State Pomona.

Just past Ajo Way, around mile 4, you exit the city. In another mile you enter the San Xavier Indian Reservation and lose the bike lane while the route locks its eyes on the bleached white building standing in the south called San Xavier del Bac and nicknamed White Dove of the Desert. The route passes the mission at about mile 9; San Xavier Plaza has a food court that sells fry bread, burritos, and cold drinks. The mission is the oldest original building in the United States, and restoration projects are ongoing. A meld of Moorish, Byzantine, and late Mexican Renaissance influences makes the old mission as captivating as it is pleasing. The mission has become a shrine church that not only sits in a very active parish but also receives visits from pilgrims from around the world, but especially from Arizona and Mexico.

From the mission, you can head back to the city the way you came or loop back to the city by turning left (east) just past MP 20 onto West San Xavier Road, then left (north) on 6th Avenue, and then left (west) on Irvington, and finally right (north) to head back on Mission Road to Menlo Park. Or, continue on this route by heading south on Mission Road.

You can gauge your distance by MPs for the next 20 miles as the route delves deep into the Sonoran Desert wilderness. This makes an excellent route to view wildflowers after a wet winter in late February and early March. The road, generally rough, has a nice atmosphere and little traffic as it courses through classic desertlands. The landscape has an extravagant show of chain fruit cholla. If you make a pit stop here, watch where you step, as these cacti shed segments coated with inch-long needles, barbed at the tips, that seem to jump onto limbs treading too close to them. This explains why they go by the name "jumping cactus."

Around MP 11, the reappearance of historic trail signs signals the end of the San Xavier Indian Reservation. Rollers add character to the road and some distinctive ridges to the mountain scenery. Gray-walled Helmet Peak lies near MP 8, and Twin Buttes at MP 5. Rolling grasslands finish the route off from MP 3 to Duval Mine Road, where you take a left (east) turn. About 1 mile later, veer right onto Continental Road, then travel 3 miles to Green Valley at I-19. From there, you may return the way you came, head south on the Frontage Road to Tubac, or continue on Continental Road under the freeway to Nogales Highway, and turn left (north) back to Tucson.

Route 89

ARIVACA ROAD
ARIVACA JUNCTION TO ARIVACA

Moderate • Experienced

♦ Travels one of the most scenic bike routes in southern Arizona
♦ Rollers, rollers, and more rollers
♦ Two lanes; no shoulder

DISTANCE: 22 miles one-way

PEAK CYCLING: October–April; early morning in warmer weather

ACCOMMODATIONS: Restaurants in Arivaca; supplies, restaurants, and lodging in Tucson

SPECIAL CONSIDERATIONS: "Share The Road" signs with a bicycle icon caution vehicles
to watch for cyclists. Nevertheless, this route has no shoulder and plenty of curves
and hills that require caution.

STARTING POINT: From Tucson, go about 31 miles south on I-19 to exit 48 (Arivaca
Junction).

Right from the start, you can tell you're on one of Arizona's most scenic
routes. The road dips and winds in seductive, rolling grasslands toward
isolated mountain ranges. Strange tales featuring unusual creatures have

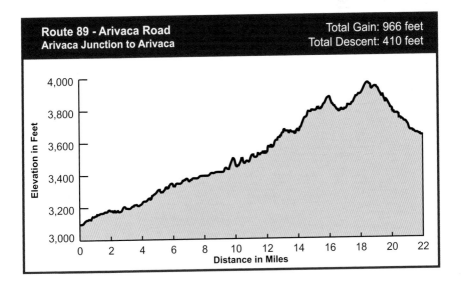

bubbled up about the first range that comes in sight, the Cerro Colorado Mountains; the more believable involve jaguars. Some claim to have spotted the treacherous *chupacabra*, the "goat-sucker," in these mountains. Said to look like a cross between the Creature from the Black Lagoon and a monkey, it sucks the blood and inner organs out of its victims—usually goats but also other mammals (perhaps people?). These mountains stay in sight for much of the ride, presenting especially rugged rock walls around MP 9.

Behind you, the Santa Rita Mountains rise like a wall across the eastern horizon. Distinctive Elephant Head, a 5,640-foot-high chunk of rock rising from the base of the range, really does look like its namesake at quick glance.

In the distant west, the Baboquivari Mountains accommodate, in Tohono O'odham cosmology, the creator, *I'itoli*. In the cosmology of rock climbers (who nicknamed this steep-walled peak Babo), the sacred mountain makes a soulful climb. These utterly dramatic mountains don't come into view until several miles into the route.

In the midst of all this legend and lore, Arivaca Road gracefully wrangles its way through quintessential ranch country. The route makes an absolutely perfect cycle ride with a destination full of character and color: the three-block-long town of Arivaca, lying only moments from the Mexican border. You might catch some cowboys sitting in a doorway shooting the breeze. Perhaps a portable Mexican grill can provide a burrito. Or you can refuel at the Arivaca Sourdough Bakery (no sandwiches, only bakery). A handful of restaurants will fulfill the more ravenous appetites.

This route ends at Arivaca, but you can continue on Arivaca Road another 12 miles through the Buenos Aires National Wildlife Refuge to AZ 286.

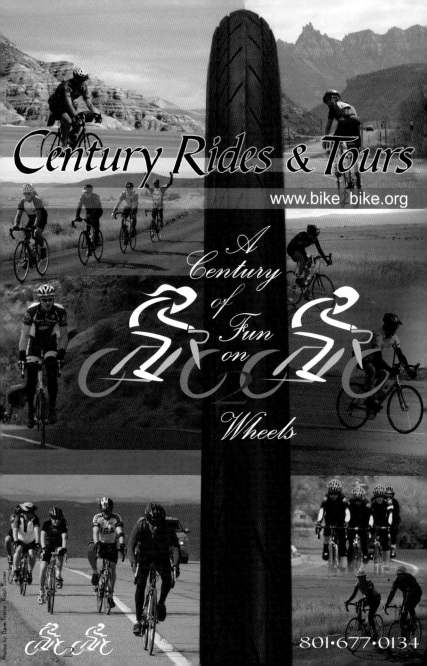

Century Rides & Tours

www.bike2bike.org

A Century of Fun on Wheels

801·677·0134

REGION 9

SOUTHEAST ARIZONA

Southeast Arizona's grasslands are interrupted by mountain ranges rising like islands in a sea, creating a landscape called the Madrean Archipelago. This is an altogether wonderful place to cycle, with rollers, mountain passes, and big stretches of open space. The romance of mining, Indians, and cowboys is alive and well all over this scenic countryside. The area is perfect for touring from small town to small town or taking day rides on a weekend getaway.

ROUTES

The road to Portal heads right to the Chiricahua Mountains.

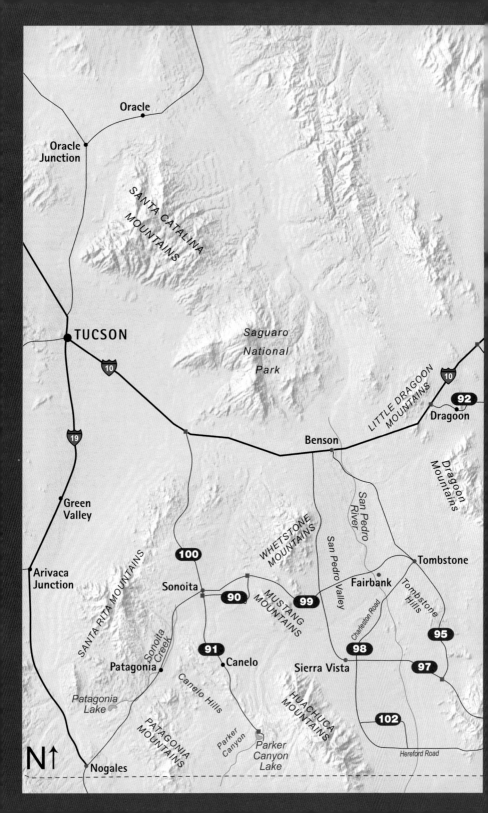

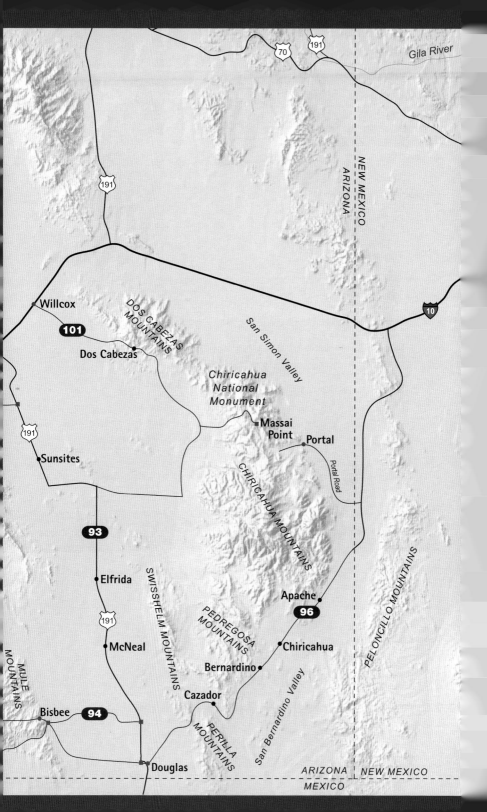

Route 90

WINE COUNTRY LOOP
AZ 83, LOWER ELGIN AND UPPER ELGIN ROADS, AND AZ 82

Moderate • Experienced

- Travels through southeast Arizona's wine country, past vineyards producing award-winning wines
- Two lanes; no shoulder

DISTANCE: 23-mile loop

PEAK CYCLING: October–April

ACCOMMODATIONS: Restaurants and lodging in Sonoita

SPECIAL CONSIDERATIONS: This road gets little traffic. However, stay aware of the little traffic you do encounter, as the locals like to zoom around these backroads.

STARTING POINT: From Sonoita, head south on AZ 83.

This route is a downright pleasant ride along the Mustang Mountains on roller-filled roads. The main ingredient to this wonderful route is the open space in which it travels, starting from the moment you begin the ride.

After starting out on AZ 83, turn left (east) onto Lower Elgin Road at about mile 4. Now you're heading into the state's premier wine country. Not only is the soil in Sonoita practically the same as in Burgundy, France, its

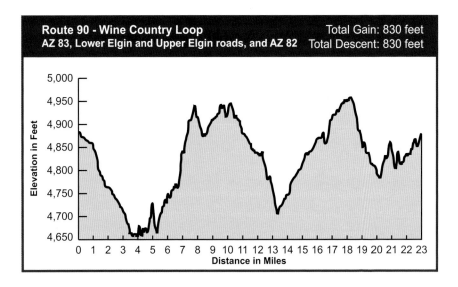

temperature matches California's Sonoma Valley. Kent Callaghan (Callaghan Vineyards) has produced wines highly rated by Robert Parker and served in the White House.

By about mile 10, you reach the tiny town of Elgin. The crossroad

community consists of a handful of houses, some cottonwood trees nestled along the banks of the dry Babocomari River, and a warm, countrified atmosphere. Several roads cross at the community, mostly unpaved; this route continues on the paved Upper Elgin Road, which heads northward. For the next 5 miles,

A pastoral and peaceful bend in the road

the route parallels the Mustang Mountains, meeting up with their northern tip where this road ends at AZ 82 (about mile 16). Cycling by the vineyards, surrounded by far-reaching panoramas and mountain ridges, could be tempting enough to repeat. If so, return the way you came. To continue this route, turn left (west) onto AZ 82 and ride 8 miles back to Sonoita.

WHEN IN ROME . . .

As a cyclist, you are entitled to use the road. You are required to ride on paved shoulders, if they exist, or as far right in the right lane as possible. You can, however, use outer lanes to pass a vehicle, prepare to turn left, or avoid objects, potholes, or debris.

Bicycle safety instructors add that when there's no shoulder you shouldn't hug the white line if the lane is too narrow for a car and bicycle to travel side-by-side safely (with a three-foot space between them). This only invites the vehicle to pass too closely. All you have to do is move into the lane. It's the motorist's responsibility to wait to pass you when the flow of traffic safely permits it.

One of the best ways to integrate well with traffic is to do as your fellow vehicles do. If you act like a car and your actions are stable and predictable, cars will tend to treat you like another car. If you're all over the place, you'll get in trouble.

Route 91

PARKER CANYON LAKE
AZ 83: SONOITA TO PARKER CANYON LAKE

Moderate to Difficult • Intermediate to Experienced

* Travels through remote and scenic Canelo Hills country to a high-desert lake
* Two lanes; narrow shoulder

DISTANCE: 32 miles one-way

PEAK CYCLING: October–April

ACCOMMODATIONS: Supplies, restaurants, and lodging in Sonoita; camping and basic food and supplies at Parker Canyon Lake

SPECIAL CONSIDERATIONS: This route crosses remote country. Bring a repair kit and enough water. A mile of this route, near Parker Canyon Lake, travels over an extremely rough surface; if conditions don't change by publication, you should be able to cycle this slowly and carefully.

STARTING POINT: From Sonoita, head south on AZ 83.

You get pretty deep into the boonies on this segment of AZ 83. Once you cycle a few miles south of Sonoita, you're pretty much on your own. During those first few miles, the road gets a little dicey in spots tread-wise,

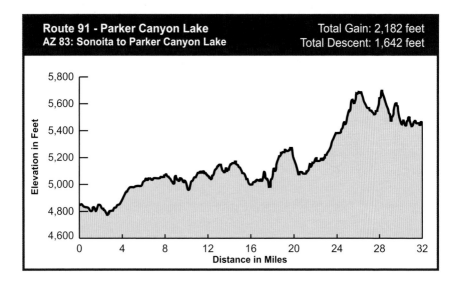

Route 91 - Parker Canyon Lake
AZ 83: Sonoita to Parker Canyon Lake
Total Gain: 2,182 feet
Total Descent: 1,642 feet

but generally it follows a delightful route that bends, dips, and swerves among stunning hillsides sprinkled with oak groves.

By MP 20, the road climbs up into the Canelo Hills, taking on a tucked-away feel as it enters the Coronado National Forest. The scenery gets so stunning here you might feel a delightful skirmish arising as to what gets your attention—the road or the panoramas. If the route didn't take on the demeanor of a rollercoaster ride rather than the persona of the peaceful country road it started with, the scenery would win hands-down.

After passing through the tiny town of Canelo next to Turkey Creek at MP 16—your only brush with civilization (and a weak one at that) until the end of this route—the route experiences some intensely remote and moody areas. Cyclists not used to isolated areas might feel a little uncomfortable here.

At around MP 14 you drop into a marshland at Lyle Canyon that takes on an unusual but cozy atmosphere. The route then passes some isolated ranches, giving an even more remote feel.

Around MP 7, a sign warns that the pavement ends. Actually, the surface is hardpacked gravel, which can be carefully negotiated by a road bike. This segment only lasts for the next 1 mile, and then the pavement returns. It's worth the trouble to traverse this section, as the road enters pretty Parker Canyon just after the pavement starts again. At MP 5, the road makes a steep climb out of the canyon and then has you screaming on your way downhill again by MP 4. Repeat.

AZ 83 ends near MP 2, and signs will direct you farther along a paved road to camping areas and a boat launch and store at the lake.

The route to Parker Canyon Lake passes through rich pastoral grasslands.

Route 92

DRAGOON ROAD
I-10 TO US 191

Moderate • Experienced

◆ Travels a roller-filled route in the Little Dragoon Mountains
◆ Several destinations of interest along the route
◆ Two lanes; narrow shoulder

DISTANCE: 13 miles one-way

PEAK CYCLING: October–April; early morning during warmer weather

ACCOMMODATIONS: Supplies, restaurants, and lodging in Benson

SPECIAL CONSIDERATIONS: This route has several blind spots.

STARTING POINTS: Western access: From exit 318 on I-10, head east on Dragoon Road. Eastern access: From the community of Cochise on US 191, go about 6 miles south and turn right (west) on Dragoon Road.

This is a fun route that twists around the Little Dragoon Mountains while skirting along the northern edge of the Dragoon Mountains. Known for their labyrinthine topography, full of hoodoos and weathered boulders balanced atop one another, these mountains provided a place for the Chiricahua Apache chief Cochise to retreat during the last years of the U.S. Army/Indian conflict.

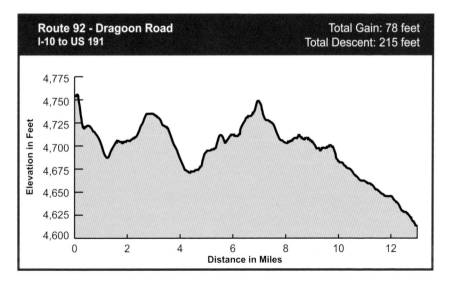

Dragoon Road is a tucked-away surprise full of scenery, orchards, and interesting businesses.

The most scenic segment of the route lies at its beginning in Texas Canyon, where a compendium of fantastic formations creates a wonderland of rock. This fabulous stretch of highway gives you great insight about the landscape of the Dragoon Mountains. Starting around MP 3, you pass the Apacheria Native Cultural Center, a guest ranch, and the Amerind Foundation. The Amerind Foundation, a museum devoted entirely to the Americas' Indians (from Alaska to South America), has one of the country's best private collections of Native American art and artifacts. A gallery/café completes the tourist section of Dragoon Road at about mile 4. Next, the route climbs into the countryside on a nice string of rollers. The dessert comes around MP 8 as a downhill starts for most of the rest of the ride. This stretch parallels fruit and nut orchards, giving the route a pleasant pastoral feel.

At route's end, you may turn north or south onto US 191 (see Route 93, p. 234) or return the way you came.

MOUNT GRAHAM HILL CLIMB

Every year in the late summer, hill-climbing cyclists head to Arizona's second-highest peak in the Pinaleno Mountains northeast of Tucson for the Mount Graham Arizona State Hill Climb. For years, Arizona cyclists Scott Price and Drew Miller jointly held the record to cycle this peak. In 2003, Miller bettered the record by 1.5 minutes, clocking in at 1:23:16, averaging 14.3 mph on the 6 percent grade.

The 20-mile, mass-start road race starts at MP 115 (elevation 3,379 feet) and winds up the Swift Trail to MP 135, near the Snow Flat campground at 9,068 feet. This 5,689-foot climb is part of the annual Arizona State Hill Climb Championships. The cyclists start climbing at 8 a.m. and reach the top between 9:30 a.m. and 11:00 a.m. Racers can finish with a ride back down the mountain by about noon.

Route 93

US 191
I-10 TO AZ 80 NEAR DOUGLAS

Easy • Intermediate

* Travels along farmlands in the Sulphur Springs Valley
* Excellent road for a two-day tour
* Two lanes; narrow shoulder

DISTANCE: 66 miles one-way

PEAK CYCLING: October–April

ACCOMMODATIONS: Basic supplies and restaurants in Elfrida and Pearce; lodging in Sunsites and Douglas

SPECIAL CONSIDERATIONS: This route travels long distances between small towns. Bring a repair kit, food, and enough water.

STARTING POINT: From exit 331 on I-10, head south on US 191; MP 66 is the first mile marker.

This route travels the tail end of a highway that runs from Morgan, Montana, at the Canadian border to AZ 80, just west of Douglas at the Mexican frontier. It's the longest highway in Arizona, traveling the eastern reaches of the state, and it passes through perfect road-touring country.

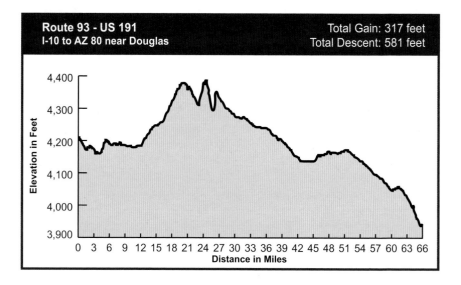

Route 93 - US 191
I-10 to AZ 80 near Douglas

Total Gain: 317 feet
Total Descent: 581 feet

Elevation in Feet vs. Distance in Miles

The ongoing open space along US 191 gives incredible panoramas, especially in summertime during the monsoon season.

This segment, basically a simple cycle route along farmlands in a wide valley, gives you some stunning panoramas. Cloud activity in the summer during the monsoon season can be spectacular. Rollers aren't big here; this route is for the cyclist who wants a tamer landscape full of fresh air and open spaces.

The route heads south from I-10 with the Dragoon Mountains rising along the western horizon. Around Sunsites (MP 48), the route approaches some scenic hills, around which it winds. Watch for the turnoff for the ghost town of Pearce around MP 46. This old mining town has some tourist appeal, and its handful of businesses might be open. If you need a pit stop or provisions, Sunsites makes a more dependable alternative.

After passing AZ 181 at MP 36, the route starts its pass through miles and miles of farm country. Elfrida, around MP 28, will provide the basics, as will McNeal, around MP 21. From there, it's all open space until route's end at AZ 80, about 1 mile west of Douglas. If you're heading to Bisbee, take Double Adobe Road (see Route 94, p. 236) around MP 11. To continue to Douglas, turn left (east) onto US 80.

Route 94

DOUBLE ADOBE ROAD
AZ 80 TO US 191

Easy • Beginner

◆ Travels a country road near Bisbee

◆ Two lanes; narrow to medium shoulder

DISTANCE: 8 miles (to Central Highway) to 15 miles one-way

PEAK CYCLING: October–April

ACCOMMODATIONS: Basic supplies, restaurants, and lodging in Bisbee

SPECIAL CONSIDERATIONS: This route is a shortcut between US 191 and Bisbee, and it
may see more traffic during typical commuter times. The route intersects with several other secondary roads, which you may want to explore to create loops.

STARTING POINT: From downtown Bisbee, go 5.5 miles east on AZ 80 to Double Adobe
Road at MP 348, and turn left (northeast).

One of southeast Arizona's most colorful towns, Bisbee makes the jumping-
off point for this cycle route. You can cycle right from downtown Bisbee
or park at the route's start at Double Adobe Road. If you start in Bisbee, add
another 5.5 miles to the one-way mileage.

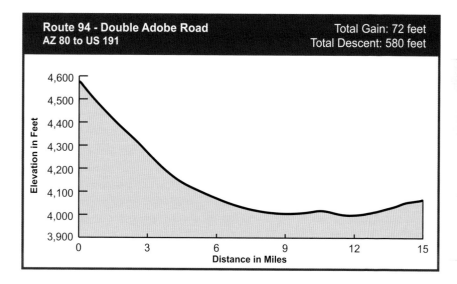

This route feels like a backroad inasmuch as it travels right into the countryside. The route starts on gradual descent from the Mule Mountains to about MP 4. Along the way, bird melodies rise from long stretches of meadows. Hawk cries drop from circling raptors looking for a meal.

Near MP 8, the route jogs left, then right, and meets up with Central Highway. For a short cycle ride, this makes a good turnaround point. To finish the route, cross the highway and continue another 7 miles to US 191.

Route 95

JEFFERSON DAVIS MEMORIAL HIGHWAY
AZ 80: BENSON TO BISBEE

Moderate • Intermediate

* Travels a roller-filled landscape of grasslands and small towns
* Two lanes; narrow shoulder

DISTANCE: 23 miles (to Tombstone) to 48 miles one-way

PEAK CYCLING: October–April

ACCOMMODATIONS: Supplies, restaurants, and lodging in Benson, Tombstone, and Bisbee; restaurants in St. David. Check out the Mimosa Market in Bisbee for gourmet food and beverages.

SPECIAL CONSIDERATIONS: This route travels long distances between small towns. Bring a repair kit, food, and enough water.

STARTING POINT: From exit 303 off I-10 (Benson), head east on AZ 80 (4th Street) through Benson, and follow it as it bends southward out of town.

Climbing the pass through the Mule Mountains into Bisbee.

It may seem odd that Arizona would have a highway dedicated to the president of the Confederate States of America. The story of its existence goes back to 1912, when a man named Carl Fisher announced his plans for the coast-to-coast

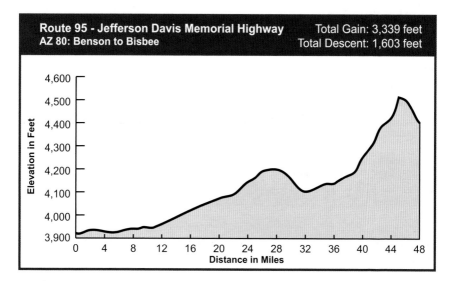

Lincoln Highway. This concept got the United Daughters of the Confederacy salivating—why not establish a coast-to-coast highway that travels through their beloved Confederacy?

The U.S. Department of Transportation reports that a proposal was submitted with the recommendation, "That the United Daughters of the Confederacy secure for an ocean to ocean highway from Washington to San Diego, through the Southern States, the name of Jefferson Davis National Highway; the same to be beautified and historic places on it suitably and permanently marked." The Feds bit.

This route, a segment of the trans-state memorial highway, starts in the town of Benson, where it travels a couple of miles before heading out on the open highway at MP 296. The route starts with a substantial shoulder as it eases down to the San Pedro River. By the time the road crosses the river (MP 299), the shoulder shrinks and the highway gets countrified as it heads into St. David. Here, the landscape turns bucolic with farms and fields. The route starts gaining altitude by MP 306, and it rolls around claylike bluffs common to this river valley.

Around MP 317, Tombstone, the "Town Too Tough to Die," makes a fun destination. The town sprawls for the next mile; then, if you don't make Tombstone your turnaround point, you're back on the open highway again by MP 318. The Tombstone Hills, where a silver strike put Tombstone on the map, rise to the west. When Ed Schiefflin staked the Lucky Cuss and Toughnut mines, the rush began and Tombstone boomed. About $1.7 billon in silver in today's dollars was mined from these hills.

After a lazy S-curve and a slow descent, the road travels like a straightedge for long stretches. Occasional curves nudge the road toward the southeast direction needed to reach Bisbee. On this stretch, surrounding mountain ranges rise abruptly from the high-desert floor, and you can understand why these ranges are called sky islands.

Around AZ 90 (MP 333), the landscape starts to take on some character as the route enters the Mule Mountains. From now until the town of Bisbee, the route entertains some animated rollers with attractive scenery.

As if the sensational silver strike in the Tombstone Hills weren't enough, yet another mineral bonanza appeared in the Mule Mountains at Bisbee. The Escabrosa Ridge, starting around MP 337, takes you to the Bisbee Tunnel. This narrow segment presents a claustrophobic moment on the route. Once through it, you have a bird's-eye view of Bisbee, the copper queen city second to San Francisco in carnal and epicurean delights during its Lavender Mine's heyday. If you want to visit the town, take the turnoff to Old Bisbee around MP 342. Otherwise, you can continue 23 more miles on AZ 80 to Douglas, or return the way you came.

If you're heading to Douglas, the road offers a nice shoulder but moderately heavy traffic. It rolls between Gold and Grassy hills along Mule Gulch. At around MP 347, the road forks: left for Double Adobe Road (see Route 94, p. 236); right for Douglas.

Route 96

ROAD TO RODEO
AZ 80 AND US 80: DOUGLAS TO PORTAL

Moderate to Difficult • Experienced

◆ Miles of open space, from the Mexican border to just inside of New Mexico
◆ Makes an excellent several-day tour
◆ An extended route travels to the town of Portal in the Chiricahua Mountains
   and beyond into scenic Cave Creek Canyon
◆ Two lanes; medium shoulder

If you like one l-o-n-g stretch of open space, this is the route for you. It makes a great century, a comfortable two-day ride, or a perfect overnight shuttle. This route is also the final segment of the Cochise County Cycling Classic. This ultracycling event, which takes place in October, offers 45-, 92-, 157-, and 252-mile events. The 252-miler starts at 2 a.m. in Douglas. Cyclists go northwest on AZ 80 through Bisbee to Benson, east on I-10 just into New Mexico, then along US 80 back south to Douglas.

DISTANCE: 49 miles (to Rodeo, New Mexico) to 58 miles (to end of Cave Creek Road in the Chiricahua Mountains) one-way

PEAK CYCLING: April–May; September–November

ACCOMMODATIONS: Supplies, restaurants, and lodging in Douglas, Portal, and Rodeo, New Mexico; camping in Cave Creek Canyon

SPECIAL CONSIDERATIONS: This route travels for a long stretch in the middle of nowhere on a road with light traffic. Bring a repair kit, food, and enough water. If you plan to stay in Rodeo or Portal, make sure you have a reservation; it's a long way to the next town. Camping in Cave Creek Canyon is first-come, first-served.

STARTING POINT: From Douglas, head north on AZ 80; MP 367 is the first mile marker.

This route follows the last segment of the event, in reverse. The quiet highway has a shoulder, but you have to white-line the very beginning of the route for a while because of a wide, bumpy safety stamp that makes it unsafe for cyclists to use the shoulder. Until MP 375, the road is ribbon straight. Then rollers and bends start to liven up the route.

Around MP 378, the road surface, while never bad, turns great. The terrain also improves, as ridges and cliffs of the Perilla Mountains put a little kick in the climbs and the bends. And though

Once it arrives at Portal, the road heads into a canyon in the Chiricahua Mountains.

you lose the shoulder in another mile, the traffic has thinned out to nearly nothing. It may take you a moment or two to notice, but one of the prevailing elements of this route is intense quiet, as if the road were wrapped in an envelope of silence.

At MP 385 the route enters the expansive San Bernardino Valley, troughing between the Chiricahua Mountains rising up to almost 10,000 feet to the west and the Peloncillo Mountains in the east. At this point, far from town sites and ranches, you are really "out there" and can start feeling mighty lonely. Grasses carpet the ground in every direction of this big, open space.

The first sign of civilization appears as the San Bernardino Valley melds into the San Simon Valley near the Price Canyon Ranch at MP 400. Next, you come to a roadside table at MP 406, with a plaque memorializing the last holdout of one of the most memorable Apaches: Geronimo. An unpaved road near the monument travels about 8 miles south to Geronimo's surrender site in Skeleton Canyon. When Geronimo described his birthplace in western New Mexico (only a stone's throw eastward) as prairie land "where the wind blew free and there was nothing to break the light of the sun…where there were no enclosures," he may as well have been describing this route.

Continuing northeastward from the roadside table, the road runs like a ruler for almost 10 miles to the New Mexico border where it becomes NM 80, an "Old West Country Trail." Tourist-tinged Rodeo, a few blocks long with a bar, motel, restaurant, and art gallery, lies 2 miles farther.

If you decide to cycle the extended route, continue north on US 80 another 2 miles and turn left (northwest) onto Portal Road (NM 533). In 2 more miles you'll return to Arizona.

Once in Arizona (MP 7), the road makes a straight shot on a constant climb to the town of Portal (MP 1) at the edge of the Chiricahua Mountains. You'll find food and lodging here. However, if you want to explore these wild and wonderful mountains, continue another 7 miles up the road into Cave Creek Canyon.

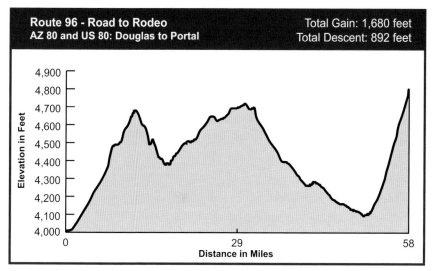

Route 96 - Road to Rodeo
AZ 80 and US 80: Douglas to Portal

Total Gain: 1,680 feet
Total Descent: 892 feet

Route 97

SAN PEDRO HOUSE
AZ 90: SIERRA VISTA TO AZ 80

Easy • Beginner

◆ Travels historic San Pedro Valley
◆ A connector road for several loops in San Pedro Valley
◆ Two lanes; medium shoulder

DISTANCE: 23 miles one-way

PEAK CYCLING: October–April

ACCOMMODATIONS: Supplies, restaurants, and lodging in Sierra Vista and Tombstone

SPECIAL CONSIDERATIONS: This route travels a remote area. Bring a repair kit and enough water.

STARTING POINTS: From the north side of Sierra Vista, head east on AZ 90.

M ost Arizona highways travel on a diagonal or straight line (albeit cluttered with curves and swerves) between two points. AZ 90 follows an unusual route. Starting at I-10 in Benson, it heads southward as a four-lane highway past Fort Huachuca to the northern edge of Sierra Vista, then turns eastward across the San Pedro Valley. This eastbound stretch makes a perfect cycle route into some wide-open spaces.

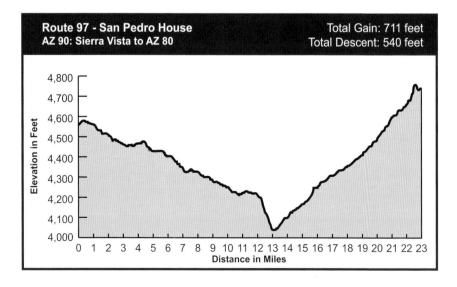

Route 97 - San Pedro House
AZ 90: Sierra Vista to AZ 80
Total Gain: 711 feet
Total Descent: 540 feet

Once you pass Avenida del Sol, between MPs 323 and 322, you're out of the business district. In another mile, you're out in the country. The road runs like a ruler riddled with rollers on a gradual descent to the San Pedro River. Just west of the waterway, around MP 326, watch for the San Pedro House. Now a gift shop and bookstore run by Friends of the San Pedro River volunteers, this 1930s ranch house is a landmark for one of the most popular accesses to the San Pedro River.

The San Pedro River has come into the national spotlight, racking up a list of important designations. The river, considered one of the most important bird flyways of the world, got the first National Conservation Area designation in 1988 and has recently been designated as a Globally Important Bird Area. The river also has made the Nature Conservancy's Last Great Places list, as one of the most important desert rivers in the world.

After climbing out of the river drainage, the road heads into some prickly countryside where mesquite trees, catclaw, and creosote feel at home. A collection of rollers gives you a great ride to the road's end at AZ 80. From here, you have several route opportunities: You can head south 9 miles on AZ 80 to Bisbee (see Route 95, p. 237) and back or make a long loop from Bisbee to Sierra Vista via AZ 92; travel 16 miles north on AZ 80 to Tombstone or continue north to make a loop back to Sierra Vista on Charleston Road (see Route 98, p. 244); or simply return the way you came.

The San Pedro House along AZ 90.

Route 98

CHARLESTON ROAD
SIERRA VISTA TO TOMBSTONE

Easy • Beginner

- Travels historic San Pedro Valley
- A connector road for several loops in San Pedro Valley
- Two lanes; medium shoulder

DISTANCE: 16 miles one-way

PEAK CYCLING: October–April

ACCOMMODATIONS: Supplies, restaurants, and lodging in Sierra Vista and Tombstone

SPECIAL CONSIDERATIONS: This route travels a remote area. Bring repair kits and enough water.

STARTING POINT: On the north side of Sierra Vista, head east on AZ 90 and follow its zigzag for about 3 miles to the intersection with Charleston Road; MP 1 is the first mile marker.

The San Pedro River Valley holds some unique history. The river has been used by several cultures for 13,000 years, starting with the mammoth-hunting Clovis Culture, continuing through farmer Hohokam and Sobaipuris cultures, proceeding through Spaniards and military occupation, and presently hosting Sierra Vista and several businesses.

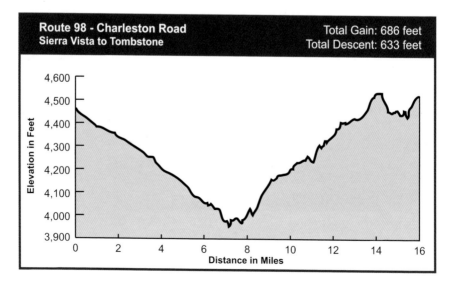

Route 98 - Charleston Road
Sierra Vista to Tombstone

Total Gain: 686 feet
Total Descent: 633 feet

Remnants of civilization lie all along the river in the form of relics and ruins. Over 250 prehistoric and historic sites have been logged in the San Pedro Riparian National Conservation Area (SPRNCA), and experts expect to find more. The Charleston Road access to the river holds

A memorial alongside the bridge over the San Pedro River.

remnants covering several strata of societies. As you cycle this route between Sierra Vista and Tombstone, you enter a historic corridor.

It only takes 1 mile to get out of town, and after 1.5 miles you pass the last stoplight and head into open space. By MP 5, you enter the SPRNCA and descend to the river within 2 miles. The bridge crosses over the Charleston Narrows, where canyon walls squeeze into the river. Hohokam Indians pecked petroglyphs into the upper rocks centuries ago. Also in the area along the river stand adobe remnants from an old mining camp reputed to be even tougher than Tombstone. This one, however, died.

If you take a moment to stand on the old metal bridge next to the highway bridge, you get a good idea of the exquisite scenic beauty and rich avian life on the San Pedro. Chances are good you will hear the chatter, squawks, whistles, and melodies of several different species of birds flitting about in the thick cottonwood-willow riparian forest, no matter what time of the day or what season. Spring and fall, however, are prime birding times. Currently, the river's ecosystem is threatened from surrounding communities.

Back on the highway, the route climbs out of the drainage on a series of rollers. The shoulder shrinks to a narrow strip. By MP 12, the road transitions through the Tombstone Hills, where the silver that made Tombstone famous was mined. At around MP 15, you can see the "Town Too Tough to Die," with its domed courthouse at the center. To visit the town, turn right (south) on AZ 80 and cycle 1 mile. From there, you can take AZ 80 south to AZ 90 to loop back to Sierra Vista, or return the way you came. As an alternative, you may head north on AZ 80 to AZ 82, then turn left (south) on AZ 90 back to Sierra Vista.

Route 99

FAIRBANK ROUTE
AZ 82: SONOITA TO FAIRBANK

Easy • Beginner

* Travels to a historic ghost town
* Crosses scenic countryside with plenty of open space
* Two lanes; medium shoulder

DISTANCE: 29 miles (to Fairbank) to 35 miles (to AZ 80) one-way

PEAK CYCLING: October–April

ACCOMMODATIONS: Supplies, restaurants, and lodging in Sonoita. Check out La Hacienda de Sonoita bed and breakfast (520-455-5308). Custom-designed as a B&B, the inn has comfortable, well-appointed rooms and the kind of hearty breakfast that can fuel an all-day ride.

SPECIAL CONSIDERATIONS: This route travels a remote area. Bring repair kits and enough water.

STARTING POINT: From Sonoita, head east on AZ 82; MP 34 is the first mile marker.

The town of Sonoita makes a great base for several cycle rides in the area. Though small in size, the town offers incredible distant views of the countryside. The massive stretch of open space, a cattleman's dream, has a

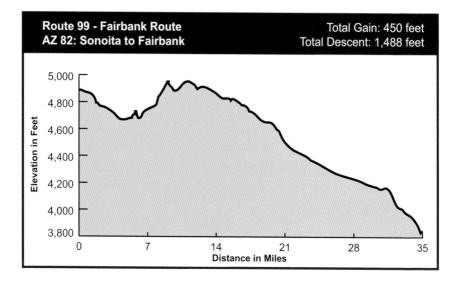

Route 99 - Fairbank Route
AZ 82: Sonoita to Fairbank

Total Gain: 450 feet
Total Descent: 1,488 feet

funny effect on city folk. Initially, urbanites may feel a bit intimidated and cocooned. But once they settle into the land, and become part of it as the rest of the area's dwellers have, life gets just as big as the views.

This route to the historic town site of Fairbank takes you across a typical landscape in southeast Arizona, where sky-island mountains rise from the high-desert floor among miles of grassland and scrub. The route heads right for the Mustang Mountains, named for the wild horses that roamed the range into the 20th century. The route skirts the northern edge of the mountains' low-rising ridges, then drops into beautiful Rain Valley around MP 46, with the Whetstone Mountains rising to the north. AZ 90, around MP 51, makes a good turnaround point for a shorter ride. To continue to Fairbank, cross the highway and continue eastward.

Though this stretch has a pancake-flat grade with a scruffy landscape for the next few miles, you return to the gentle rollers typical of this corner of the state by MP 57. The ribbon of green in the distance is the cottonwood-willow forest following the San Pedro River. The route reaches the San Pedro Riparian National Conservation Area near MP 63; Fairbank stands on the east side of the river.

A railroad, used by mines and passengers, kept the town site alive. Several stamp mills along the tracks, which followed the San Pedro River northward, supplied freight. The mills pounded day and night and literally shook the earth around them. You can continue another 6 miles of rolling country-side to AZ 80 (which would bring the mileage total to 35 from Sonoita), or return the way you came.

Relaxing along the San Pedro River at Fairbank on a spring day.

Route 100

PATAGONIA-SONOITA SCENIC BYWAY
AZ 83 AND AZ 82: I-10 TO NOGALES

Moderate • Intermediate

* Travels a scenic byway through beautiful rolling grasslands surrounded by mountains
* Makes an excellent two-day route or enjoyable century
* Two lanes; narrow shoulder

DISTANCE: 27 miles (to Sonoita), 39 miles (to Patagonia) or 52.5 miles (to Nogales) one-way

PEAK CYCLING: October–April; morning in warmer weather

ACCOMMODATIONS: Supplies, restaurants, and lodging in Tucson, Sonoita, Patagonia, and Nogales

SPECIAL CONSIDERATIONS: The first half of the route, I-10 to Sonoita, crosses remote country. Bring a repair kit and enough water.

STARTING POINTS: AZ 83 and I-10 (exit 281); MP 58 is the first mile marker. If you plan to cycle from Tucson to Sonoita, take Houghton Road south from I-10 about 7 miles to Sahuarita Road; turn left (east) and go about 7 miles to AZ 83. This will start you at about MP 55.

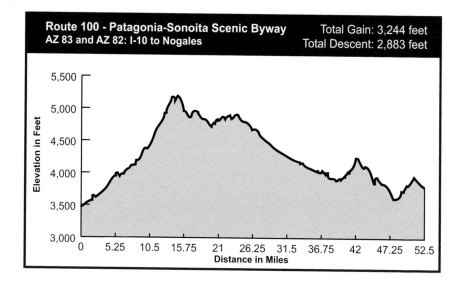

Part of this route, AZ 83 to Sonoita, is one of the popular long rides for Tucsonans. The whole scenic byway makes a truly enjoyable two-day cycle ride or a scenic century.

Starting from I-10, the route enters one of the state's most scenic landscapes, full of rolling hills, long-reaching views, and hawks riding thermals that keep them aloft almost forever as they peruse golden hillsides of dried grasslands that turn gemstone green after wet weather. The road meanders in a fun way up and down and around these hills.

Riparian forests fill the roadsides around Sonoita Creek.

Around MP 44, you see the peaks of the Santa Rita Mountains tilt haphazardly along the range's powerful shoulders. The mountains rise in the west close enough to get their foothills in on the roller action. Across a valley to the east, the Whetstone Mountains rise from a rippled landscape eroded like folds of shifting sand after a windstorm. Oak trees gather in crevices, mirroring the coastal wine country in California, and indeed some of the world's top wines grow in vineyards located about a dozen miles south near the town of Sonoita.

From Sonoita, the route turns right (southwest) onto AZ 82 at MP 32. Within a couple miles, the route squeezes between the Santa Rita Mountains and Canelo Hills. The beautiful grassland hills filled with groves of oaks, smooth road, long rollers, and wide shoulder equal a cyclist's dream. This ranch country has lured Hollywood producers to use it as a movie set and movie stars to seek it as a retreat. Highly charismatic with laid-back manners, the place grows on you.

The route enters tiny Patagonia at MP 21. The creekside habitat of cottonwood, willow, and Arizona walnut trees reaches into the roadsides where the route rubs shoulders with Sonoita Creek. The creek chatters with birdlife all year long, becoming especially active in spring and fall during migration times. Birders come from around the world to catch sight of some of the avian traffic that passes through the area—about 300 different species. In November, the riparian habitat colors with gold.

The road wends around the Patagonia Mountains, following Sonoita Creek for several miles. At a roadside rest area, about MP 16, watch for a shrine located in a hillside grotto on the east side of the road. The shrine, honoring those who served in the armed forces, has been tended by locals and visitors for half a century.

A little farther south of the shrine, the road parts company with the creek and enters a desert landscape. Though the route leaves the mountains by MP 14, some rollers remain with the road all the way to Nogales. If you're interested in visiting Patagonia Lake, watch for its turnoff around MP 12.

Nogales comes into view at MP 3, and the highway doubles to four lanes within 0.5 mile. When you reach Nogales, you can take Old Tucson Road north to Rio Rico or return the way you came.

Route 101
DOS CABEZAS
AZ 186: WILLCOX TO CHIRICAHUA NATIONAL MONUMENT
Moderate • Intermediate to Experienced

◆ Travels a variety of landscapes, from rolling mountains to the open space of the Sulphur Springs Valley
◆ Passes through a scenic ghost town full of adobe ruins
◆ Extended route ends in a national monument full of Arizona's most unique geology
◆ Two lanes; medium to no shoulder

DISTANCE: 33 miles (to AZ 181) to 43 miles (to end of road in Chiracahua National Monument) one-way

PEAK CYCLING: September–May

ACCOMMODATIONS: Supplies, restaurants, and lodging in Willcox; camping in Chiricahua National Monument

SPECIAL CONSIDERATIONS: This route travels in a remote area. Bring a repair kit, food, and enough water.

STARTING POINT: From I-10 (exit 336) in Willcox, go east to S. Haskell Ave. and turn left; drive through Willcox to AZ 186, and turn right (south); MP 329 is the first mile marker.

Dos Cabezas, Spanish for "two heads," refers to a pair of peaks in a mountain range with the same name. Someone with a good imagination might think the pinnacles look like large heads from afar. This route skirts along this range and gets a good look at the twin peaks. But there's more. This

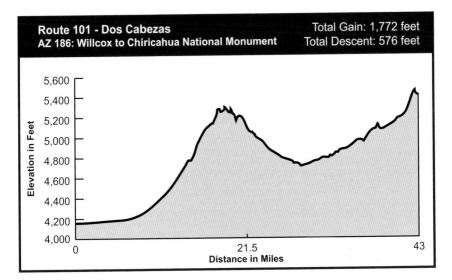

Route 101 - Dos Cabezas
AZ 186: Willcox to Chiricahua National Monument

Total Gain: 1,772 feet
Total Descent: 576 feet

route also takes you into some beautiful, rolling hill country, through a ghost town, and to one of the most unusual collections of rock pinnacles, totems, and spires in the Southwest: Chiricahua National Monument.

The route hits the open road after wending through Willcox for about 1 mile; then get ready to start a nonstop climb into the foothills of the Dos Cabezas Mountains. The twin-peak formation appears on the scene right away.

By MP 335, the roadsides become crowded with mesquite trees and the shoulder, already weed-wracked, narrows and looks more like an obstacle course than a safety strip. Since this road has relatively little traffic, it's better to avoid the shoulder at this point.

In the ghost town of Dos Cabezas (MP 342), you enter a bit of Arizona mining history. (A cluster of mines is located just above the town site in the mountains.) At the north end of town, a handful of tourist shops with arbitrary (if any) opening hours looks inviting enough to check out. But watch out for the family of dogs at Muddy's Mine. They have an unpredictable nature, and, what's worse, they can slink under the fence and into the street. A bit further into the mile-long town, a string of ramshackle adobe buildings rises along the roadsides.

Once out of town, the road unwinds into a landscape full of rollers that have the pavement rippling and swaying over beautiful high-desert terrain. Watch for Helen's Dome rising in the southeast in the Chiricahua Mountains. Once called Cow Peak, and sometimes called Helen's Doom by salty old-timers, the mountain was named for a military man's wife named Helen. The Dos Cabezas Mountains meld seamlessly with the Chiricahua Mountains as the road pulls away from the ranges on a more southerly route. At MP 347, a hilltop view gives you an expansive look at the Sulphur Springs Valley.

The road settles down to a relatively even grade with a few token rollers. The cemetery at MP 357 belongs to the Erickson family, who settled in the area in the late 1880s and discovered the wonderland of rocks that eventually became Chiricahua National Monument. The route reaches the turnoff for the park around MP 359.

For an extended cycle ride, turn left (east) at the signed turnoff for Chiricahua National Monument. You'll be traveling a few miles on AZ 181 to the entry gate. Once in the park, you can cycle 8 miles on Bonita Canyon Drive to a beautiful overlook.

The route (two lanes with no shoulder) climbs quickly into the park in a sunny forest of juniper and oak trees. Within a mile, you get glimpses of strangely sculpted hoodoos and balanced rocks—the trademark landscape of the park.

Ever climbing, the route ducks under the shade of Arizona cypress and piñon trees for a spell. Keep watch for wildlife here; you might see black bear, deer, or coatimundi. By about mile 4, the road opens up as it starts an arduous climb up the ridge to some fabulous views. This is a very steep climb with very precipitous dropoffs in a very scenic area. If you want to gawk at the scenery, find a safe place to stop and look.

The road ends at Massai Point, where an overlook gives you an extraordinary view of this special park. As you look upon the congregation of totems, hoodoos, and pinnacles, you can understand why the Apaches called them "standing up rocks." The Chokonen Apaches lived in and around the Chiricahua Mountains. Cochise, the leader of this band of Apaches, along with his fellow Apache leader Geronimo, colored the final pages of warfare against the pioneer settlements on their land, which they revered as the very special place it is.

Entering Chiricahua National Monument.

MIRACLE VALLEY LOOP
AZ 92 AND HEREFORD ROAD

Easy • Beginner to Intermediate

* Travels scenic stretches along the Huachuca Mountains
* Alternate route, Buffalo Soldier Trail, has a 7-mile-long bike path
* Two lanes; medium shoulder

DISTANCE: 7 miles one-way (Buffalo Soldier Trial) or 35- to 49-mile loop

PEAK CYCLING: October–April

ACCOMMODATIONS: Supplies, restaurants, and lodging in Sierra Vista. The San Pedro
House Bed and Breakfast (888-257-2050, 8933 S. Yell Lane) in Hereford is located
along the San Pedro River, on of the best birding spots in the country. The serve
big, wonderful breakfasts that local running and riding groups indulge in.

SPECIAL CONSIDERATIONS: You can just take Buffalo Soldier Trail bike path for
a 14-mile round-trip. Or, you can whittle 14 miles off the full loop route
by starting from AZ 92 where Buffalo Soldier Trail ends.

STARTING POINTS: Buffalo Soldier Trail and AZ 92; MP 324 on AZ 92. Or follow the
Buffalo Soldier Trail south from AZ 90 in Sierra Vista (see Special Considerations,
above).

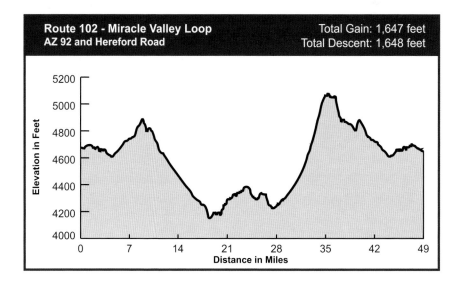

Route 102 - Miracle Valley Loop
AZ 92 and Hereford Road

Total Gain: 1,647 feet
Total Descent: 1,648 feet

Though this route starts on the outskirts of southeast Arizona's largest city and never quite travels far enough from the clutches of civilization to feel entirely remote, the scenery does have an overwhelming personality, strong enough to make you feel a tad dispensable. This is because the route closely parallels the Huachuca Mountains, whose massiveness evokes a perceptible grandeur that turns poetic as the route travels in rolling hills with oak groves. Mexico lies within eyesight to the south.

AZ 92 narrows from four to two lanes but keeps its wide shoulder between MPs 328 and 329. It runs close enough to the Huachuca Mountains to feel the effects of some long rollers. The route finally breaks free of Sierra Vista by MP 331 and looks straight at the Mexican border, only a few miles away, and at the montane countryside of the Coronado National Memorial that rises before it. The turnoff for the memorial comes up at MP 335, and just afterward the road bends left (east) and enters Miracle Valley.

This ethereal stretch of land, reminiscent of the oak-groved hills of Santa Barbara, has a colorful past. It received its name from a faith-healing evangelist named Asa Alonzo Allen, who purchased 2,400 acres, held tent revivals here and around the country, started a church and bible college (a 15-building complex), and employed 175 people who sold his books, tapes, and prayer cloths, managed radio programs on 70 stations, and handled his 300,000-member mailing list. Miracle Valley's woes started when Allen died in 1970 (of, according to an autopsy, acute alcoholism), then were exacerbated in 1978 when a religious group from Chicago moved in. For the next decade, tensions between rural Cochise County and citified black church members escalated into fights and deaths, provoking visits from Jesse Jackson and then-governor Bruce Babbitt. Today, a sojourn through this beautiful grassland would never let on about the valley's controversial history.

Palominas Road, about MP 340, makes a nice turnaround point if you want to review the striking mountain scenery. You can rest and refuel at Palominas Trading Post (a restaurant with homemade pies) or the Morning Star Café. You can continue another 12 miles on AZ 92 to the town of Bisbee, dropping in and out of the San Pedro River drainage and traveling rollers that lead to the Mule Mountains. Or, to continue on this loop, turn left (north) on Palominas Road. This country road parallels the San Pedro River for the next 4 miles. At Hereford Road, turn left (west).

This relatively flat road travels about 8 miles through a pastoral landscape accented with a few mild rollers before rejoining AZ 92. Turn right (north) to return to Sierra Vista.

Hereford Road, the last segment of the Miracle Valley route, travels a pastoral landscape back to Sierra Vista.

REGION 10

WESTERN ARIZONA

Traveling the lowest elevations in the state, routes in western Arizona take you into a drought-prone land, influenced by two different deserts, that quenches its thirst with the lower Colorado River. The landscape rumbled with volcanism eons ago, and that created the dramatic ridgelines along which these routes travel. If you decide to tour this part of Arizona, remember it's the place of choice for the RV set and snowbirds in the wintertime.

ROUTES

The ridgelines get dramatic along the lower Colorado River near Parker Dam.

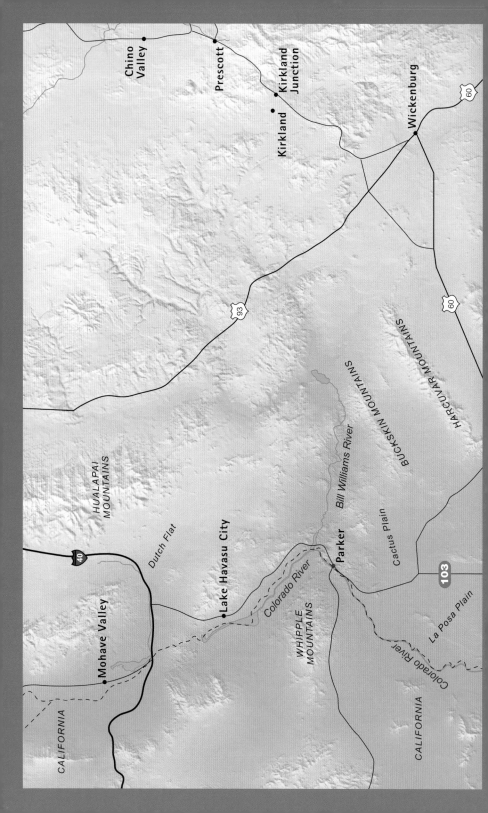

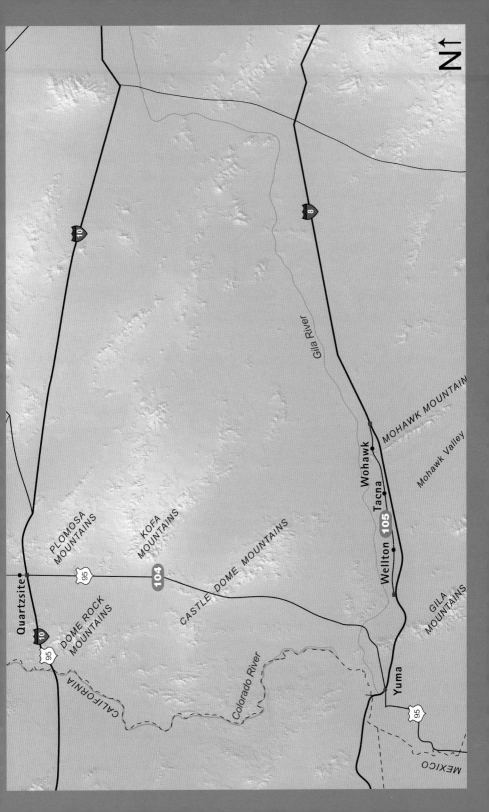

Route 103

WESTERN BORDER–NORTHERN ROUTE
AZ 95: I-40 TO PARKER

Easy • Intermediate

* Travels the western edge of Arizona along the lower Colorado River to Parker Dam
* Profuse shows of wildflowers in February and March after a wet winter
* Two to four lanes; wide to narrow shoulder

DISTANCE: 19 miles (to Lake Havasu City), 38 miles (to Parker Dam), or 57 miles
(to Parker) one-way

PEAK CYCLING: October–April

ACCOMMODATIONS: Supplies and restaurants in Lake Havasu City and Parker. Check
out the Agave Inn (866-854-2833), with the best views of London Bridge
in Lake Havasu City.

SPECIAL CONSIDERATIONS: Though winter would seem the best season to travel this
route, it's also when the barrage of recreational vehicles take over the highway.

STARTING POINT: From exit 9 on I-40, head south on AZ 95;
MP 202 is the first mile marker.

Western Arizona has developed into a multifaceted destination. As one
of the warm spots of choice for "snowbirds" and a magnet for whale-
sized recreational vehicles in the winter, Lake Havasu City then turns raucous

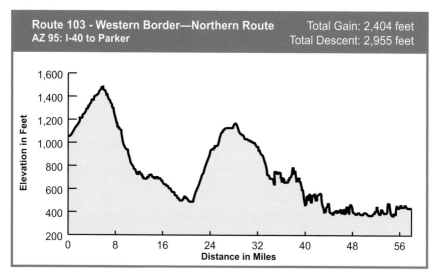

Route 103 - Western Border—Northern Route   Total Gain: 2,404 feet
AZ 95: I-40 to Parker   Total Descent: 2,955 feet

The Lower Colorado River near Parker Dam.

in the springtime, and the party atmosphere spreads down the whole lower Colorado River in summer. In the late fall, the area catches its breath. A window of quiet opens up where the roads, restaurants, and hotels see less traffic. This makes the perfect time to cycle western Arizona.

Rollers and scenic ridges start the route out and never really leave during the whole time you make your way down the edge of the state. Shark-tooth-shaped peaks and notched hilltops rise right along the road. By MP 191, the route enters Lake Havasu City's limits and the road widens to four lanes. At London Bridge Road a multiuse bike path comes on the scene, which might be a good alternative when the town's traffic gets intense. Take McCullough Boulevard to get to London Bridge. The span from the interstate to Lake Havasu City makes a good day route of 19 miles one-way.

Lake Havasu City sprawls quite a bit down the edge of the state, and the route finally gets free of the business traffic around MP 180. At the Special Activity and Recreation Area (SARA) Park at MP 177, check out the riverside with its razorback ridges, tilted peaks, totems, and hoodoos. All this scenery follows you as the route winds southward in the Aubrey Hills. You can stop at the scenic overlook at MP 170 to take in the dramatic landscape.

At Cattail Cove State Park (MP 168), the river is close enough to the road to catch glimpses of its teal-colored flow between the ridges and peaks. Self-contained cyclists should note that this park is a good place to camp. A few miles later, the route drops down to the reed-choked mouth of the Bill Williams River in its namesake wildlife refuge. The refuge sees hundreds of migratory birds in the spring and fall, as well as year-round waterfowl. The reeds, especially, make a favorite hangout for rails.

At MP 159 the route passes the turnoff for Parker Dam. This makes a good turnaround point for a shorter route, for a total of 19 miles one-way from Lake Havasu City or 38 miles from I-10.

The route continues along the river for several miles in a roller-ladened landscape. After passing Buckskin Mountain State Park, the route enters a particularly scenic stretch of wild and rugged mountain country for a few miles before reaching Parker.

Route 104

WESTERN BORDER—SOUTHERN ROUTE
AZ 95 AND US 95: PARKER TO YUMA

Easy • Intermediate

- Travels the lower desert along scenic volcanic rock mountains
- Profuse shows of wildflowers in February and March after a wet winter
- Two to four lanes; wide to narrow shoulder

DISTANCE: 35 miles (to Quartzite) to 115 miles one-way

PEAK CYCLING: October–April

ACCOMMODATIONS: Supplies and restaurants in Parker, Quartzsite, and Yuma. The
    Hampton Inn & Suites in Yuma (928-329-5600) is relatively new and nice. In
    Yuma, check out Lutes Casino for the western border's best hamburger and the
    River City Grill for fish.

SPECIAL CONSIDERATIONS: Though winter would seem the very best season to travel this
    route, it's also when the barrage of recreational vehicles takes over the highway.

STARTING POINT: In Parker, take AZ 95 south; turn left on California Avenue to continue
    on AZ 95; MP 143 is the first mile marker.

Where the northern segment of AZ 95 never strayed far from the lower
Colorado River, this southern segment travels inland. The road stays
on a fairly straight line due south, but the river bends westward, straying
from the highway's side for dozens of miles until the route bends westward
to ends its course at
the river's side.

For the first 9
miles, the route travels
through the Colorado
River Indian
Reservation. The route
follows the Arizona &
California Railroad
from Parker until
about MP 132, where
the railroad heads east
along AZ 72. To con-
tinue on AZ 95, follow

*Several mountain ranges along US 95 keep scenic panoramas a
constant on this ride.*

it as it turns sharply south. The Plomosa Mountains, up until now strung across the distant southern horizon, now appear to the southeast, and the route runs like an arrow across the La Posa Plain. This flatland has occasional ripples as it travels oh-so-slowly downhill toward Arizona's low point.

But first, the route passes through Quartzsite (MP 111), Arizona's answer to Calcutta come gem-show time in January and February. A sea of RVs spreads like a white wave over the little town. If you pass through during those months, it will turn into a project to make your way across town on this highway. Quartzsite lies 35 miles from Parker.

Once past Quartzsite, the route (now designated US 95) enters an unusual segment of Arizona. Here the route doesn't get another look at the more civilized assets of life (such as gas stations, restaurants, and lodging) for several dozen miles. Make sure you have all the provisions you will need.

The route continues in a generally flat manner, interspersed by gentle rollers, with the Dome Rock Mountains in the west and Plomosa Mountains in the east. At MP 96, the beautiful Kofa Mountains take over in the east. For the next 50 miles, the mountainscapes make the journey. The ridgelines' distinctive profiles and ruddy color add an attractive feature to this outback countryside.

After traveling through the La Posa Plain for so long, it feels good when the route flirts with the hills of the Middle Mountains between MPs 70 and 59. By MP 55, any hint of a grade wanes, and at MP 41 the farms surrounding Yuma start. These farms feed the nation. This great agricultural area produces alfalfa, which brings wintering geese; lettuce, which brings migrant workers; and dates, which produce luscious milk shakes. Citrus trees perfume the roadway in the spring. Watch for a little roadside chapel built by a farmer around MP 39.

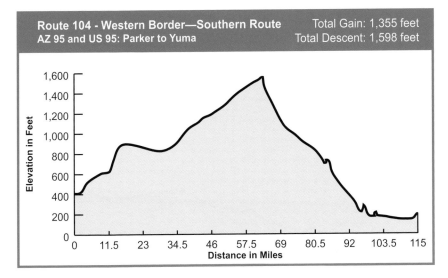

Route 104 - Western Border—Southern Route
AZ 95 and US 95: Parker to Yuma
Total Gain: 1,355 feet
Total Descent: 1,598 feet

The Gila Mountains add a little character to the route as it nears its end. As the route bends westward near MP 34, it continues in the midst of farmland. Flat and four-laned, the road has emerald fields bordered by date palms on both sides. Yuma's city limits (80 miles from Quartzsite) start at MP 25.

Route 105

OLD HIGHWAY 80
HIGHWAY 80 NEAR YUMA

Easy • Beginner

* Travels through a long, rural stretch of land on a little-used road
* Two lanes; medium to wide shoulder

DISTANCE: 34 miles one-way

PEAK CYCLING: October–April; early morning in warmer weather

ACCOMMODATIONS: Supplies, restaurants, and lodging in Yuma; check out Chretin's Mexican Food

SPECIAL CONSIDERATIONS: This route has remote sections. Bring a repair kit, food, and enough water.

STARTING POINTS: From Yuma, travel east on I-8 to exit 21, go 1 mile east to Old Highway 80 and turn right (east). Or, start partway through the route in Wellton: Take Old Highway 80 to California Street and turn left (north); go a block farther and park at the town's park.

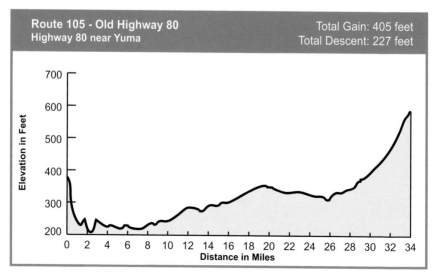

Route 105 - Old Highway 80
Highway 80 near Yuma
Total Gain: 405 feet
Total Descent: 227 feet

This route travels part of the North End Classic road-bike event that takes place in late February or early March. It's one of the first pro events of the year and draws more than 400 participants from all over the world.

Ricky and Jane Rinehart of Yuma organized the event for years. The husband-and-wife cyclists recall one year taking several foreign riders to Chretin's Mexican restaurant for dinner. Many didn't quite know how to order, and an Aussie ordered a burrito with eggs. The restaurant is famous for the margaritas it serves, and the cyclists "liked that," Ricky recalls.

The North End Classic starts and finishes in the town of Wellton. This route starts at I-8 for cyclists who want to get in some extra miles. Otherwise, do as the Classic's cyclists do and start at Wellton's town park.

Once on the old highway, now bypassed by I-8, you get a feel of the grassroots side of America, with farms on one side of the road and the Southern Pacific Railroad on the other—both iconic industries from the 20th century still hard at work. The real beauty of this route is its long stretch of uninterrupted road that sees very little traffic.

Though it doesn't have any remarkable scenery, the route exudes a comfortable aura that keeps you compelled to continue. After Wellton (mile 10), the route has some interesting features. Watch for an old junkyard full of vintage tractors around mile 17. The several-blocks-long town of Tacna (mile 21) has some restaurants and a mini-mart at a gas station. If you need anything, get it at Tacna. The road ends at the next town of Mohawk in its namesake mountains, and there are no services here.

Route 106

DOME VALLEY ROAD
DOME VALLEY ROAD NEAR YUMA

Easy • Beginner

- Travels through quintessential Americana farmland with fresh earthen air
- Two lanes; no shoulder

DISTANCE: 13 miles one-way

PEAK CYCLING: October–April; early morning in warmer weather

ACCOMMODATIONS: Supplies, restaurants, and lodging in Yuma

SPECIAL CONSIDERATIONS: Watch for farm vehicles on this route.

STARTING POINTS: **North access:** From Yuma, travel north on US 95 to MP 40, and then turn right (east) on Dome Valley Road. **South access:** Travel east on I-8 to exit 21, go 1 mile east to Dome Valley Road, and turn left (west).

This route zigzags through one of the nation's food sources, thanks to water supplied via irrigation from the lower Colorado River. This flat, silt-rich land produces loads of fruits and vegetables. The area runs a bit cooler because of the humidity hovering around the well-watered fields, and

Emerald fields splay before a farmer's estate in Dome Valley.

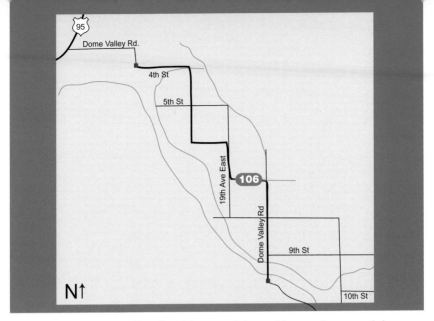

it has a rich loamy smell. Palatial homes cloistered by eucalyptus and date trees look like mini-oases surrounded by rich dirt or fields of greens (lettuce is big here).

The Muggins Mountains make a serrated backdrop for this emerald scene. Food crops start in October and get harvested in early spring. This flat, easy ride is an intriguing one, with its mountain scenery on the edges and rural farm life at the center. Simply follow the signed route for Dome Valley Road and enjoy the green.

JUST ADD WATER

It doesn't matter what the season, or the location. You can cycle all year long in Arizona. Just be sure to add water.

Phoenecian Eric Prosnier, who cycles 25 miles one-way to and from his job each day and describes himself as a "cyclist from my mother's womb," always keeps himself "topped off." He constantly drinks water when he's at work, and he hydrates before starting a cycle ride.

Eric explains that most cyclists do not drink enough water. He recommends cyclists develop a system, such as taking a drink every 10 or 15 minutes. After hydrating before he starts, he drinks a pint of water during his hour-long commute.

Wherever you go, always take more water than you think you need, and drink it. Never mind the extra weight. Cyclists die from dehydration in the Arizona heat. Extra weight becomes meaningless if you don't have enough water.

Be sure to hydrate even in cold weather. Without enough fluids, your blood can thicken. When that happens, your circulation slows, your heart pumps harder, and fatigue plays with your pluck.

Appendix A—Route Finder

Regions & Routes	Page Number	One-Way/Loop (L) Mileage	Ratings	Rollers	Steep Climbs	Level Grade	Forests	Meadows	River/ Lakes	Scenic Vistas
Region 1: Northern Arizona										
1. North Rim Parkway	16	33-45	M/B	X	X		X	X	X	X
2. Cape Royal Road	18	20	M/I	X			X	X		X
3. Big Water	20	15	M/I	X					X	X
4. Lake Shore Drive Loop	22	10 L	E/B						X	X
5. Jacob Lake Half-Century	24	14-55	M/I	X	X		X			X
6. Hermit Road	26	8	E/B							X
7. AZ 64 East	28	54	M/I-Ex	X	X		X	X	X	X
8. AZ 64 North	30	18-58	M/Ex	X	X		X	X		X
9. Perkinsville Road	32	11-24	M-D/Ex	X	X		X	X		
10. US 89	34	136	M/Ex-I	X			X		X	X
11. Sunset Crater Loop	36	36-46 L	M/I	X	X		X	X		X
12. San Francisco Peaks Scenic Road	39	51	M/Ex	X			X	X		X
13. Snow Bowl Road	41	7.5	D/Ex		X		X			X
14. Mormon Lake Loop	43	7-15 L	M/B				X	X	X	
15. Lake Mary Road	45	15-55	M/I	X			X	X	X	X
Region 2: The Navajo Nation										
16. Coppermine Road	50	14.5	M/B	X						X
17. Navajo Mountain Scenic Road	52	36-66	M/Ex	X	X					X
18. US 160	54	72	M/Ex	X						X
19. Monument Valley	56	29	M/I	X						X
20. Navajo National Monument	58	9.5	M/I							X
21. Navajo Mountain Road	60	25.5	M/I		X					X
22. Antelope Point	62	10-11	E/B	X					X	X
23. Road to Leupp	64	37	M-D/I	X	X				X	X
Region 3: North Central Arizona										
24. White Spar Road	70	13-61	M-D/I-Ex	X	X		X			
25. Lynx Lake	73	10	M/B	X			X		X	X

#	Route	Page	Miles	Rating					
26.	Prescott Peavine Trail	75	4.6	E/B			X		X
27.	Williamson Valley Road	77	22-38	M/I					X
28.	Iron Springs Road	79	26	M/I				X	X
29.	Jerome-Cottonwood-Clarkdale Scenic Road	81	29	M/I					X
30.	Mingus Mountain Scenic Road	83	32	D/Ex				X	X
31.	Red Rock Crossing	85	5.5	M/I					X
32.	Page Springs Road	87	7	E/I				X	X
33.	Mogollon Rim West	89	156	M-D/I-Ex				X	X

REGION 4: PHOENIX AREA

#	Route	Page	Miles	Rating					
34.	Cave Creek Bikeway	94	8	E/B	X		X		
35.	Arizona Canal Bikeway	96	13.5	E/B	X		X	X	
36.	Indian Bend Bikeway	98	12	E/B	X		X	X	
37.	Skunk Creek	100	4.75	E/B	X		X		
38.	Summit Road	102	6.5	D/Ex					X
39.	San Juan Road	105	5.5	M/B	X				X
40.	Papago Salado Loop	107	12 L	E/B			X		
41.	Phoenix Sonoran Bikeway	109	38	E-M/B-I			X		
42.	Bartlett Dam Road	111	14	D/Ex	X			X	X
43.	Bush Highway	114	6-15	M/B-I	X			X	X
44.	Tortilla Flat	117	16-21	D/Ex	X			X	X
45.	Rio Verde Drive	119	12	M/I	X			X	X
46.	McDowell Mountain Route	120	14	M/I	X				X
47.	Pecos Road	122	7	E/B			X		
48.	Pima Road	123	18	M/B-I	X				

REGION 5: CENTRAL ARIZONA (DESERT)

#	Route	Page	Miles	Rating					
49.	Lake Pleasant	130	16.5-17	M/I	X				X
50.	Sun Valley Parkway	132	28.5	E/B			X	X	
51.	Old Highway 80	134	39	E/B	X				X
52.	Wickenburg to Tonapah	136	10-42	M/I	X				X
53.	Wickenburg	139	47	M/I	X				X
54.	Pinal Pioneer Parkway	141	42	M/Ex	X				X

Ratings: E (easy), M (moderate), D (difficult), VD (very difficult); B (beginner), I (intermediate), Ex (experienced)

APPENDIX A—ROUTE FINDER (CONTINUED)

Regions & Routes	Page Number	One-Way/Loop (L) Mileage	Ratings	Rollers	Steep Climbs	Level Grade	Forests	Meadows	River/ Lakes	Scenic Vistas
REGION 6: CENTRAL ARIZONA (MOUNTAINS)										
55. Road to Globe	146	32-55	M-D/I-Ex	X	X					X
56. Mining Country Route	148	32	D/Ex	X						X
57. El Capitan	150	36	D/Ex	X						X
58. Black Hills Run	152	43	M/I	X						
59. Roosevelt Dam	154	35	M-D/B-Ex	X	X				X	X
60. Young Highway	156	27	D/Ex	X					X	X
61. Coolidge Dam	158	13	M/B	X	X					
62. Point of Pines	160	50	D/Ex	X	X		X	X	X	X
63. Salt River Canyon–South Route	162	29	D/Ex	X	X				X	X
64. Salt River Canyon–North Route	164	48	D/Ex	X	X		X		X	X
REGION 7: EASTERN ARIZONA										
65. Mogollon Rim East	170	56	M/Ex	X	X		X	X		X
66. Hawley Lake	172	9.5	M/I	X			X	X	X	
67. Road to Greer	174	5	E/B				X	X	X	
68. Big Lake	175	23	M/I	X			X	X	X	X
69. Lyman Lake	177	17-29	E/I	X				X	X	X
70. Concho Route	179	34-45	M/I	X				X	X	X
71. Cerro Montoso	181	45	D/I	X	X			X		X
72. Coronado Trail	183	123	M-D/I-Ex	X			X	X		X
73. Three Way Near-Century Loop	186	93 L	M-D/I-Ex	X					X	X
74. Old West Highway	188	118	M/I	X	X					X
75. Swift Trail	191	21	VD/Ex				X			X
76. Road to Fort Grant	194	10-28	D/I	X	X					X
REGION 8: TUCSON BASIN AND BEYOND										
77. Oracle Junction	198	25	M/I	X						
78. Ventana Canyon Loop	199	14 L	M/I	X	X					
79. Bear Canyon	201	20 L	E/I	X						X

No.	Route	Page	Miles	Rating							
80.	Christie Hills Loop	203	4.7 L	M/B							X
81.	Rillito River Park	205	7.5	E/B			X		X		
82.	Sky Island Scenic Byway	207	30	VD/Ex			X		X		
83.	Oro Valley Loop	209	18 L	M/B							
84.	Avra Valley Loop	211	19.5 L	E/B					X		X
85.	Cactus Forest Drive	212	8 L	M/B	X			X	X		X
86.	Old Spanish Trail Loop	214	35 L	E/I	X				X		X
87.	Gates Pass Loop	216	34 L	D/Ex	X				X		X
88.	Anza Trail	219	9-35	E/I					X		X
89.	Arivaca Road	221	22	M/Ex					X		X

REGION 9: SOUTHEAST ARIZONA

No.	Route	Page	Miles	Rating							
90.	Wine Country Loop	228	23 L	M/Ex			X		X		X
91.	Parker Canyon Lake	230	32	M-D/I-Ex	X	X	X		X		X
92.	Dragoon Road	232	13	M/Ex				X	X		X
93.	US 191	234	66	E/I					X		
94.	Double Adobe Road	236	8-15	E/B					X		
95.	Jefferson Davis Memorial Highway	237	23-48	M/I					X		X
96.	Road to Rodeo	239	49-58	M-D/Ex					X		X
97.	San Pedro House	242	23	E/B				X	X	X	
98.	Charleston Road	244	16	E/B				X	X	X	
99.	Fairbank Route	246	29-35	E/B				X	X	X	
100.	Patagonia-Sonoita Scenic Byway	248	27-52.5	M/I				X	X		X
101.	Dos Cabezas	250	33-43	M/I-Ex					X		X
102.	Miracle Valley Loop	253	35-49 L	E/B-I		X		X	X		X
	(Buffalo Soldier Trail bike path)		7	B/E							

REGION 10: WESTERN ARIZONA

No.	Route	Page	Miles	Rating							
103.	Western Border—Northern Route	260	19-57	E/I				X	X		X
104.	Western Border—Southern Route	262	35-115	E/I			X		X		X
105.	Old Highway 80	264	34	E/B					X		
106.	Dome Valley Road	266	13	E/B			X		X		X

Ratings: E (easy), M (moderate), D (difficult), VD (very difficult); B (beginner), I (intermediate), Ex (experienced)

APPENDIX B

BICYCLE ADVOCACY GROUPS, USER GROUPS, AND REGIONAL CYCLE GROUPS

ARIZONA BICYCLE CLUB
P.O. Box 7191
Phoenix, AZ 85011-7191
602-264-5478
www.azbikeclub.com

COALITION OF ARIZONA BICYCLISTS
480-893-3159
(for road-bike handling and riding classes, contact
Matt Radar at radarmatt@aol.com)
www.cazbike.com

GREATER ARIZONA BICYCLING ASSOCIATION
www.bikegaba.org
www.sportsfun.com/gaba

LEAGUE OF AMERICAN BICYCLISTS
1612 K St. NW, Suite 800
Washington, DC 20006
202-822-1333
www.bikeleague.org

NATIONAL CENTER FOR BICYCLING AND WALKING
1506 21st St. NW, Suite 200
Washington, DC 20036
202-463-6622
www.bikewalk.org

THUNDERHEAD ALLIANCE
P.O. Box 3309
Prescott, AZ 86302
928-541-9841
www.thunderheadalliance.org

APPENDIX C

BIKE MAPS

BIKE WAYS–METROPOLITAN PHOENIX AREA
Maricopa Association of Governments
602-254-6300
www.mag.maricopa.gov

CITY OF PRESCOTT BICYCLING OPPORTUNITIES MAP
Prescott Bicycle Advisory Committee
928-777-1560

CITY OF TEMPE BIKEWAY MAP
480-350-2775
www.tempe.gov/bikeprogram

MESA BIKE MAP
City of Mesa Transportation Division
480-644-2160
www.cityofmesa.org

TUCSON BIKE MAP
Pima Association of Governments
520-792-1093

INDEX

ABOUT THE AUTHOR AND PHOTOGRAPHER

CHRISTINE MAXA

A Lowell Thomas Gold and International Regional Magazine Association award-winning freelance travel writer, Christine has authored four books and has written articles for *Chicago Tribune, Christian Science Monitor, National Geographic Traveler*, and *Southwest Art*, among other national and regional publications. She has been featured on National Public Radio and local television. Barnes and Noble featured her as Author of the Month.

DAVID A. JAMES

A road biker for several decades, David shoots in many different formats with his Hasselblad, Canon, and digital cameras. His landscapes have been published in guidebooks, environmental publications, and as posters. His photography has been exhibited at galleries in Phoenix and Flagstaff, Abravanel Hall in Santa Barbara, Music Academy of the West in Los Angeles, and the Museum of Contemporary Art–Washington, D.C. David has published travel and outdoor photography in *AAA Highroads, Phoenix Magazine*, and *Arizona Highways*.